POLICING SEX AND MARRIAGE IN THE AMERICAN MILITARY

Studies in War, Society, and the Military

POLICING SEX AND MARRIAGE IN THE AMERICAN MILITARY

The Court-Martial and the
Construction of Gender and
Sexual Deviance, 1950–2000

KELLIE WILSON-BUFORD

University of Nebraska Press
Lincoln and London

This book is derived in part from "From Exclusion to Accep-
tance: A Case History of Homosexuality in the U.S. Court of
Military Appeals," in "Evolution of Government Policy Toward
Homosexuality in the U.S. Military," special issue, *Journal of
Homosexuality* 60, nos. 2–3 (February–March 2013): 250–72,
doi:10.1080/00918369.2013.744671, http://www.tandfonline.com/,
copyright by Taylor & Francis; reprinted as *Evolution of Govern-
ment Policy Towards Homosexuality in the US Military: The
Rise and Fall of DADT*, ed. James E. Parco and David A. Levy
(New York: Routledge, 2014).

∞

Library of Congress Cataloging-in-Publication Data
Names: Buford, Kellie Wilson, author.
Title: Policing sex and marriage in the American military:
the court-martial and the construction of gender and sexual
deviance, 1950–2000 / Kellie Wilson-Buford.
Description: Lincoln: University of Nebraska Press, [2018] |
Series: Studies in war, society, and the military | Includes
bibliographical references and index.
Identifiers: LCCN 2017050526
ISBN 9780803296855 (cloth: alk. paper)
ISBN 9781496208705 (epub)
ISBN 9781496208712 (mobi)
ISBN 9781496208729 (pdf)
Subjects: LCSH: Military law—Social aspects—United States.
| Families of military personnel—Legal status, laws, etc.
—United States. | Military offenses—Law and legislation
—United States. | Sex crimes—United States. | Soldiers—
Family relationships—United States. | Soldiers—Sexual
behavior—United States.
Classification: LCC KF7270 .B84 2018 | DDC 343.73/014—dc23
LC record available at https://lccn.loc.gov/2017050526

Set in Minion Pro by E. Cuddy.

For
Diego and Baylie

CONTENTS

TABLES

This book would never have been possible without the support of Professor Margaret D. Jacobs, whose research, work ethic, and super woman–like ability to balance motherhood and academia continue to inspire me. She shared the vision I had for this project from the beginning, and her belief in me never waivered, even when I doubted myself. Nor would this book have been possible without the expertise and critical insights of Professor Emeritus Pete Maslowski, who graciously welcomed me into the world of military history in a memorable graduate research seminar at the University of Nebraska–Lincoln. Always eager to critique drafts and push me to become a better writer, his wisdom and encouragement are on every single page of this book. Professors Tim Borstelmann, Jeannette Eileen Jones, and Professor Emerita Helen Moore offered invaluable feedback on the original manuscript, while Professor Maureen Honey offered friendship and inspiration. I am indebted to Adam Hodge, Nate Probasco, and Lisa Maurer for the support and encouragement along the way that only fellow graduate students can provide, as well as to Professors Will Thomas and Professor Emeritus John Wunder for encouraging me to keep writing and publishing my work. I am eternally grateful for the University of Nebraska–Lincoln's generous financial support through the Othmer and Fling Fellowships that made the majority of the research for this book possible.

My teachers at the University of North Carolina–Greensboro, especially Professors Pete Carmichael and Lisa Levenstein and Professor Emeritus Karl Schleunes, helped sharpen my research and writing skills and unknowingly set me on the path toward completing a doctoral degree in history. Professor Emeritus Loren Schweninger took me under his wing on the Race and Slavery Petitions Project from 2004 to 2006 and inadvertently transmitted his love for legal documents and court transcripts to me.

I am immensely grateful to Elizabeth L. Hillman for her inspiring work *Defending America*, which saved the *Court-Martial Reports* from decades of scholarly neglect and laid the groundwork for this book. She provided insights and suggestions on my work that only a scholar well versed in these courts-martial transcripts could, and I am grateful for her guidance. I am also indebted to anonymous readers who graciously took time out of their busy schedules to provide invaluable feedback on this book.

Ploughing through revisions would not have been possible without the support of my colleagues in the History Department at Arkansas State University. J. Justin Castro offered not only feedback on portions of the book but also advice on the publishing process. His unwavering support was a lifeline for me as I struggled to bring this book to life despite the many demands of my job. In addition to providing feedback on last-minute final drafts of the introduction, Joe Key provided comic relief and moral support that kept me focused on the big picture of publishing this book. Cherisse Jones-Branch graciously provided feedback on the introduction in its final stages despite competing demands on her time. Ed Salo supported me from the outset by inquiring about my progress and offering words of encouragement. I also owe a special thanks to Gina Hogue, LaQuita Saunders, Pamela Hronek, Phyllis Pobst, and Gary Edwards for taking my family and me under their wings and helping us make Arkansas home. I also thank my graduate students who, in a memorable summer reading seminar called Sex, Gender, and War, asked questions that made me think about some of my arguments in new ways. And to Timothy Richmond, my graduate assistant and friend who lightened my teaching load after multiple back surgeries and carried on my work in my absence—thank you.

Bridget Barry, Sara Springsteen, and the rest of the staff at University of Nebraska Press have been incredibly gracious and patient in guiding me through the publishing process. I also owe a special thanks to Vicki Chamlee for her fierce copyediting skills. This book would not have been possible without them.

Last, I owe thanks to my wonderful family without whose support this book could not have been written. My parents played a huge role in the evolution of this book by teaching me the values of hard work and commitment. Growing up on military bases around the world as an air force brat, I was fortunate to live in many places, to immerse myself in different cultures, and to learn military traditions. The questions that stemmed from my exposure to military culture, particularly those related to gender and sex, ultimately planted the seed for this book. My sister, Kacey, was a lifeline for me through the writing process, though she might not realize it. On good days and bad, she was always just a phone call away. And only as a sister can, she knew exactly what to say to help me keep moving forward. Though distance separated us, her presence made the writing of this book—and the years leading up to it—a lot less lonely.

For the endless joy and companionship they brought to my life as I worked on this book, I owe a huge thank you to Pixie, Izzie, Maddie, Huxley, Nina, Nya Willow, Draco, and "Mighty" Tank. Whether curled up at my feet, on my lap, or around my head, they shared the moments of elation after finishing a chapter and the moments of despair when I thought I would never finish this work. Especially on those sleepless nights when I just could not quite fit the pieces together, they were there by my side.

But I owe the biggest thanks to my partner Petree and our two children, Diego and Baylie, who sacrificed so much on a daily basis to help me bring this book to life. Always willing to take care of the kids, cook dinner, clean the house, run errands, or lend an ear or a word of encouragement, Petree did whatever needed to be done without complaint to give me the time and space I needed to write. His steady reminders of why I started this project in the first place anchored me through many storms of doubt and frustration. Diego and Baylie, meanwhile, rarely gave up "mommy time" willingly and without complaint, but their never-ending supply of hugs, questions, laughter, and vibrant energy infused my life and writing with purpose and motivated me to keep going. For giving so much and asking so little in return, it is to them that I dedicate this book.

AUTHOR'S NOTE

A note on methodology and the racialized nature of the courts-martial transcripts is in order here. First, my arguments and evidence in chapters 2–5 are based on my analysis of sexually deviant crimes that appeared in the *Court-Martial Reports* from 1950 to 1975. Consequently, these chapters are a useful starting point for scholars interested in the legal and social history of marriage regulation, adultery, bigamy, sodomy, prostitution and pandering, consumption of pornography, indecent exposure, public masturbation, and window peeping in the U.S. military in the third quarter of the twentieth century. My arguments and evidence in chapter 6 are based on a smaller sample of cases I selected from the digitized collections of the *Military Justice Reporter* from 1976 to 2000. The chapter is not intended to serve as a comprehensive analysis of all courts-martial in the given period but rather as a summary overview of major shifts and patterns in the courts' prosecution of sexual deviance crimes in that period. Indeed, an exhaustive analysis of these cases would require multiple volumes. However, scholars interested in pursuing further research based on the evidence in chapter 6 will find the endnotes especially helpful.

Second, in the early Cold War, military courts normalized "whiteness" by noting only the races and ethnicities of accused service members who deviated from this norm. Whiteness was implied through the transcript's silence on a defendant's racial makeup. In contrast, the courts explicitly characterized African

American defendants as either "colored" or "Negro." This practice was most prevalent in the 1950s and, in response to the civil rights movement, steadily decreased until 1975 when legal officials all but abandoned the custom of noting the racial backgrounds of nonwhite defendants.

Consequently, this body of case law poses a frustrating challenge for scholars of race relations. As fascinating as it would be to offer valid statistics about the rates of comparative convictions and punishments for whites and persons of color, the courts-martial reports involving crimes of sexual deviance in the post–World War II military evade this type of inquiry.[1] In the few instances where the race or ethnic background of defendants is noted, I have offered analyses of how racial or ethnic identity influenced the proceedings and sentencing outcomes. Available comparisons of cases featuring white and nonwhite service members whom the courts prosecuted for the same crimes of sexual deviance suggest that the defendants' racial backgrounds sometimes adversely affected their sentences. But sometimes, white defendants received equal, if not more severe, punishments for committing the same crimes of sexual deviance as African American and Hispanic service personnel. Though too small a number to make generalizations, these few cases illustrate the Court of Military Appeal's ambiguous role in protecting the rights of minorities to fair trials amid a culture of racial hatred and suspicion.[2] However, comparing only the outcomes of cases authorities chose to prosecute risks underestimating the influence of command discretion in investigating and charging that was likely the more salient cause of racially disparate outcomes.

Finally, the court records and primary sources I analyze in this book neither prove the guilt or innocence of the defendants nor the guilt or innocence of the U.S. military justice system and that of the armed forces. Rather, I use these legal documents to trace the evolution of military law on crimes of sexual deviance to shed light on the gendered nature of the military as an institution as well as on the role and function of its justice system in policing sex and marriage. To protect the privacy of plaintiffs, defendants, and witnesses involved in the courts-martial analyzed, I use only first initials of first names (where available) and last names.

ABBREVIATIONS

ABR	Army Board of Review
ACMR	Army Court of Military Review
AFBR	Air Force Board of Review
AFCMR	Air Force Court of Military Review
AFOSI	Air Force Office of Special Investigations
AFR	air force regulation
AR	army regulation
CAAF	Court of Appeals for the Armed Forces
CCA	Criminal Court of Appeals
CGCMR	Coast Guard Court of Military Review
CMA	Court of Military Appeals
CMR	*Court-Martial Reports*
COMNAVPHIL	commander, U.S. Naval Forces in the Philippines
DADT	don't ask, don't tell
JAG	judge advocate general
MCM	*Manual for Courts-Martial*
MJ	*Military Justice Reporter*
MP	military police
NBR	Navy–Marine Corps Board of Review
NCMR	Navy–Marine Corps Court of Military Review
NCO	noncommissioned officer

OSI	Office of Special Investigations
ROTC	Reserve Officers' Training Corps
SECNAV	secretary of the navy
UCMJ	Uniform Code of Military Justice
USFK	U.S. Forces Korea
WAC	Women's Air Corps

POLICING SEX AND
MARRIAGE IN THE
AMERICAN MILITARY

Introduction

On June 23, 1951, Staff Sgt. M. Snyder of the U.S. Marine Corps Reserve was tried by general court-martial in Camp Lejeune, North Carolina, for attempting to entice three servicemen to engage in fornication, or illicit sexual acts with a woman not their wife. The evidence established that Snyder, accompanied by a woman and her two children, ages six and four years old, were occupying a table at the Noncommissioned Officers (NCO) Club. When Chief St. Sing entered the facility, Snyder called him over to the table and, using "vulgar terminology" in the presence of the woman and children, invited St. Sing to engage in sexual intercourse with the woman. Undeterred by St. Sing's rebuke and departure, Snyder extended the same offer in "equally lewd language" to Master Sergeant Loewig upon his entry into the club. Loewig also rebuked Snyder and departed. Later that afternoon, Snyder took the woman (without the children) to a barracks and made a similar proposal to Staff Sergeant Schick, who was asleep on his bunk. The pair departed after a warrant officer who had observed the woman's presence and overheard Synder's "indecent invitation" ordered them to leave the barracks. Witnesses testified that Snyder never mentioned a price for his offers and was "quite sober" during his rendezvous.[1]

The original review board convicted Sergeant Snyder on three counts of attempting to entice other servicemen to engage in fornication in violation of Article 134 of the Uniform Code of

Military Justice (UCMJ) and sentenced him to a bad conduct discharge, forfeiture of all pay and allowances, and confinement at
hard labor for one year. A convening authority and subsequent
review board in the Office of the Judge Advocate General (JAG),
U.S. Navy, reduced Snyder's sentence to six and then four months
of confinement on the grounds that the charge for which Snyder
was convicted—attempting to entice persons in fornication—was
not specified under Article 134. Stemming from British military
law and incorporated into every issue of the army's Articles of
War since 1775, the general article's purpose was to "prevent the
possibility of a failure of justice in the army" by criminalizing
noncapital offenses not made punishable by other existing articles but recognized as crimes in federal civil courts. Article 134's
scope included "all disorders and neglects to the prejudice of
good order and [military] discipline and all conduct of a nature
to bring discredit [on the armed forces]." Snyder appealed his
case to the U.S. military's supreme court, the Court of Military
Appeals (CMA), on the grounds that his crimes were not "prejudicial to good order and discipline."[2]

The CMA had to determine if the act of attempting to entice
persons to fornicate constituted a punishable offense under Article 134. Historically crimes that fell under the purview of Article
134 included insubordination, drunkenness, profanity, fraud,
wearing an improper uniform, use of indecent language to a
female, uncleanliness in person, gambling, neglect or evasion of
job duties, pandering, and other vaguely defined acts of immorality. The court could not classify Sergeant Snyder's actions as
pandering because he did not stand to profit financially from
his solicitations. It determined his actions did not equate to fornication because neither Snyder himself nor the three servicemen he approached actually engaged in sexual relations with the
unnamed woman. Was an unsuccessful attempt to entice persons
to fornicate a punishable offense?

The court's answer to this question significantly expanded the military justice system's jurisdictional authority to prosecute vaguely defined "immoral" acts not specified under Article 134. The presiding CMA judges unanimously agreed that Snyder's immoral conduct compromised the "good order" of the military community by evincing to his fellow corpsmen "a wanton disregard for a moral standard generally and properly accepted by society." The moral standard to which the judges referred recognized the sanctity of the marital bed between one man and one woman as the only acceptable space for sexual relations in 1950s America. Marriage—particularly heterosexual, monogamous marriage, as this book illustrates—was central to the courts' concept of "good order," which was defined as a "condition of tranquility, security and good government." Sex out of wedlock would not have disturbed the public peace, national security, or America's democratic system of government in any real, measurable sense unless citizens were physically harmed. But the moral disorder that would ensue if premarital and extramarital sex became the new standard was considered just as threatening to good order as violent uprisings, the communist menace, or nuclear war. Though Congress had "not intended [for Article 134] to regulate the wholly private moral conduct of an individual," the judges' decision to expand its scope in *Snyder* transformed the general article into a legal blank check that granted the courts unprecedented authority to police the private, intimate lives of the service community.[3]

This book began as an investigation into the history of rape and sexual assault committed by American service members in the second half of the twentieth century. In spite of the countless work scholars conducted on the history of the Korean, Vietnam, and Cold Wars, one must search the literature diligently to find even a footnote referencing American servicemen's acts of sexual violence abroad and at home in this era.[4] Assuming that courts-martial were the ultimate arbiter of acceptable behavior in the U.S. military, I turned to the *Court-Martial Reports*, the official annual publication of the Judge Advocate General Corps of the armed forces since 1951. The comprehensive compilation included reports of all military crimes originating in general and special courts-martial in the army, navy, air force, marine corps, and coast guard. The reports also contain transcripts of all cases whose petitions were accepted for review by the newly established Court of Military Appeals. Spanning a hundred volumes and more than one hundred thousand pages of original documents, these transcripts provide an unparalleled window into the historic criminalization of sexually deviant and violent acts committed at the hands of American servicemen around the world from 1950 to 2000.[5]

A surprising trend emerged from the *Court-Martial Reports* that shifted my investigative focus beyond rape cases. Alongside courts-martial for sexual assault were a significant number of trials for crimes of sexual *deviance*, a term I use to describe sexual offenses that undermined the sanctity of heterosexual, monogamous, and racially homogenous marriage, which served as the moral linchpin of the post–World War II military community. These crimes included adultery, bigamy, sodomy, pandering and prostitution, pornography consumption, indecent exposure, public masturbation, and window peeping, and their prosecution occurred into the twenty-first century. Though sometimes the commission of sexually deviant crimes involved violence and dual charges of rape, carnal knowledge (statutory rape), assault with a dangerous weapon, robbery, and homicide, often these crimes only involved the perpetrators and their pornographic films or consensual sexual partners.[6] That the military justice system existed to protect the public from hard-core rapists and murderers was a given. Less apparent was why the courts concerned themselves with the intimate private lives and the consensual sexual relationships of service members.

The predominance of courts-martial for crimes of sexual deviance—what the courts referred to as "crimes of moral turpitude"—raised intriguing questions about the fundamental purpose of military law under the newly established Uniform Code of Military Justice.[7] Why, in the midst of an international arms race with the Soviet Union and a supposed impending nuclear holocaust, were military courts ridding the ranks of troops who consumed pornography and hired prostitutes for sexual pleasure? Why, at the height of the Cold War when the U.S. military was expanding to the farthest reaches of the globe to reconstruct war-torn countries as potential democratic allies, were American service members being court-martialed, dishonorably discharged, and imprisoned for cheating on their wives? Why, during an era in which many Americans were seeking comfort and security through marriage and family, were troops court-martialed for disobeying orders forbidding them from marrying without command approval any non-American women living in occupied territories? And why, as the U.S. military's mission shifted from containing communism to fighting the global war on terror in the last decade of the twentieth century, were military judges dismissing troops for engaging in "unnatural" sexual acts such as oral and anal sodomy with consenting adult partners despite these troops' invaluable contributions to the mission?

In the absence of a comprehensive study on this topic, this book seeks to answer these questions.[8] This research contributes to a growing literature on state surveillance of the intimate, private lives of American citizens in the twentieth century and illustrates how the U.S. military, as an arm of the state, policed sex and marriage from 1950 to 2000. I argue that the U.S. military's public international strategy of communist containment, its systematic buildup of weapons, and its territorial occupations across the globe depended on its internal and often less visible strategy of policing its respective members' private lives and intimate relationships. The military justice system, under the UCMJ, waged a legal assault against all forms of sexual deviance that supposedly threatened the moral fiber of the military community and the nation from 1950 to 2000. The UCMJ, legal historian Elizabeth Lutes Hillman argues, was the "greatest reform in the history of American military law" because it granted service members basic legal protections such as their rights to due process, to have access to counsel, and to appeal unfavorable decisions to the Court of Military Appeals, an appellate court of presidentially appointed civilian judges.[9] In an attempt to humanize what many veterans and politicians condemned as an archaic and undemocratic implementation of justice prior to 1950, the UCMJ streamlined the laws and legal procedures of the various service branches to more closely reflect those of U.S. civil law. But the broad discretion that the UCMJ granted commanding officers to define and prosecute conduct both unbecoming of an officer (Article 133) and prejudicial to good order and discipline (Article 134) inadvertently transformed review boards and the CMA into the military's police task force for enforcing accepted notions of morality, decency, and deviance in the military community on a global scale.

Policing marital relationships was the primary means by which the U.S. military in the post–World War II world punished moral and sexual deviance. Because the strength of the nation and the military seemingly depended on the service community's commitment to creating and sustaining functional and lasting marriages, the services endorsed heterosexual, monogamous, and ethnically homogenous marriage as the antidote to political and sexual radicalism. Protecting the nuclear family, of which the marital union between husband and wife was an integral part, served the dual purpose of projecting an international image of stable democracy while channeling the soldiers' sexuality into the wholesome influences of family and marriage. Enforcing heterosexual marriage theoretically minimized the soldiers' use of prostitutes, cutting back on rates of venereal disease, interracial mixing, and illegitimate pregnancies. Married soldiers were less likely to commit sexual crimes against host women and children in the international arena and thus improved civil-military relations abroad by boosting the international reputation of the United States. But, most important, marriage provided a powerful check on homosexual tendencies by providing soldiers with an outlet that enabled them to fulfill their sexual needs without endangering their health or masculinity.

In the process of policing sex and marriage, legal officials constructed and enforced gendered ideals of masculinity and femininity by which men and women in the military were judged. Service members who committed adultery, same-sex sodomy, and bigamy deviated from the military's gendered status quo, which idealized masculine troops as married, heterosexual, morally righteous breadwinning soldiers who were as committed to protecting their country as they were to preserving their monogamous relationships with their wives. Troops who engaged in prostitution or pandering, indecent exposure, consuming pornography, and window peeping not only threatened the sanctity and stability of their relationships by pursuing sexual pleasure outside of their marriages but also undermined the credibility and moral righteousness of the U.S. military to both the citizens back home and the international community. Through the creation and enforcement of laws and regulations aimed at protecting heterosexual, monogamous, and racially homogenous marriage, military courts policed gender and played an important role in aligning military masculinity and femininity with traditional family values in the post–World War II era.

But efforts to police sex and marriage were not unique to the postwar era. Military officials regulated prostitution, for example, as far back as the 1870s on frontier army posts, in the Philippines during the Spanish-American War, and in nearly every location where American troops landed during World War II and the Cold War to protect troops from venereal disease.[10] At the same time, officials attempted to control and often prevent the troops' decisions to marry native women in occupied territories. The military's initial commitment to policing the troops' intimate lives became an increasingly harrowing task as the military grew in size and function in the twentieth century, often leading to embarrassing public spectacles that portrayed the armed forces as hothouses of homoeroticism and sexual sin.[11] The federal and state governments also had a long history of regulating their citizens' marital and sexual choices prior to World War II to preserve a patriarchal social structure rooted in laws of coverture.[12] By the time the UCMJ streamlined the ways in which the different service branches regulated sex and marriage in 1950, the stakes for policing venereal disease and enforcing monogamy and heterosexuality were much greater as the U.S. military began expanding to the farthest reaches of the globe in the second half of the twentieth century.

In many ways, what is most interesting about this study is the extent to which the armed forces' surveillance efforts diverged from similar state-sponsored heteronormative maneuvers to endorse monogamous and racially homogenous marriage in U.S. civilian society. For instance, in the 1950s the paranoia of the lavender scare, which saw the nationwide state-sanctioned purge of alleged homosexuals from U.S. government agencies, buttressed the legitimacy of the military's homosexual exclusion regulations that harkened to post–World War I hunts for servicemen who committed same-sex sodomy.[13] The courts inadvertently challenged the homophobic cultural norm of the times by upholding suspected homosexuals' due process rights, thus paving the way for alleged homosexuals to demand fair treatment in civil courts from the 1960s onward. Although the courts were at the forefront of the gay rights movement in the 1950s, they still enforced traditional views of marriage and family that circumscribed women to the home and idealized men as breadwinners. By tenaciously clinging to heterosexual, monogamous marriage as the fundamental organizational unit of military society into the new millennium, the courts rejected the liberalizing effects of relaxing sexual mores in civilian society. At the same time, they redefined sexual deviance to meet the demands of the digital age, establishing the military justice system as one of the leading enforcers of federal statutes that prohibited the sexual exploitation of children.

Chapter 1 lays the foundation for this book by examining the gender ideologies and discursive constructions of desirable masculinity and femininity embedded in U.S. military laws and regulations and promoted by prescriptive literature of the post–World War II era. Equating what pioneering scholar Cynthia Enloe calls responsible masculinity with specific traits—such as loyalty, bravery, responsibility, self-sacrifice, and honor—the military's official regulations, UCMJ, field service manuals, and propaganda coded the prototypical masculine soldier as a married white heterosexual man who was both a provider for and a protector of his family and country. This brave breadwinner maintained high moral standards in his private life by refraining from extramarital sexual activities that could threaten his marriage. Respectable military wives, meanwhile, were homemakers and helpmates to their soldier husbands and devoted mothers to their children. Much like their civilian counterparts, they achieved feminine respectability in the military community by meeting their husbands' physical and emotional needs, by nurturing their children, and by managing their households without complaint or question. Both the breadwinner and homemaker/helpmate prototypes not only normalized heterosexuality and monogamy but also rendered any variations unnatural, deviant, and morally suspect. Mapping these masculine and feminine ideals is crucial for understanding the gendered context in which military courts prosecuted crimes of sexual deviance in the second half of the twentieth century.

Chapters 2–5 analyze how the courts policed crimes of sexual deviance through the lens of traditional gender roles from the beginning of the Korean War to the fall of South Vietnam. Taken together, these chapters illustrate that the courts' construction and criminalization of sexual deviance during the third quarter of the twentieth century were part of the military's ongoing production of gender ideology. Chapter 2 turns to overseas military installations to deconstruct the military's historic regulation of "international" marriages (or what many commanders viewed as the problematic, resource-consuming, morale-lowering, and morally tainted unions between American troops and citizens of the host countries). Those non-U.S. citizens whom service members chose to marry while stationed abroad carried weighty implications for the racial, ethnic, political, and sexual security of the nation; the morale of the military community; and the civil-military relations in the host countries where these marriages took place. For these reasons, single service members stationed abroad after World War II were subjected to regulations requiring them to obtain command approval before consummating unions with non-U.S. citizens of the host countries or territories. Military courts endorsed such regulations as vital command necessities to maintain discipline and to prevent hastily arranged marriages that usually ended in divorce; however, in reality the regulations served to reflect and reinforce the nation's strict immigration quotas, which theoretically protected the nation from political and sexual radicalism. Whether commanders deemed potential wives to American servicemen as worthy depended largely on the women's perceived physiological and moral characteristics. Conversely, those servicemen whom commanders deemed fit for the particular challenges of international marriage had to exhibit physical and job competence, as well as the financial means to support a family.

In addition to regulating whom single service members married in the global arena, the courts policed the intimate sexual relations of married service members to protect the sanctity of the marital bond between husband and wife as the moral bedrock of the military and the nation's social order. Utilizing the vagueness and elasticity of Articles 133 and 134, legal officials criminalized acts such as wrongful cohabitation, adultery, and bigamy. The courts' unwavering enforcement of monogamy is the focus of chapter 3. Legal officials also policed sexual relations among both married and unmarried couples in an attempt to prevent the commission of "unnatural" and perverse sexual acts including oral and anal sodomy and bestiality. So dangerous was the perceived threat that sodomy posed to the moral righteousness of the military community that the authors of the UCMJ created Article 125 for the sole purpose of criminalizing and prosecuting acts of sodomy.

Aside from rape and carnal knowledge, crimes so serious and violent that they warranted the creation of their own article (Article 120) for prosecution purposes, sodomy is the only other crime of a sexual nature for which the UCMJ contains a specific article.[14] Notably however, the majority of the sodomy crimes that the courts prosecuted in the second half of the twentieth century were consensual acts committed by same-sex partners. As chapter 4 illustrates, the courts wielded Article 125 as a weapon to target and oust suspected homosexuals from the ranks in an effort to codify heterosexism and so-called natural sexual relations into military law. In their efforts to normalize heterosexism, however, legal officials laid the groundwork for legal reforms that allowed LGBTQ service members to serve openly in the twenty-first century.

Chapter 5 explores the courts' regulation of sexually deviant crimes of moral turpitude, or "moral misdemeanors," with Articles 133 and 134. Though this category of crimes rarely involved physical violence, legal officials treated them as dangerous violations of a widely accepted moral code that contained sexual expression within the private confines of one's residence (and ideally within the confines of legal marriage). Interpreting crimes of moral turpitude in terms of marriage and the nuclear family, the courts prosecuted behaviors that undermined both the attitudes about loyalty and morality that gentlemen were expected to exhibit toward their relationships with women and children in public, as well as the justice system's endorsement of natural sexual relations between a man and a woman for procreation rather than for pleasure. Perverse and indecent acts such as the communal consumption of pornographic and obscene matter, indecent exposure and public masturbation, window peeping, and prostitution-related activities eroded both the military's international reputation as a morally righteous fighting force and the courts' efforts to channel sexual conduct into the marital unit. In their rigorous attempts to preserve the boundary that relegated sex to the private realm, however, the courts blurred these distinctions even more.

Chapter 6 analyzes major trends and patterns in the courts' prosecutions of crimes of sexual deviance among the military community from 1976 to 2000. It reveals the increasing commitment of military courts to endorse heterosexual monogamous marriage and privately contained sexual expression as the primary means by which service members were validated as normal and desirable members of the military community in this era. The statistics alone are revealing. The number of prosecutions for crimes of sexual deviance—particularly sodomy and adultery—more than doubled in the last quarter of the twentieth century in comparison to prosecution rates from 1950 to 1975. While President Ronald Reagan's conservative revolution in the 1980s fueled this conservative shift in military courts, the U.S. military's emergence as the world's single most formidable police force after the Soviet Union's demise catapulted military social issues to the forefront of national and international news. As national security concerns shifted from containing communism to preventing terrorism in the post–Cold War era, military justice officials tightened their grip on the intimacies of the service community to preserve the social order and protect the armed forces' reputation for being as morally upright as they were mighty. This shift stood in stark contrast to the civil courts' general retreat from regulating citizens' intimate lives.

Examining the ongoing interactions between law, criminality, sexual deviance, and normalcy during the Cold War implicates the court-martial as a key site where gendered ideals about what constituted respectable military men and women were constructed and contested. The courts' efforts to police the marital and sexual relationships of service members constructed a new category of military criminal—the sexual deviant—whose presence in turn necessitated an expansion of the justice system's responsibilities and resources to regulate its boundaries. By turning a gendered lens on the inner workings of the military justice system under the UCMJ, we can detect another "militarized maneuver," a phrase Enloe coined to explain the subtle yet pervasive ways the process of militarization is normalized and made to seem a part of the natural landscape.[15] Backed by the ultimate authority of the UCMJ, the justice system's surveillance apparatus gave legal officials unprecedented access to the most intimate spaces in service members' lives—their bedrooms and personal relationships. Though the specter of legal repercussion undoubtedly dissuaded many service members from challenging gender and sexual norms, it did not dissuade all of them. At the height of its power and global reach, the military's project of policing the intimate proved too challenging to completely control.

The courts' construction and systematic enforcement of moral and sexual normalcy illustrate the dual purposes of military law under the UCMJ. While ensuring both the safety of the larger populace and the procedural rights afforded to accused service members, the courts harnessed the power and legitimacy of the UCMJ to preserve the military's existing social order against the democratizing effects of class, racial, and sexual diversity as the military morphed into a standing professionalized establishment in the immediate postwar years.[16] The process by which standards of marital and sexual decency were codified into military law and legal practice was a complex one brimming with contradictions and challenges. The court-martial, Hillman argues, exposed the deep tensions underlying the military justice system's competing goals of upholding the procedural rights of accused service members while simultaneously preserving the military's "cherished culture."

In more cases of sexual deviance than not, the courts forfeited their commitment to cultural preservation as they sought to protect defendants' rights to due process, though exceptions certainly occurred. The Court of Military Appeals played a particularly significant role in reversing guilty sentences that resulted from intentional or accidental miscarriages of justice. But where no evidence of a miscarriage of justice was readily evident, appellate review boards (also called convening authorities) and the CMA commonly upheld the original guilty sentences, reaffirming the criminality of actions that deviated from and threatened normative standards of moral and sexual responsibility embedded within the UCMJ and legal precedent.

The process of constructing and enforcing appropriate expressions of masculinity, femininity, and sexual desire had international implications for the United States' status in the second half of the twentieth century. Monitoring the boundaries of acceptable masculinity and femininity in the military community was central to the institution's efforts to stamp out perceived weakness during an era in which the country's international reputation depended heavily on its armed forces' portrayal of strength, courage, honor, and virility. Troops who engaged in sexually deviant activities in the presence of citizens of occupied countries and territories could trigger doubt about the moral righteousness of U.S. democracy. These incidents had the potential to poison friendly civil-military relations as the United States scrambled to win the ideological battle between capitalism and communism. Crimes of sexual deviance committed on the home front could have the equally adverse effect of poisoning patriotism and public support of the military's permanent presence in American society.

The military justice system assumed the responsibility and expense of exercising jurisdiction over crimes of sexual deviance because these moral judgments both helped define what the armed forces stood for and allowed it to control the most intimate aspects of service members' lives. Bringing the surveillance of service members' intimate experiences—particularly those of suspected adulterers, bigamists, alleged homosexuals and sodomites, voyeurs, exhibitionists, panderers, and consumers of pornography—to center stage provides a more complete understanding of the ways in which the U.S. military's ongoing production of gender ideology drove changing constructions of deviance and justice in the second half of the twentieth century.

1

Engendering Military Marriages

In 1959 U.S. Army sergeant H. Woolridge was court-martialed for forging his wife's signature on four of her allotment checks without her permission. W. Woolridge, upon marrying the defendant in 1942, received a monthly class Q allotment from the army for basic necessities of life including food, clothes, and maintenance of the family home. When her husband transferred to Fort Devens, Massachusetts, W. refused to accompany him for undisclosed reasons, though the trial transcript mentions that Sergeant Woolridge likely used the money to "sustain an extramarital relationship." W. chose to stay in St. Louis instead, where she had established a career.[1] Following the precedents established in both civil and military courts protecting the wife as an injured party when a husband's forgery was involved, the original U.S. Army Board of Review (ABR) convicted Woolridge of forgery in violation of Article 123 on the grounds that the allotment checks were strictly his wife's property and that she suffered injury to her personal rights when he cashed them.[2] Dissatisfied with the outcome, Woolridge appealed his case to the Court of Military Appeals on the grounds that the law officer committed prejudicial error by violating his right to the *husband-wife privilege*, or the long-standing common law practice of preventing one spouse from testifying against the other except in cases where the witness-spouse sustained personal injury.[3]

In a stunning reversal of both civil and military precedent, the CMA overturned the decision. It reasoned that "the husband [Woolridge] is still head of the household, and he is entitled to establish a new place for the family domicile. . . . As a person having an interest in the check[s], the accused had implied authority to change the check into cash and to use the proceeds for the establishment and maintenance of a home."[4]

In no uncertain terms, the military high court ruled that in cases where wives voluntarily chose not to join their husbands (and thus failed to uphold their obligations as homemakers and helpmates who received financial support from the military), service husbands could legally withhold and endorse their wives' allotment checks without their permission. Not only did this precedent deprive military wives (and, by extension, their children) of critical financial support without regard for the reasons that motivated them not to relocate to new duty stations with their husbands (in the court-martial transcripts of this era, adultery was the most commonly cited motivation for military wives' refusal to move with their husbands), but it also decriminalized forgery in all cases where military wives chose not to domicile with their active duty husbands.[5] More important, the *Woolridge* case illustrates how court decisions about justice and criminality were inseparable from gendered ideas about what constituted respectable military wives and service husbands.

In the post–World War II era, U.S. political, legal, and social institutions idealized nuclear families as the antidote to political and sexual radicalism. Insecurities abroad motivated many Americans at home to seek stability and happiness through marriage, parenthood, and traditional gender roles.[6] Validated by a political culture that idealized the nuclear family and contained sexual expression within the safe confines of marriage, many Americans conformed to this domestic ideology of containment in further pursuit of the American dream.[7] Conservative politicians played on the anticommunist hysteria to control and contain sexually deviant behavior that undermined the nuclear family and threatened to unravel the nation's moral and social fabric. This domestic ideology provided a buffer against those disruptive political and sexual tendencies, and it served as a response to Americans' concerns about national security beginning in the home.

Ironically, at the same time that many Americans were "homeward bound" in the 1950s, the U.S. military began expanding its presence around the world.[8] Fighting to win the loyalties of democratic allies in the fight to contain communism, American service members arrived in occupied countries not only with guns but also with their families as a sign of the United States' peaceful intentions.[9] Service members and their spouses stationed overseas were not immune to the domestic containment ethos that pervaded the political and cultural discourses of the postwar era. To the contrary, official and unofficial military publications, regulations, and laws echoed the domestic containment ethos by establishing (and enforcing) gender roles for servicemen and their wives to perform while stationed overseas. As "unofficial ambassadors," military officials perceived this gendered performance as a critical component of winning the loyalties of wartorn countries. By showcasing nuclear family values as the moral bedrocks of the U.S. military and the nation it defended, military families sought to demonstrate that U.S. democracy was superior to Soviet communism.

U.S. military wives played a critical role in sustaining this domestic ideology through their adherence to specific gender-encoded habits of thought and action. These traditional gender roles were essential to constructing the image of democratic marriage as the antidote to immorality and as the bulwark of democracy. Embedded within the model of Christian marriage were socially acceptable gender and sexual expectations that ordered military society. The type of family the military endorsed was a specifically heterosexual union between a man and a woman in which the man was the head of household and breadwinner and the woman's role was rooted in the singular desire to please and assist her husband and care for their children. The military's model of heterosexual marriage, which promoted powerful masculinity and dependent femininity, was the sacred medium through which service husbands and their dependent wives transmitted cherished beliefs about morality, responsibility, and social obligation to younger generations of military children.

Service guidebooks targeting military wives idealized heterosexual marriage and the nuclear family by promoting exacting standards of behavior for women in the military community. From the beginning of World War II through the end of the Vietnam War, the U.S. armed forces sanctioned the sale of prescriptive literature in their base and post exchanges around the world that instructed American service wives on how to behave so they would be supportive of both their husbands and the wider military community. Popular enough among military wives to warrant multiple editions, guidebooks periodically appeared in the *Stars and Stripes* (the U.S. military community's main international newspaper both historically and currently) in advertisements that showcased the latest editions. Educating wives on the details of achieving the domestic homemaker and helpmate ideal was essential to the success of military marriages; thus, behavioral guidebooks aimed to incorporate service wives into the military family by controlling and conditioning the affective realm of intimate husband-wife relations. Just as American consumers in the postwar economy gained acceptance in the dominant political culture by purchasing American-made products and embracing the domestic containment ethos, American service wives earned recognition as respected members of the global military community by embracing the quintessential homemaker and helpmate roles espoused in the prescriptive literature.[10]

Regulating the behaviors of service wives was a critical component of the postwar military's attempts to police the private, intimate lives of service members and their families because, military leaders believed, a wife's misconduct could easily threaten troop morale, discipline, and ultimately the armed forces' mission. Wives who rejected these standards (and many did) faced public censure and legal or financial punishment (as in the case of W. Woolridge); thus, they served as infamous examples to the military community of what happened to women whose questionable conduct threatened the moral fiber of their families and communities. The most extreme examples were those military wives who were convicted of murdering their husbands in occupied Germany and Japan between 1948 and 1953. Characterized by domestic violence, extramarital affairs, financial difficulties, drug and alcohol abuse, and loneliness and despair, these cases revealed a darker side of military marriage that wives endured on overseas tours. Two of the five homicide cases ultimately worked their way to the U.S. Supreme Court and successfully challenged the constitutionality of the military courts' jurisdiction over dependent family members outside U.S. territory.[11]

Homemakers and Helpmates: Constructing the Ideal Military Wife

In 1941 Nancy Shea—an experienced military wife and pioneering author of the first guidebook for service wives, *The Army Wife: What She Ought to Know about the Customs of the Service and the Management of an Army Household*—affirmed to doubtful military wives that they were "an important though silent member of the team."[12] Setting the behavioral standard for service wives during World War II and the Cold War, Shea argued that service wives should be helpmates to their soldier-husbands and fulfill the dual roles of homemakers and career enhancers.[13] Being a successful mobile homemaker meant that wives must be expert housekeepers, financial managers, and mothers. Good homemaking infused the wives' more public role as their husbands' career enhancers. Central to boosting their husbands' careers was the concept of feminine respectability, with the service wives' ladylike appearance, manners, and comportment improving their husbands' public image and morale.

Refraining from gossiping and complaining, participating in social functions and the obligations of wives' clubs, and accepting military protocol without question were also crucial aspects of wives' comportment to ensure their husbands' promotions. On overseas military bases after World War II, service wives took on the added role of unofficial ambassadors, modeling respectable American womanhood to fledgling democratic countries to enhance the appeal of democracy. In an era that witnessed a dramatic increase in the number of women who entered the workforce, service wife guidebooks generated a striking discourse about wives' domestic responsibilities that echoed Victorian era separate sphere ideology.

Fulfilling all these roles meant that service wives had to forgo establishing their own careers, enjoying sexual freedom, pursuing their own interests, and leading settled lives. Yet containing their behavior within the military nuclear family and the home seemed an appropriate way to incorporate new wives into the military community without threatening established gender roles and traditions.[14] Guidebook authors pressured wives to conform to behavioral standards through censure, as Ester Wier illustrates in her comment, "Any cause you give for criticism or censure does both the Army and your husband a real disservice."[15] Encouraging young service wives to seek male validation for all their domestic efforts, the guidebooks offered a cheap way to ensure that soldiers had silent, personalized laundresses, cooks, homemakers, and entertainers who provided sexual pleasure and emotional support while still remaining financially and emotionally dependent on their husbands. Controlling female behavior within the military community through guidebooks that pressured service wives to conform to traditional gender roles mirrored a broader containment ethos in the 1950s that both restricted women to their prewar domestic roles and reinforced heterosexual, monogamous marriage as the foundation of U.S. democracy.[16]

For service wives, conforming to the domestic homemaker ideal had its benefits. Accepting the domestic support role earned wives recognition, respect, and lifetime membership in the official military community. The service wives' membership in the official military community afforded them access to military benefits and a chivalrous society where they (ideally) felt honored, protected, and respected, all of which in turn were born out of their ability to maintain enriching, decorous homes amid a constantly changing environment. Embracing the transient homemaker ideal also gained them access to the underground sisterhood of service wives—"a world-wide fellowship of valiant and courageous women"—through which lifetime friendships and support networks were built.[17] That military wives continue to publish (and that base and post exchanges on military bases around the world continue to sell) behavioral guidebooks illustrates their popularity and significance in maintaining gendered boundaries in the military community.[18]

Despite discouraging women from participating in official military business, guidebooks legitimized the supreme authority of service wives in their households' affairs. Calling for a gender balance based on mutual respect and independence within their appropriate spheres, guidebook authors carved out an autonomous space for service wives in the home by granting them full authority in domestic decisions, including those involving financial affairs. Yet these guidebooks also conveyed contradictory messages: they called for women's independence in the home while still insisting they must seek their husbands' validation of their appearance and behaviors. Such messages exemplified the struggle military wives waged in the postwar era to fit into a culture that theoretically relied on women's subservience to men to sustain militarized masculinity yet required that wives be independent and adaptable enough to maintain the home front while their husbands were away at war.[19] By cloaking their readers' domestic independence within a broader discourse that promoted feminine subservience to men, guidebook authors neutralized the potential threats to the military's gendered social structure, which depended on wives' conformity to traditional gender norms.[20]

Transient Homemakers

In 1942 as American soldiers began traveling abroad to fight for the Allied cause, guidebook authors were pressuring soldiers' wives to study homemaking as though it were a business.[21] Warning service wives that "your home is the way to ensure you keep your husband," Shea discouraged wives from seeking employment in order to retain their marital status. Working outside the home would not only annoy husbands who found a "slapdash sort of housekeeping" unacceptable but also rob service wives of the opportunity to make their homes "passionate reflections of [their] character."[22]

Clella R. Collins, author of *Army Woman's Handbook*, expanded on Shea's homemaking argument in 1942 by suggesting that wives should take pride in providing a cheerful, supporting home environment for their husbands as the ultimate war contribution. For Collins successful mobile homemaking required owning a homemaking chest with essential items such as chintz curtains, scatter rugs, good linens, personal trinkets, and photographs for adding the "homey touch" in any living situation. In return for good homemaking, wives could enjoy "natural protection" against the vices of the civilian world, where newly liberated women struggled to earn legitimacy and respect in male-dominated workplaces. By accepting the homemaking ideal, wartime wives acquiesced to the military's desire to keep women out of men's public sphere.[23] By the war's end, guidebooks across all of the military branches instructed service wives to "be good helpmates to the men they marry."[24]

Throughout the Cold War, guidebooks echoed the homemaking directives established by World War II authors. In 1951, for instance, Shea instructed all air force wives to give their husbands "congenial, happy home lives" by being "gentle, understanding and quiet when it would be more fun to be sharp, questioning, and feline."[25] Marine corps wives were encouraged to feel honored because their homemaking efforts kept their husbands' lives stable and secure.[26] Then the 1960s saw wives' honorary homemaking roles infused with a sense of moral purpose. Mary Kay Murphy and Carol Bowles Parker, authors of *Fitting in as a New Service Wife*, captured this sentiment when they argued that good homemaking should be a service wife's top priority because it strengthens and stabilizes the family unit "amid all the chaos and confusion which the transient life often metes out."[27]

As late as 1973 behavioral discourse emphasized the importance of dedicated homemakers to the military's mission. Heloise Bowles's *Hints from Heloise: From the Air Force to Air Force Wives*, which was published in 1973 to acknowledge officially the air force wives' contributions to their husbands' performance in combat, best exemplifies this focus on perfecting women's homemaking skills for the military's benefit. Aimed at providing household hints to ease the wives' home burdens so they would have "even more spare time to devote" to their husbands, this official gift from the U.S. Air Force echoed earlier messages that wives were useful primarily because their ability to "maintain the right kind of environment at home makes any man a better worker and more valuable in his job."[28] By establishing homemaking as their primary responsibility both to their husbands and their country, World War II and Cold War guidebooks established a behavioral standard that circumscribed military wives' activities and influence to the domestic sphere and their thoughts and ambitions to the approval of their husbands.

Persuasive wartime propaganda bolstered the guidebooks' positive images of homemaking. Catherine Redmond, in her *Handbook for Army Wives and Mothers and All Other Dependents*, justified the domestic obligations of service wives as a necessary price to pay "to help protect American women's personal and intellectual freedom, equality in domestic life, in politics, or in business."[29] Contrasting American women's freedom to be homemakers with the forced employment of Nazi and "Oriental" women, Redmond invoked powerful stereotypes of masculine German women under the Third Reich and Chinese women as products of tyrannical dictatorships and communism that robbed women of their womanhood by making them work. While "women's lot in the Orient has never been enviable," and Nazi women's main function was "to breed and rear children, who, from the moment of conception, are regarded as the property of the state," American women remained feminized through their ties to homemaking and motherhood.[30] By highlighting the masculinizing effects that forced employment had on fascist and communist women, Redmond made an enduring connection between American service wives and "true womanhood" that pressured many to conform to the military's domestic expectations.

The greatest reward for being a successful transient homemaker was the honor of being "both buffer and bulwark of strength for her busy husband." Collins's symbols of "buffers" and "bulwarks" underscored all the guidebooks' arguments that male validation was the ultimate reward for military wives' behavior. Indeed, a wife's ability to support her husband—to march "stanchly [*sic*] beside him in all life's battles short of war"—was the high point of her life.[31] As late as 1973, for example, wives were told that "the Air Force is the best part of your future."[32] Regardless of their personal or professional aspirations outside of their husbands' careers, the U.S. Air Force Recruiting Service Directorate of Advertising promoted the idea that wives were valuable to the military primarily as domestic servants to their husbands. Endorsing such traditional gender roles suggests that military officials benefited from the pervasive rhetoric of male validation that permeated guidebooks, perhaps because containing wives in the domestic sphere enhanced the service members' self-perceptions as masculine fighters and protectors.

Expert housekeeping was central to the homemaking ideal. Likening home management to an "important business [that] requires just as capable handling as any career," Shea established bed making, dishwashing, meal planning, marketing, and preparing meals as paramount objectives for a daily routine. Maintaining an efficient daily housekeeping routine was an important component of pleasing husbands since military men "like feminine women but they like functional houses." Functionality from the masculine point of view meant furnishing homes with man-size chairs, solidly built furniture, good reading lamps, their own personal studies to read books, and a well-stocked liquor cabinet. Since wives shared bedrooms and bathrooms with their husbands, authors encouraged them to paint these rooms "in a monotone accented by a masculine color."[33] Despite their obligation to consider the masculine point of view before decorating, the wives' authority in making the final decisions on how to decorate and organize their homes and what meals to prepare granted them a significant amount of autonomy and respect within the domestic sphere.

If efficient housekeeping was necessary to please husbands during World War II, well-kept homes were essential for receiving praise from the military community during the Cold War. In 1958 Wier instructed wives that "keeping up the neat appearance of your home and grounds is extremely important," since women were "judged by outward appearances" in the military community.[34] Shea's sister publications for air force and marine corps wives in the 1950s reiterated the connection between the wives' well-kept homes and their reputations in the military community.[35] Bowles stressed the importance of efficient housekeeping to air force wives in 1973 when she urged them to "think before you clean" and to eliminate clutter, a housekeeper's biggest foe. Reminding wives of the "glorious feeling" they would get the next time they "opened the drawer and found what they were looking for immediately," Bowles stressed "simplicity [as] the answer to our problems."[36] Her inclusion of a blank section for notes in the back of the pamphlet emphasized the expectation that wives should study homemaking like a business. Writing down tips to make their household routines more effective reflected the significant amount of pride women took in their homes. As creative reflections of their own characters, houses were one of the few spaces that did not require husbands' approval.

Managing the family's finances was an equally critical aspect of household management because husbands could be absent for years at a time. In 1941 Shea established the principle of "good husbandry" for service wives to follow regarding money matters. Good husbandry was "a matter not only of spending the income wisely but also of making husband[s] feel happy, both about the income and about that for which you spend it."[37] Echoing Shea's financial management expectation, sixteen years later Wier and Dorothy Coffin Hickey reminded wives that the ability to budget and spend their husbands' earnings was an honor to be treasured and taken seriously because it indicated "his complete trust in you." Because indebtedness reflected poorly upon a soldier's integrity and character, the authors encouraged wives to spend frugally and wisely to protect their husbands' reputations. Instructing service wives that "your husband's entire credit reputation is in your hands," Wier and Hickey cautioned them to "be most careful never to undermine your husband's confidence in the way you spend money."[38] Losing their husbands' confidence would not only reflect poorly on their characters as respectable service wives but also create conflict at home that could "lessen the efficiency of officers" and enlisted personnel in battle.[39]

Guidebooks published in the 1960s and 1970s echoed earlier calls for sound financial management. Murphy and Parker devoted an entire chapter to instructing wives on how to "plan to keep your spending within the limits of your husband's earnings." Covering topics such as pay allotments, insurance coverage, and different types of bank accounts, they acknowledged that "such a responsibility will call for your best efforts," but the financial security in the long run "will be your medal, your security, your trophy."[40] Bowles encouraged service wives to save money by advocating making homemade Halloween costumes, baby toys, and cleaning agents, as well as recycling plastic bags to use in gardens and as stuffing for homemade pillows.[41] Instructing service wives in responsible budgeting habits, guidebooks established sound financial management as a critical component of wives' homemaker roles.

Handling the family income granted women a measurable amount of authority and autonomy. Not only could wives decide on what to buy for their home furnishings, meals, and clothes but also they could do so with little accountability for what they purchased because they controlled the checkbooks and pay stubs. Encouraging wives to establish joint banking accounts with their husbands to ensure automatic access to their husbands' paychecks while they were absent, guidebook authors spurred wives to gain equal access to money and authority in deciding how to spend it. Shea established an even higher standard for wives' financial independence by counseling them to open their own separate savings accounts so they would have something to fall back on in case of emergencies.[42] Marrying a military man was a financial risk for many women because their frequent moves made it difficult for them to establish their own careers and long-term support networks. Building a private savings account was one means by which women could protect themselves and their children. By cloaking their language on budgeting instruction in the rhetoric of male validation, however, guidebook authors assured potential male audiences that they were not encouraging wives to spend money independently.

Disciplined yet affectionate mothering, more so than efficient housekeeping and good husbandry, was the service wives' ticket into the realm of successful homemaking and feminine respectability. Raising disciplined children who were instructed "to respect Army traditions and to comply with Army customs" was integral to respectable military mothering during World War II because children were seen as reflecting their parents' values.[43] Central to good parental values in the military were the fathers' leadership and discipline skills. The unspoken reality, however, was that while the mothers assumed the leadership and disciplinarian roles while their husbands worked and were away at war, the fathers received the credit for their children's good behavior. Throughout her various guidebook publications between 1941 and 1955, Shea argued this point and urged the military mother to remember that any of her children's misbehavior "can cause their father to suffer official humiliation" because poor manners would reflect a deficiency in their father's leadership and discipline qualities.[44]

The message that wives should be affectionate but disciplined mothers for the benefit of their husbands' public image reverberated throughout the guidebooks of the late 1950s and 1960s. Wier captured the ultimate goal of military mothering when she instructed mothers to "guide your children's behavior so that no lack of training on their part reflects discredit upon you or your husband."[45] Murphy and Parker stressed women's responsibility to provide "the security of unfailing love, unharried care, and unreserved acceptance" for their children, similar to the love, care, and acceptance wives were expected to provide for their husbands.[46] Betty Kinzer and Marion Leach, in *What Every Army Wife Should Know*, suggested that mothers combine unconditional love with firm authority in the home to enhance their husbands' promotion prospects.[47] In reality, wives often made autonomous decisions regarding their families' well-being, granting them significant control in shaping their children's behavior to reflect positively—or poorly—on their husbands.

In 1969 Mary Preston Gross applied similar expectations to enlisted wives in *Mrs. NCO*. Instructing them to ensure that their children saluted the flag, stood at attention when adults entered the room, picked up after themselves, and said "yes, sir" and "no, sir" to their fathers and other men, Gross acknowledged that corporals and airmen would not respect a sergeant "if the sergeant's own children don't respect him.[48] Despite other equally legitimate reasons (that did not depend on male validation) for service wives and mothers to raise decent children, prescriptive literature conceptualized the well-behaved military child as the gold standard against which successful homemaking was ultimately measured. Some criticized this female influence on male children, however, and argued against the emasculating effects of affectionate mothering.[49]

Career Enhancers

"While a wife is a partial contributor to her husband's success," Wier warned, "she can be the principal cause of his failure."[50] Good wives enhanced their husbands' careers, and central to boosting their husbands' career prospects was the concept of feminine respectability, in which ladylike manners and appearance improved their husbands' public image and morale. Refraining from gossiping and complaining about the military lifestyle, accepting military protocol without question, dressing appropriately, and participating in social functions—all were crucial to boosting their husbands' morale and subsequently to ensuring their promotions. As noted previously, wives on overseas military bases in the postwar era assumed the added role of unofficial ambassadors by modeling respectable American womanhood to native inhabitants to enhance the appeal of democracy and their husbands' career prospects. Service wives' "unwritten efficiency reports," in which the military community made informal judgments about their domestic efficiency and ladylike behavior, pressured them to conform to guidebook standards of respectability.[51]

Refraining from gossiping and complaining was central to achieving feminine respectability. According to Shea in 1941, "complaining suggests a lack of restraint, self-control, plain common sense, and maturity," or the essential characteristics of respectable ladies. Gossiping even more strongly indicated a lack of restraint because it reflected poorly on a husband's "happiness in his work—and on his choice of a chatterbox for a wife."[52] Pye and Shea warned navy wives about "Lady Commodores, who lessen the efficiency of officers by family squabbles, financial worries, rumors, and taking over the helm."[53] Antithetical to feminine respectability, lady commodores and their counterparts in other services symbolized the unrestrained woman who stirred up trouble for hardworking men by vocalizing their opinions indiscreetly. Through their domineering personalities and independence, which blurred traditional gender roles and undermined their husbands' patriarchal authority, lady commodores posed a fundamental threat to the gendered foundations of the military community. By establishing a crucial connection between the wives' verbal restraint and their husbands' public image, Shea set the verbal standard of silence that endured for nearly sixty years.

Other wartime guidebooks expanded the expectation for female restraint. Stating that "a wife can make or break her husband," Collins juxtaposed tactful and courteous wives with those overbearing nags who were "spiteful, dictatorial, and constantly critical of officers, their families, [and] the conduct of affairs on the post." Such tactless criticism could "injure her husband's reputation, as well as her own." Providing examples of good officers who were not promoted "entirely because . . . the wife was indiscreet in her speech or showed too plainly a lack of knowledge of military customs," Collins raised Shea's standard for a culture of verbal restraint by cautioning wives that the consequences of their unruly tongues could cost their husbands' careers.[54]

Postwar guidebooks strengthened the call for verbal restraint. In 1958 Wier invoked patriotism to pressure wives to refrain from gossiping and negative discourse. Complaining was disloyal to the military because it could create "lasting and unfavorable impressions of service life as a whole." Since their manners, actions, and appearance influenced the impression their husbands could make on superiors, Wier urged readers to reflect their husbands' work ethic and patriotism through respectable physical comportment and dress.[55] In *Something on Protocol*, Virginia Greiner and Charlott Bedrick expanded Wier's notion of loyalty and verbal restraint by arguing that a wife's gossiping and complaining reflected disloyalty to her husband. Since "loyalty is part of an officer's code of conduct," they argued, "part of a wife's loyalty to her husband is in observing his loyalties."[56] Gossiping and complaining also undermined the morale that was crucial to the military's mission. Because "High Army officials pay Army wives the compliment of depending upon them to help maintain the morale of the Army communities and to contribute to their well-being," guidebooks articulated an uncompromising stance on verbal restraint that strengthened over time.[57]

Verbal restraint was part of a larger culture of silence that guidebook authors endorsed to incorporate wives into the military community without threatening male authority. Fearing the challenge to traditional gender roles that could result from women exchanging ideas about their experiences, authors encouraged them not to question the military hierarchy. Articulating the standard message of World War II guidebooks, Shea instructed wives to "accept the Army on blind faith, pull your weight in the boat and in every way to uphold the fine traditions of the Army."[58] In the late 1950s and 1960s, authors continued to encourage service wives to "conform to established rules and customs," implicitly acknowledging wives' potential to undermine the military's gendered social structure if they questioned its stance on females' inferiority.[59]

Nonverbal restraint was an equally critical component of service wives' roles as career enhancers. Through their dress and appearance that signified them as respectable ladies, the wives could enhance their husbands' public image and their own reputations. In keeping with ideals of feminine respectability, Shea dictated that "bare midriffs, slacks, shorts, or bikini bathing suits are not considered good taste."[60] Detailing a wardrobe list of "what Army men like," including "dainty, attractive organdy aprons, lacy effeminate collars and immaculate cuffs, and sleek fit which shows off the figure," Shea encouraged women to select their clothes in accordance with their husbands' tastes. Likewise, avoiding shorts, slacks, and tight blouses on military installations ensured making a good impression on superiors.[61] Especially on military installations, wives were urged to dress modestly and wear hats and gloves at all times.[62] This modest dress code starkly contrasted with the sex appeal of those women whose images frequently appeared on airplanes and in popular magazines.

The reward for dressing like a lady was making husbands proud. Redmond promised service wives that "your husband will be proud of your good behavior, of the fact that you have fit yourself into his new world and that you wear your most becoming clothes and sweetest smile to send his rating sky high with others." Promoting wives as trinkets to be shown off and in constant need of male validation, Redmond concluded that "he may be too shy or too long married to put it into words, but his eyes will tell you when he thinks you are a credit to him—and can you ask for more, in war or peace?"[63] Basing women's wardrobe choices on their husbands' tastes, guidebook authors established a strict standard of modest and sensible dress for service wives who sought to boost both their husbands' careers and their own reputations as ladies.

Maintaining an appropriate ladylike appearance was intimately connected to service wives' responsibilities as their husbands' social secretaries. When arriving at a new base, Collins instructed wives to "put on your best looking street frock, your hat, and your gloves, then sally forth at your earliest opportunity to begin properly your family's social army career at this new post."[64] Central to properly starting a sociable service career was having poise and grace. "By combining good manners with a consideration for others," Wier directed, "your social poise is assured."[65] Participating in wives' clubs and official military functions was another critical aspect of service wives' social roles. In outlining traditions such as the military's calling system in which guests left engraved cards for their hosts and hostesses and the hierarchical seating arrangements at dinners, where the guests seated themselves in descending order according to rank, guidebooks pressured women to represent their husbands in all social activities that could enhance their career prospects.

The wives' participation in social activities boosted their husbands' careers by symbolizing an interest in and dedication to the military lifestyle. Collins argued that a wife's socializing was important "in maintaining a reputation for culture, intelligence, and hospitality in the community" and for establishing "her family on a footing that has increasing value to her husband and her children as the years pass."[66] Sixteen years later, Wier advocated service wives' engagement in social clubs because "joining clubs reveals that you have an interest in your husband's service."[67] As late as 1969 Gross called for greater involvement in social functions by NCO wives since the military would be their husbands' "most recent recommendation and reference" for future jobs.[68] Participating in social functions as well-dressed and well-mannered ladies thus enabled wives to contribute to their husbands' careers in subtle but important ways. Equally significant, club activities widened their sphere of influence from the home into the military community and exposed them to other women who shared common experiences. Social networking enabled women to build female support groups and friends who could aid each other in adapting to the challenges of the military lifestyle.[69]

While guidebooks exhibited a striking continuity in presenting wives' expected roles as homemakers and career enhancers, the rise of the postwar unofficial ambassador role expanded their domestic influence to the international arena. As the military obtained bases overseas to thwart the spread of communism, women who accompanied their husbands abroad became the quintessential icons of American womanhood. The international stage magnified domestic expectations as wives strove to impress upon native inhabitants the democratic ideals that enabled them to be such respectable ladies. Historian Donna Alvah provides a nuanced analysis of service wives' performance of their ambassadorial roles in *Unofficial Ambassadors*. Drawing largely upon issues of *U.S. Lady*, a magazine published by and for service wives living abroad between 1955 and 1968, Alvah illustrates that many wives embraced their ambassadorial roles because they believed they were helping to uplift downtrodden native women who were forced to work outside the home.[70] Yet Alvah's work does little to analyze the guidebook rhetoric that pressured wives to fulfill the ambassadorial role. When did this new role emerge, and what did fulfilling this role entail and mean for military wives?

The expectation that wives would serve as informal diplomats first emerged in the third edition of Nancy Shea's popular guidebook, *The Army Wife*. Published in 1948, three years after the end of World War II and during an unprecedented expansion of U.S. military bases abroad, Shea claimed that "the Army wife is truly a diplomat without portfolio . . . when her husband serves on a mission to a foreign country." Instructing the army wife to be on her best behavior abroad because "she is the focus of all eyes . . . and in a very real way she is representing the United States of America," Shea told her to fulfill this international role "with charm, sincerity, and dignity." Because military wives "have tremendous influence overseas," Shea expanded on this theme and reminded her readers, "we should be extremely careful in our dress to leave a good impression of the American way of life."[71] In 1951 Shea reinforced her message in her book for air force wives by reminding them that "each American is an ambassador to the American way of life."[72] Wier and Hickey refined Shea's ambassador expectation in 1957 by claiming that air force wives abroad were representatives of "American womanhood" who at all times should "put [their] best foot forward as a representative of the United States. Learning the language and customs of the host country, developing patience with locals, and avoiding wearing casual sports attire, shorts, slacks, tight sweaters, curlers or head bandanas, or going barelegged" were a few fundamental ways American women overseas could make a respectable impression. Being a good ambassador also meant striking a balance between accepting local customs while retaining an American identity. "Don't confine yourself to the American colony," instructed Wier and Hickey, "but don't go native [and] remember to remain an American."[73]

Guidebooks in the late 1950s and 1960s coached goodwill ambassadors to be respectful of local laws and customs as a means of befriending natives and converting them to democratic ideals. Organizing programs that explained "the American way of life" and participating in clubs that "improve our relations abroad" were essential aspects of good ambassadorship. Equally important was striking a balance between "conform[ing] to the customs and manners of the host country" while retaining one's American identity. Likening the military bases to "American Islands," authors encouraged wives to travel to the foreign country's interior to show native inhabitants that democratic countries enabled their women to fulfill the true ideal of womanhood as homemakers and helpmates.[74] Their ultimate goal in fulfilling the unofficial ambassador expectation was not only to "try to be a good American in thought, word, and deed" but, more important, to make their husbands proud. By conforming to the ambassador ideal, authors promised women, "you'll be an Army wife your husband will be proud to have had as a helpmate on assignment overseas."[75] The emergence of the international ambassador ideal in postwar guidebooks symbolized the extent to which the country's shift from an isolationist to an internationalist approach was highly gendered. The presence of service wives abroad signified the peaceful intentions of the United States in the Cold War era, and the women's "soft imperial" tactics played a significant role in boosting the occupied countries' opinions of the United States.[76]

Significantly, the guidebooks further normalized heterosexuality (and marginalized same-sex relationships among women) and constructed an ideal of feminine respectability for military wives that hinged upon their appropriation of the homemaker and helpmate roles. Implicit in these roles were a fidelity and submission to one's husband in word and deed, meaning that (among many other things) wives were expected to forgive their husbands' extramarital indiscretions and to suffer in silence when they became victims of domestic violence. When women appeared as witnesses, victims, accomplices, or defendants at courts-martial as W. Woolridge did, judges and review boards measured the women's trustworthiness and credibility according to how closely they represented this ideal.

Providers and Protectors: Legal Construction of Military Masculinity

Ideals of military masculinity were in the making long before guidebooks for military wives articulated an ideal of feminine respectability that was contingent upon a woman's marital status and homemaking capabilities. These feminine characteristics that situated military wives in the home starkly contrasted with the masculine warrior ideals to which military training programs ascribed. Political scientist Joshua Goldstein's exhaustive book on how gender relates to war documents countless examples of how militaries enact rites of passage that force men to prove their masculinity by renouncing weakness, sadness, feminine traits and characteristics, and other qualities that typically were viewed as feminine. As Goldstein notes, "Masculinity often depends on an 'other' constructed as feminine."[77] Cynthia Enloe has long argued that the military needs women—military wives, nurses, girlfriends, and mothers—to legitimize and justify the military's ongoing production of masculine soldiers.[78] The guidebooks targeting service wives are a powerful example of a genre that constructed an ideal military wife to help justify the military's creation of "real" military men characterized by warrior mentalities, mental and physical toughness, and a renunciation of the feminine. As I argued previously, guidebooks for military wives conversely built an ideal of femininity that renounced "masculine" traits such as financial independence and assertiveness and instead encouraged women to merge their identities into the shadows of their husbands' soldier identities. This renunciation of the masculine in establishing the ideal of military femininity and the renunciation of the feminine in molding the masculine characterize the majority of the literature on gender and the military.[79]

I argue in this section that the UCMJ and military courts worked together in the post–World War II era to construct a definition of masculinity that idealized servicemen as providers for and protectors of their wives and children. As the legal code that has governed the definition and prosecution of criminal behavior in the U.S. military from 1950 to the present, the UCMJ has done more than any other doctrine, document, or regulation to codify specific ideals and behaviors associated with masculinity into military law. But what the UCMJ said and how the courts used it to prosecute different cases were two different things. In theory the UCMJ idealized troops as family men who provide for and protect their families. In reality the outcomes of many cases reinforced a definition of masculinity that fell far short of the ideal. Though many of the UCMJ's punitive articles are gender neutral and can be applied equally to active duty servicemen and women (Article 123, for example, criminalizes forgery), others define appropriate expressions of masculinity quite specifically.[80] Article 133 of the UCMJ, for instance, defines the ideal military officer and gentleman as one who conducts himself with honesty, integrity, respect for one's self and others, and self-discipline. His self-control and loyalty to his family mean that he holds himself to the highest standards of moral conduct in public, barring his participation in any crimes of moral turpitude and illicit sexuality. Meanwhile, his loyalty and responsibility to his family mean that he is both a "provider" who supports his wife and children with the daily necessities that a comfortable life requires and a "protector" who ensures the physical and emotional safety of his family against foreign intruders. In doing so, he abides by Article 134, which criminalizes conduct (vaguely defined) that is prejudicial to good order and discipline and could disgrace the armed forces' reputation of being a morally righteous fighting force.[81]

The courts enforced the code's articles by interpreting and applying their meaning to cases involving servicemen who deviated from their normative definitions of masculinity. Through the criminalization of same-sex sodomy, for example, as explored in chapter 4, the courts reinforced an avowedly heterosexual masculine ideal that prized traditional marriage as the foundation of a democratic society.[82] Similarly, prosecutions of marital infidelity and crimes of moral turpitude enforced character traits such as loyalty, decency, self-discipline, and moral righteousness as legally permissible expressions of masculinity.[83] By constructing definitions of gender deviance and criminality in response to behavioral violations that challenged cherished notions of masculinity, the military justice system revealed one of its main functions in the postwar era—that is, to preserve the gendered social structure that channeled men's and women's emotional and sexual needs into the safe confines of the marital union.

For example, the military justice system consistently enforced the provider role for service husbands and fathers by policing the means by which dependent wives received their monthly government allotments. Recall the *Woolridge* case, where the CMA found Sergeant Woolridge not guilty of forgery despite his admission that he had forged his wife's signature on her allotment check to punish her for choosing not to accompany him to his new duty station. The *Court-Martial Reports* have abundant similar cases. Unlike *Woolridge*, however, in the majority of these cases the courts sided with the dependent wives, who complained that their husbands fraudulently endorsed their monthly allotment checks to keep the money for themselves and not provide for their families.[84] These cases highlight the courts' commitment to bolstering the provider role for married servicemen *so long as* the dependent wives dutifully embraced their roles as homemakers and helpmates. Upholding the breadwinner ideal also extended to commanders of overseas duty stations who prohibited servicemen stationed abroad from marrying "aliens" (non-American citizens), or women native to the host countries, when the servicemen failed to provide evidence of their financial ability to support a new wife.[85]

The courts also reinforced the protector role by prosecuting service husbands and fathers who physically and sexually abused and killed their own children and stepchildren. Sadly, the case law is saturated with courts-martial featuring prosecutions of service fathers accused of victimizing rather than protecting their children. Though an analysis of these cases in their entirety is outside the scope of this project, a handful of them appear in the book.[86] Legal officials also prosecuted husbands for murdering their wives, though they very rarely prosecuted the domestic violence that preceded such crimes unless it occurred in public.[87] In a notable case in which a service member was prosecuted for publicly assaulting his own wife, a general court-martial found Lt. Col. Donald E. Downard of the army guilty of "scandalous" public conduct that was unbecoming an officer and a gentleman by cursing, kicking, and hitting his wife in front of fifteen people outside of the U.S. Army Field Forces Officers' Mess at Fort Monroe, Virginia, in 1950. Though Downard justified his actions by testifying that his wife had instigated the incident by flirting with another officer at the party, the legal officials (one major general and seven colonels) presiding over his trial sentenced him to dismissal from the service. The Court of Military Appeals reversed the decision a year later on the grounds that Downard's right to a fair trial had been violated when the law officer instructed the court that dismissal was mandatory if the officials found him guilty.[88]

Other programs reinforced the justice system's ongoing construction and enforcement of responsible masculinity. Commanding officials created the U.S. Army's Character Guidance program (with similar variations available in the other services) for the sole purpose of instilling servicemen with moral values such as responsibility, loyalty, integrity, and an appreciation for family. Providing mandatory monthly counseling to all active duty personnel to strengthen "those basic moral, spiritual, and historical truths which motivate the patriot and which undergird the Code of Conduct," the Character Guidance program taught soldiers "an acceptance of social obligation," "an awareness of individual responsibility," "an understanding of the dignity of man," "the logic of self-discipline," "a respect for lawful authority," and "a patriotic response to our democratic foundations." The foundation of these "truths" was a moral and social obligation to family and cultural heritage—that is, the "wholesome influences . . . from which stem our esprit, and strength as a free nation."[89]

Conclusion

If the strength and esprit of the United States as a free nation depended on the wholesome influences of family and cultural heritage, producing and enforcing gender ideologies that buttressed these wholesome influences were critical steps for protecting America's "democratic foundations." Prescriptive literature instructing military wives on how to fulfill their homemaking duties to the best of their abilities positioned women at the center of this effort. As military families began following active duty service members to the farthest reaches of the globe after World War II, the wives' performance as the homemaker and helpmate took on international significance because it helped show the world why U.S. democracy was supposedly superior to Soviet communism.

By being efficient homemakers, housekeepers, financial managers, mothers, social entertainers, morale boosters, unofficial ambassadors, and respectable ladies in appearance, manners, and comportment, military wives embodied the compromise that military officials had to make by incorporating marriage and these women into the Cold War mission to fight political and sexual radicalism at home and abroad. Their presence, so long as their behavior was conditioned to buttress the dichotomous gender roles the military supported, enhanced the efficiency and morale of military communities by deterring servicemen from committing adultery or other sexual crimes. In turn, the leadership of service wives overseas exemplified to host populations that in the United States, women were treated with dignity and respect (at least in public most of the time)—a true measure of a country's progress.

Meanwhile, legal codes, courts-martial, and character guidance programs constructed a definition of masculinity that complemented that of military wives as homemakers and helpmates. Idealizing servicemen as the courageous protectors and loyal providers of their families, the Uniform Code of Military Justice did exactly what its name implied: it codified into military law a set of rules and values aimed at achieving uniformity in thought and action among members of the military community. The foundation of these rules and values stemmed from the same wholesome influences of family and cultural heritage that served as the guideposts of the services' character education programs and the behavioral guidebooks targeting military wives. Mapping these masculine and feminine ideals is important for understanding the gendered context in which the courts prosecuted crimes of sexual deviance in the second half of the twentieth century by establishing baselines of gendered behavior against which suspected criminals and their accomplices or victims were judged. By constructing and enforcing definitions of criminality and deviance to prevent conduct that threatened the wholesomeness of the family—especially sexual conduct that officials deemed immoral—the military justice system played a leading role in the ongoing production of gender ideologies that channeled service members' sexual and emotional needs into the safe confines of the marital unit. As chapter 2 reveals, however, the courts sometimes undermined their own efforts at preserving the marital unit by denying service members in overseas locations the basic right to choose their marital partners when these international unions supposedly threatened Americans' morality or racial purity.

2

Policing International Military Marriages

In 1956 in West Germany, Private Reese's frustration as a boy-friend and soon-to-be father reached a boiling point after his army commander repeatedly denied him permission to marry A, his pregnant German girlfriend. Reese had "sought vigorously and repeatedly to obtain permission to marry and legitimize his child," but his commander consistently denied his requests "solely because he did not have the $500 which was required by an unspecified 'Command' directive, before a United States soldier could marry a woman with two children." Because A was unable to support their baby in addition to her older child, a German welfare agency took the baby and placed him under permanent custody with an American foster family. After the first sergeant of Reese's unit callously advised him to "resubmit his letter in about five years—it would take him five years to save approxi-mately $18.50 a month to save enough money to get married"— Reese "lost interest" in the army and began to drink excessively. The humiliation, demasculinization, and grief Reese experienced after being denied the opportunity to marry the mother of his child and raise his own son ultimately led to the behavior that resulted in his court-martial.[1]

In Reese's case, the U.S. Army Board of Review—the interme-diate appellate authority over general courts-martial—questioned the arbitrary command policy that denied Reese (and other similarly situated service members) the opportunity to marry and "legitimize his offspring," arguing that it contradicted the army's historic commitment to encouraging and supporting the legitimation of soldiers' children through marriage. In a persuasive call for imposing limits on command discretion of overseas marriage regulations, the board urged:

> We can readily perceive that there are numerous valid, and even compelling reasons why the United States Army must exercise some supervision over marriages of military personnel to nationals of foreign lands. However, we are unaware of any military reason, or any recognized national or social policy, which would preclude or frustrate a soldier's commendable desire to marry the mother of his child and legitimatize his son, unless he could demonstrate "financial responsibility. . . ." We know of no civilized nation which requires such a condition or qualification for the marriage of persons otherwise competent to contract matrimony.

The arbitrary nature of the financial requirement that precluded the soldiers' marriage to German nationals was summarily "so contrary to general moral standards and public policy" that the ABR modified Reese's sentence because of its negative impact on his morale.[2] But despite the board's condemnation of the arbitrary and unreasonable nature of the financial requirement in Reese's case, its decision to uphold the legality of the marriage regulation legitimized (and encouraged) other commanders' attempts to prevent cross-cultural marriages.[3]

As early as 1888, the U.S. Supreme Court recognized marriage as "the most important relation in life and the foundation of the family and of society without which there would be neither civilization nor progress." As a public institution, marriage had "more to do with the morals and civilization of a people than any other institution."[4] Because of the state's power through marriage restrictions to transmit the moral values necessary for preserving a democratic nation, legal officials in U.S. civil law readily acknowledged the state's inherent interest in regulating the boundaries of marriage.[5] For the same reason, the U.S. military had a vested interest in the marital status of its troops. Just as the sexual conduct of married military couples after World War II garnered the sustained attention of legal officials whose goal was to endorse monogamous marriage as the foundation of "wholesome" families, so too did the cross-cultural and interracial relationships between American GIs and native women of occupied countries.

From Germany, Korea, and the Philippines to the Panama Canal Zone, the intimate choices of service members about when and whom they should marry in overseas locations carried weighty implications for the service missions involved. According to a 1981 pamphlet titled "Commander's Guide to Marriage Counseling" distributed for use among U.S. Forces Korea and the Eighth U.S. Army, these cross-cultural unions not only often ended in divorce but also created financial and psychological problems that spilled over into servicemen's jobs.[6] Because the severity of such personal problems tended to lower service members' morale, to degrade their duty performance, and generally to draw resources away from the critical goals of the mission, the army, air force, and navy instituted overseas marriage regulations during and after World War II requiring service members to apply for and receive command permission before consummating their marriages with non-U.S. citizens. During the Allied occupation of West Germany in 1945, for example, the U.S. military's official policy of nonfraternization between GIs and German civilians proved so difficult to enforce that commanders instituted marriage regulations by December 1946 that allowed GIs to marry their German girlfriends and legitimate their children. By the end of the occupation period in 1949, military commanders had approved approximately twelve thousand marriages between American GIs and German women. But gaining approval of these cross-cultural marriages was a harrowing process. Commanders instituted cumbersome procedures to protect "innocent" GIs from "crafty" German women who supposedly wanted to take advantage of the U.S. standard of living.[7] In reality, as the *Reese* case illustrates, these attempts to protect servicemen often compromised the military's mission by lowering the troops' morale and loyalty to the armed forces.

Many service members who bypassed the application approval process received dishonorable discharges and hard labor confinement for violating command orders. Though a handful of service members challenged the legality of these regulations from 1950 to 1975, military courts consistently upheld the constitutionality of these directives into the twenty-first century as "reasonably necessary" measures that aimed to maintain discipline and morale in overseas commands. And though legal critics insisted that service members should be able to choose when and with whom they would marry without command interference, the courts' momentum in derailing this logic drowned out their voices.[8]

The services cited multiple justifications for creating and implementing overseas marriage regulations. Initially, efficiency was the primary rationalization for prohibiting international and interracial marriages. When ensuring the "efficiency" of the troops during wartime failed to persuade a skeptical postwar public of the necessity of exerting command control over international marriages, the services argued that the "morale, discipline, and good order of the command require control of overseas marriages."[9] Offering the rationale that the military sanctioned such intervention to "minimize, if not eliminate wholesale divorce and broken homes which would result if large numbers of alien spouses failed to qualify for admission to the United States," postwar service regulations portrayed Cold War military officials as paternalists with benevolent intentions.[10] In addition to questions of security that arose with military marriages that crossed international and interracial borders, issues of immigration eligibility, state statutes nullifying interracial marriages, and parental dissatisfaction with young service members who married across national and racial boundaries validated the services' unyielding stance on granting overseas commanders the discretion to prevent such marriages.

Though "not intended to prevent marriage, but rather to protect both aliens and the United States from the possible disastrous effects of an impetuous marriage entered into without appreciation of its implications and obligations," overseas marriage regulations enabled commanders to do precisely what the regulations claimed they were not intended to do—that is, to prevent cross-cultural marriages between American GIs and "alien" women of the occupied territories. As the integrity and democratic ideals of the United States were intimately connected to ideals of racially homogenous marital unions and stable nuclear families, commanders believed preventing American GIs from marrying non-white, non-American women of questionable moral, mental, and physical backgrounds was a surefire way they could maintain the "wholesomeness" of military families and the efficiency, morale, and cohesion of their troops while safeguarding the nation from "undesirables." Military officials policed marital vows in overseas commands because alien spouses who were granted U.S. citizenship potentially threatened the moral fiber of the country with antidemocratic and sexually promiscuous beliefs and behaviors, while American service members who abandoned their illegitimate children from these cross-cultural relationships undermined their country's international reputation. In the process, the stereotypes that the regulations perpetuated about potential alien brides as sexually promiscuous, disease ridden, and dangerous buttressed the prescriptive literature's conceptualization of the ideal military wife as the moral linchpin of her family.

The military's overseas marriage regulations contributed to the federal government's ongoing construction of the categories "legal" and "illegal aliens" since the passage of the 1924 National Origins Act. As Mae Ngai masterfully illustrates, restricting immigration through numerical quotas and requirements concerning national origins created new categories of racial difference that immigration officials used to justify the exclusion of "undesirables" (typically non-Europeans) from entering the United States.[11] Military commanders were on the frontlines of immigration control after World War II, wielding overseas marriage regulations as weapons to deter interracial marriages and the conferral of U.S. citizenship to women in host countries. But commanders were not entirely successful in fortifying the nation's borders against foreign women in the name of national security. Indeed, foreign war brides embodied the dilemma of citizenship and the national security state in the postwar world.[12] This chapter presents overseas military marriages as an issue where competing ideas about race, gender, and citizenship were contested and intimately connected to the rise of the national security state after 1945.

History of Military Marriage Regulations, Pre-1950

The well-known aphorism "If the Army wanted you to have a wife, it would have issued you one" reflects the U.S. military's historic struggle to incorporate marriage—and military wives—into its mission. Worried that the troops' competing loyalties to their wives and their country would undermine the efficiency of their wartime service, the army and the navy (and later the air force) established a long tradition of discouraging marriage, which officials believed would hinder personnel from their obligation to commit to the military's transient and dangerous lifestyle.[13] The settled lifestyle of typical nineteenth-century American families was antithetical to the mobility and unit loyalty that were critical to the soldiers' success in the army. As early as 1847 a federal law attempted to reconcile these competing loyalties by preventing married men and fathers from enlisting altogether, though the onset of the Civil War illustrated the law's futility in the face of manpower needs.[14]

Frontier army officials made little progress in reconciling the tension between marriage and mission. From the Revolutionary War through the Indian Wars on the western frontier, military wives were camp followers who received no official acknowledgment or support from the services.[15] Afforded no housing, medical care, or social services, frontier military wives often took jobs as laundresses for the troops so they could support themselves. Between 1870 and 1880, frontier army officials debated the benefits and drawbacks of keeping laundress wives as part of the official army. While some officers argued that the feminizing influence of laundress wives maintained morale and good behavior among the troops, others felt that the laundresses' behavior violated Victorian norms of feminine respectability in a way that undermined the army's mission.[16] The eventual expulsion of laundress wives from the frontier community signaled the army's negative attitude toward wives who supposedly hindered the mission with their familial drama.[17]

As army officials voted to rid its ranks of laundress wives, military justice officials ruled that soldiering should in no way hinder a man's natural right to pursue the marital union. In 1876 U.S. Army judge advocate general W. M. Dunn articulated one of the first known statements regarding the military's uneasy stance toward incorporating married troops and their dependents into the mission when he condemned a commanding officer for prohibiting the marriage of a soldier on the grounds that the army had no authority to interfere in the soldier's private marital business. Without an official statute or regulation, Dunn reasoned, "no officer can be authorized to prohibit the soldiers of his command from taking wives, or to bring them to trial if they do so without his permission."[18] Allowing soldiers to marry without command interference not only bolstered the institution of marriage as a fundamental social unit, it undermined (at least in theory) the appeal of same-sex relationships by channeling soldiers' sexual needs into the sanctuary of heterosexual, monogamous marriage.

Succeeding JAGs supported Dunn's determination that the army had no statutory authority to police the marital contracts of its soldiers. In the 1879 court-martial of a sergeant who was charged with violating General Article 134 for marrying in spite of his commanding officer's prohibition, the judge advocate general outlined the limits of the commanding officers' authority to punish soldiers for marrying:

> A military commander, authorized to grant or refuse passes or furloughs to his command, may of course refuse permission to leave the post to a soldier whose purpose is to become married. A commander may also, if the interests of discipline require it, exclude the wives of soldiers from a post under his command at which their husbands are serving. But while the Army Regulations forbid the enlisting (in time of peace without special authority) of married men, there is no statute or regulation forbidding the contracting of marriage by soldiers, any more than by officers, while in the service. So held that, under existing law, a military commander could have no authority to prohibit soldiers, while in his command, from marrying; and that the contracting of marriage by a soldier (although his commander had forbidden him, or refused him permission, to marry) could not properly be held to constitute a military offense.[19]

This policy was reaffirmed in 1912 when the acting JAG reminded commanding officers that they lacked the authority to punish soldiers who married without their express permission.[20]

When the United States entered the First World War, the military began observing stricter marriage policies. In 1917 for the first time in U.S. history, the army expressly prohibited female members of the U.S. Army Nurse Corps to marry because it determined the women's marital obligations were incompatible with their job responsibilities. Those who tried to integrate marriage into the corps's mission were dishonorably discharged for violating command orders.[21] Though the army placed no similar prohibitions on the servicemen's ability to pursue marriage during the war, whom they chose to marry did become a matter of increasing importance to commanding officers and military justice officials. In response to the apparently alarming rate at which servicemen married prostitutes and sexually promiscuous women, the army criminalized these unions in 1918. Thereafter, servicemen who willfully entered into the bonds of matrimony with a prostitute could be court-martialed for conduct that brought discredit on the armed forces in violation of Article of War 96.[22] The army cited the supposedly deleterious effects of venereal disease and moral vice stemming from marital unions between servicemen and sexually promiscuous women as necessitating its construction of a crime that had never before existed.

The matter of whom servicemen married became increasingly important in the interwar years. In the face of severe immigration quotas of the 1924 National Origins Act, which curtailed immigration to an all-time low to protect the United States from radical and antidemocratic ideas, "alien brides" who married American servicemen posed an unprecedented obstacle for commanding officers. Many brides were ineligible for immigration to the United States, leaving their servicemen-husbands with the unfortunate options of divorce, long-distance marriage (which typically resulted in bigamy courts-martial), or separation from the service and their families to move to their wives' countries of origin. Even brides who were eligible for entry were not guaranteed admission. For those newlywed couples fortunate enough to arrive in the United States together, state miscegenation laws forbidding interracial marriages threatened to undermine the legality of these unique international unions. In response to these challenges, the army instituted a service-wide policy in 1935 requiring all service members—both male and female—to acquire command permission before marrying non-U.S. citizens.[23] The punishment for violating this regulation was denial of reenlistment in the service. The transition from a mostly single to a mostly married force during World War II forced officials to acknowledge service wives as a legitimate, and potentially powerful, segment of the military community. In an effort to draw in more recruits, to retain experienced service members, and to maintain a large standing force during and after World War II, all service branches incorporated married servicemen and women into their ranks, albeit "grudgingly," as historian Elizabeth Hillman notes.[24] But this incorporation came at the expense of the freedom of unmarried service members stationed overseas during and after the war to marry when and whom they pleased.

Upon joining the Allied cause in 1941, the U.S. War Department issued a service-wide directive granting the commanding generals of all overseas commands the discretionary authority to prohibit all marriages between American GIs and citizens of the occupied countries. When the commanding general of the Caribbean Defense Command invoked his regulative authority to prohibit one such marriage in 1942 (premised upon army regulation [AR] 600-780, the revised version of the original 1935 rule), Maj. Gen. Myron Cramer upheld the legality of AR 600-780 and reversed all prior opinions in the interests of military efficiency when he dictated the following: "If in the opinion of the Secretary of War the military efficiency of foreign commands requires the prohibition of marriages by members of those commands except with special permission, a regulation [to that effect] would be subject to no legal objection. To the extent that prior opinions of this office express a contrary view, they are hereby overruled." By ruling that "military efficiency of foreign commands requires the prohibition of marriages by members of those commands except with official permission," Cramer granted American commanders in the global arena unprecedented power to police the private lives and relationships of their unmarried troops during the war.[25]

On the heels of Cramer's landmark ruling, the War Department issued circular number 179 to codify into law the regulation that Major General Cramer ruled "would be subject to no legal objection." This service-wide regulation established that "no military personnel on duty in any foreign country or possession may marry without the approval of the commanding officer of the United States Army forces stationed in such foreign country or possession."[26] Despite such formidable obstacles, American service members married non-U.S. citizens, both European and Asian, by the thousands during the Second World War. Responding to public criticism of the harsh immigration restrictions that prevented American GIs from bringing their foreign spouses and children home after the war, Congress enacted the War Brides Act of 1945.[27] During the three-year life of the act, roughly ninety-six thousand wives, husbands, and children of American GIs entered the United States.[28] To accommodate service members who became engaged to non-U.S. citizens during the war, Congress passed the Alien Fiancées and Fiancées (or GI Fiancées) Act of 1946, admitting more than five thousand intended spouses of American service members before it expired in 1984.[29] With these congressional acts, commanders retained their authority to prohibit marriages between American GIs and foreign nationals with apparently little resistance from their troops.

As the U.S. military expanded to various regions throughout the postwar world to contain communism and assist potential allies in rebuilding their war-torn countries, incidences of interracial encounters between American servicemen and native women multiplied at an exponential rate. When American GIS' requests to marry Asian women reached an all-time high during the Korean conflict, commanders faced an unprecedented dilemma. The existing national immigration quotas made no provisions for the Asian wives and fiancées of American servicemen. In response to the marital dilemma these servicemen faced in Korea, President Harry Truman urged Congress to pass a new immigration law that would "remove all barriers against Asians."[30] Because the current U.S. immigration law made it nearly impossible for American GIS to take their alien brides to the United States, commanders attempted to avoid the problem altogether by denying the marriage requests of most intended newlyweds.

Servicemen who surmounted command obstacles faced the heartache of leaving their spouses behind, frequently in countries where their brides were ostracized by their families and communities for marrying American "foreigners," when their tours of duty ended.[31] Partly in response to Truman's request, Congress enacted the Immigration and Nationality Act of 1952, which removed the barrier prohibiting most Asians from entering the United States. In an attempt to quell any misinterpretations of what the new immigration policy meant for service members stationed overseas, the services issued a single joint directive the following year to affirm that the new immigration policy had no bearing on the commanders' authority to prohibit international marriages.[32]

As intended, the new requirements of AR 600-240 matched the admissibility criteria contained in the Immigration and Nationality Act of 1952. The worthiness of aliens as potential marriage partners and U.S. citizens depended on their moral and physiological health. Upon receiving a soldier's application requesting permission to marry an alien, a commander conducted "mandatory personal investigations," which often amounted to humiliating invasions of privacy, to determine the sexual history, political beliefs, and moral character of the potential spouses. Not only did potential alien spouses undergo extensive medical screening to determine if they had venereal disease, tuberculosis, leprosy, and other "contagious diseases," they were also interrogated regarding their political affiliations with communism and anarchy. Evidence of sexual promiscuity, political radicalism, or (vaguely defined) immorality could result in their automatic denial of permission to marry an American GI. AR 600-240 explicitly addressed these issues.

> [The] mental and physical health of the alien spouse, as well as character, morals, and political beliefs and affiliations, are matters of primary importance since individuals in certain categories may be inadmissible to the United States for permanent residence. These categories include aliens who are feeble-minded, insane, or have had attacks of insanity; afflicted with psychopathic personality, epilepsy, or a mental defect; narcotic addicts or chronic alcoholics; afflicted with tuberculosis in any form, or leprosy, or any dangerous contagious disease; paupers, professional beggars, or vagrants; those who have been convicted of a crime involving moral turpitude; polygamists or persons who practice or advocate the practice of polygamy; prostitutes or persons who have engaged in or profited from prostitution; and anarchists, opposers of organized government, advocates of violent overthrow of government, or persons who are members of or affiliated with the Communist or any other totalitarian party or association.[33]

To weed out potential national security threats, overseas commanders invoked their regulative authority to ensure "proper screening and counseling" of marriage applicants. Such applications were considered incomplete when they lacked character references for the alien spouse in question and physical exam results proving that the alien spouse was free from "active tuberculosis and infectious venereal disease." Since the procedures for soldiers to marry alien spouses were "substantially similar to the processing of request for entry of alien spouses," commanders in the U.S. military's postwar empire established the first line of defense between the American public and the sexually promiscuous (and racially inferior) alien women in the postwar world.[34]

Under the provisions of the 1952 Immigration and Nationality Act, visas were typically denied to alien spouses and children who were convicted of crimes of moral turpitude and prostitution. Upon being denied permission to marry by the commander, the potential alien spouse could file an I-601 application, or the Application for Waiver of Grounds of Excludability, to the attorney general of the United States and request an individual waiver for a visa. The attorney general consequently weighed the inadmissibility of proposed alien spouses based on their individual merits and denied all applications "where entrance of such alien dependents would be contrary to the national welfare, safety, or security." Additionally, the applicants had to show that "extreme hardship would result to a U.S. citizen or lawful resident of the U.S. should his or her alien dependents be excluded from the United States" as a precondition for approval.[35] Alien spouses who were excluded from obtaining visas because of "mental retardation, a history of mental illness, or affliction with tuberculosis" but who were otherwise eligible could also apply for visa waivers. Alien spouses whose mental illnesses or physical conditions were manageable with treatment and did not compromise their otherwise good moral characters were automatically granted waivers because their afflictions were not considered moral in nature or threatening to the security or welfare of the nation.[36]

Commanders also initiated private investigations into the applicants' moral, emotional, sexual, and financial stability. Prior to approving a marriage application, commanders required applicants to undergo counseling with the base chaplain to determine their work ethic and moral character.[37] Commanders often denied permission to service members whom they perceived as lacking emotional maturity, moral conviction, and social and financial responsibility. Because a soldier-husband's ability to provide for and protect his prospective wife and children depended upon his breadwinning capabilities, a commander could delay and deny marriage applications in a case where, according to AR 600-240, the active duty applicant failed to "present satisfactory evidence of ability to prevent the spouse from becoming a public charge."[38] This evidence consisted of pay stubs, bank account information, and any other pertinent income records that could establish his ability to support a family.

Without a universal definition of "financial stability," however, commanders' decisions varied. While some prohibited these unions altogether (recall the *Reese* case at the beginning of the chapter) to prevent alien wives from becoming social welfare recipients, others denied the marriage requests temporarily and instructed the prospective breadwinners to save more money and apply again at a later date.[39] The underlying and often inaccurate assumption that alien wives were incapable of providing for themselves and their children after obtaining U.S. citizenship complicated this process by reinforcing stereotypes of alien women as logistical burdens to the communities that supported them.

Commanders could also deny the marriage requests of all service members whose questionable moral characters raised doubts about their ability to fulfill marital or parental commitments, though the boundary between acceptable and unacceptable moral standards was fluid and lacked a uniform interpretation. The services justified their endorsement of such a policy by contending that a lack of command approval was simply "indicative of probable unfavorable action of the U.S. Counsel and Commission of Immigration and Naturalization." Though rhetorically, "all active duty personnel of the Armed Forces basically ha[d] the same right to enter marriage as any other citizen of the United States in the same locality," in reality commanders could use evidence of moral degeneracy or deviance to prevent servicemen from marrying the spouses of their choice while assigned to an overseas command.[40]

No one questioned this disparity between rhetoric and reality until the precedent-setting court-martial of Seaman Apprentice P. Nation Jr. in 1958. The U.S. Navy–Marine Corps Board of Review (NBR) convicted Nation of violating Article 92 (failure to follow a lawful order or command directive) of the UCMJ because he disregarded the provision set forth in navy personnel regulation (NAVPERS) 15858 (its version of AR 600-240) that he had to obtain his commanding officer's written permission to marry a noncitizen of the United States. Nation's commander of the U.S. Naval Forces, Philippines on April 7, 1955, instituted a procedure that all members of his command had to follow in order to obtain his official permission to marry Filipino nationals. In addition to the general provision that service members must apply for permission to marry noncitizens and submit to mandatory personal investigations, the commander established a six-month postponement after applications were submitted before considering the permissibility of the proposed marriage. Justifying it as a "cooling-off" period aimed to "prevent ill-considered marriages between U.S. military personnel and aliens," the commander granted waivers of the postponement period in three exceptional circumstances: when the applicants' prospective spouses were pregnant, when the applicants were parents of children born out of wedlock (assuming the prospective spouse was also the other biological parent), and when "both prospective spouses" were "of the same race and nationality."[41]

Though Nation's case did not meet the exceptional circumstances whereby the commander could waive the six-month waiting period, he waited six months and three days from the date he submitted his application on July 16, 1956, to get married. On January 19, 1957, Nation married a Filipina national in Quezon City without the commander's written permission. A special court-martial found Nation guilty of violating Article 92 by disobeying NAVPERS 15858 and sentenced him to a bad conduct discharge, partial forfeiture of pay and allowances, confinement at hard labor for six months, and reduction in rank to seaman recruit. A navy review board dismissed Nation's charges and sentence, however, on the grounds that NAVPERS 15858 was not a lawful order. To establish the legality of the regulation, the navy appealed the case to the Court of Military Appeals and asked it to reconsider the NBR's decision to dismiss the charges against Nation.

CMA judges Ferguson Quinn and George Latimer affirmed the NBR's dismissal of Nation's guilty sentence on the grounds that the six-month waiting period was both arbitrary and unreasonable: "For a commander to restrain the free exercise of a serviceman's right to marry the woman of his choice for six months just so he might better reconsider his decision is an arbitrary and unreasonable interference with the latter's personal affairs which cannot be supported by the claim that the morale, discipline, and good order of the command require control of overseas marriages." Especially in cases such as Nation's, where the prospective spouses had known each other for eleven months before considering marriage, the six-month cooling-off provision seemed particularly "broad, unreasonable, and arbitrary" because it made no allowance for marriage of couples "who have known each other long enough, in the normal course of events, to arrive at a deliberate decision to marry."[42] The judges found the waiting period provision was an abuse of command discretion since it granted the commander an inestimable time to forestall the service members' future marriage plans without assurance that his action would be either expeditious or favorable to the applicant and alien spouse in question.

Though the CMA condemned the arbitrary waiting period as unlawful, it upheld the general legality of NAVPERS 15858 regarding the question of "whether the right of servicemen to marry while serving overseas is the proper subject of reasonable control and regulation by appropriate military commanders."[43] Requiring servicemen to obtain command permission to marry fell within the purview of "reasonable control and regulation" since general regulations were lawful if "reasonably necessary to safeguard and protect the morale, discipline and usefulness of the members of a command and . . . directly connected with the maintenance of good order in the services."[44] The assumption that obtaining written permission to marry aliens safeguarded the soldiers' morale, discipline, and general usefulness overseas, however, remained unsupported by evidence. Arguably, the opposite could be true since the likelihood of disciplinary problems arising from soldiers engaging in acts of prostitution, adultery, sodomy, and sexual assault was extremely high among single troops in stressful overseas environments. The commander's denial of permission for American soldiers to marry the spouses of their choice could lead to disciplinary problems among servicemen who resented the military's intrusion into their private affairs, as Private Reese's case illustrates.

The most significant aspect of the *Nation* case, however, was not the CMA's determination of what provisions of NAVPERS 15858 were illegal in the Philippines command but of what provisions remained unchanged. The exceptional circumstances that enabled the commander to consent immediately to certain marriages suggest that preventing divorce was only one motivation for regulating marriages between American GIs and Filipinas.[45] Maintaining ideals of racial and sexual purity among American married couples motivated command decisions as well. Marriage requests from service members who had impregnated alien women were urgently considered (though the *Reese* case exemplified the opposite) not only because the birth of illegitimate children undermined the sanctity of marriage as the appropriate institution in which procreation took place but also because children born out of wedlock were at higher risk for becoming what the military termed a "public charge," or wards of the state. The incidences of racially mixed children born out of wedlock to American GIs and Filipinas (and German women as Reese's case shows) suggested to both the American public and the host populations that American service members were defying the moral standards that they professed to uphold and protect. American servicemen who abandoned their children also undermined the international reputation of the United States as a nation of integrity and responsibility.

Spc. 2nd Class W. Guidry's case exemplifies the complications the military faced in trying to protect the country's international reputation by attempting to control the sexual and marital affairs of GIs in the Philippines. Guidry entered the army in 1951 and met Miss M. Carey, the daughter of an American soldier and a Filipina, in September 1953 when Guidry was stationed in the Philippines. He maintained a regular, though "illicit," relationship with Carey (they were not married) until the fall of 1954 when Carey became pregnant. Prior to his next assignment to Okinawa, Guidry and Carey were married by Domingo P. Aquino, a Catholic priest in Manila. The marriage contract, which was in English, was filed with the local civil registrar on December 13, 1954.

Guidry later claimed, however, that he had never married Carey in the Philippines despite impregnating her and providing continual support for her and their son. He argued that on December 4, 1954, he and Carey had consulted Carey's brother-in-law, who was a lawyer. Speaking in a language Guidry did not understand, the lawyer had advised them to "step into a little room" and sign a paper.[46] Guidry asserted that he did not understand what it was that he had signed; he thought it was "just something M could show her mother in order to get back in her mother's good graces." According to Guidry, because he did not think he was getting married, he did not go through official command channels requesting permission to marry Carey. He did maintain written contact with her and his son, however, as he completed his tour in Okinawa and started another tour at White Sands Proving Ground, New Mexico.

While in New Mexico, Guidry met Miss M. Duncan, a civilian employee at the military post. They married in November 1955 at Las Cruces. Their marriage was apparently a happy one until she discovered a letter Guidry had written to Carey in the Philippines bearing the salutations "My Dearest Wife and Son" and "Your Loving Husband Willie Guidry" and containing "repeated expressions of conjugal devotion."[47] Having doubts about Guidry's background, the former Miss Duncan wrote to his commander, who initiated an official investigation into the matter.

Guidry was court-martialed for bigamy in 1957 as a violation of Article 134. Drawing on the "mistake of fact" precedent established in preceding bigamy trials (wherein military courts held that bigamy was not a crime where the accused service member could prove that the bigamous marriage was contracted "in good faith upon a reasonable and non-negligent belief that the prior marriage had ceased to exist"), Guidry argued that he honestly did not know he had legally married Miss Carey in the Philippines when he entered into a marriage contract with Miss Duncan in New Mexico.[48] Since the prosecution clearly established that Guidry had married Carey in 1954, it was incumbent upon him, in asserting mistake of fact, to show that his mistake was both honest and reasonable. The U.S. Army Board of Review ruled that Guidry's mistake was unreasonable and dishonest both because the salutations in his letter to Carey indicated that he was well aware of his marital status and because the original marriage contract between himself and Carey was written in English, making it impossible for him not to understand what he had signed in Manila on December 4, 1954. With Guidry's guilt established, he was sentenced to a dishonorable discharge, total forfeiture of pay and allowances, and confinement at hard labor for nine months. Had Guidry been found innocent, he could easily have been court-martialed for failing to follow a command order by not gaining command approval to marry in the Philippines.

Guidry's case illustrates the tenuous hold official service regulations retained on the complicated private lives of service members in the postwar world. By ignoring the service regulations that required him to obtain command approval before marrying a foreign national, Guidry challenged the military's authority to regulate his private affairs overseas. Ironically, his private affairs spilled into public view when his second wife discovered evidence indicating that he was already married. Guidry's illicit sexual relations with Carey in the Philippines also epitomized one of the key issues that the U.S. military services' overseas marriage regulations sought to address—that is, protecting the U.S. military's international reputation and strengthening its democratic alliances abroad. By late 1956, according to U.S. Army judge advocates Reitzel, Lancefield, and Ayars, "the number of children fathered by American soldiers in Britain, Germany, Italy and other countries has created social problems there; and has led to criticism by the press in these countries, and to no little concern in this country."[49] Impregnating local women put the integrity of American troops at risk by creating friction in the host communities surrounding international U.S. military bases.[50]

The irony of regulations that sought to prevent servicemen from fathering illegitimate children, Hillman contends, is that those well-intentioned service members who wanted to legitimize and support their offspring by marrying the mothers of their children were often prevented from doing so because of the services' micromanagement of their marital affairs in the global arena.[51]

By 1960 the military justice system had fully legalized "reasonable" marriage regulations in all overseas commands. In the only three challenges that servicemen posed to the regulations in the decade, the courts reaffirmed the commanders' authority to prohibit marriages between American GIs and non-U.S. citizens. In the first of these cases, Spc. G. Jordan challenged the legality of memorandum number 78—the official marriage regulation for all soldiers stationed at U.S. Army Headquarters of Caribbean Command at Fort Amador, Panama Canal Zone—as an infringement on his right to choose when and with whom he should marry. At trial army judge advocates Crook and Love endorsed the services' absolute right to prohibit marriages between American servicemen and foreign women to uphold discipline and morale. In their opinion, service members in the postwar military had a duty to renounce some of their personal freedoms, including marrying nonwhite, non-American women while overseas, in exchange for the privilege of serving their country. The judges wrote:

> Those in the military services must submit to many restraints on their personal liberty unknown to civilians, and many of these restraints vary from time to time and place to place. We do not think that the right to marry stands on an essentially different plane from the other fundamental rights of a citizen. . . . [Marriage], like the right to possess and use property, is subject to temporary diminution by the necessities of military service, and that it is not necessarily unreasonable to demand that a soldier while stationed overseas

postpone the immediate gratification of his desire for matrimony if his proposed marriage would adversely affect his organization, his usefulness as a soldier, or the prestige of the United States.[52]

In consideration of "the impact on tightly knit military communities in overseas commands when one of its members contracts a poorly advised marriage with an alien resident," the ABR argued that alien wives were "undesirables" who would threaten the close bonds of the military community with their potential security risks or physical, mental, or moral "unfitness." Not only would "the addition of dependent wives to an overseas command increase the burden and responsibilities of the commander" but also "if the bride [was] incapable of assimilation, the burden imposed on the command [would be] greater because of the morale problems generated by the presence of an undesirable." The logical outcome of a service member marrying one of these undesirables would be the inevitable loss of an "efficient and useful soldier as a result of his marriage."[53]

While Jordan was challenging the constitutionality of the Canal Zone marriage regulation, the commander of the U.S. Naval Forces in the Philippines (COMNAVPHIL) in Subic Bay court-martialed Pvt. 1st Class H. Levinsky of the U.S. Marine Corps for violating COMNAVPHIL 5800.1E 60. The purpose of the regulation was to "promulgate information, policy, guidance and procedural assistance . . . to prevent hasty and ill-considered unions followed by abandonment of wife or children who thereupon may become public charges." In the typical scenario, Levinsky had married a Filipina woman by the name of A. Hernandez in San Narciso, Zambales, without the commander's written permission. Levinsky appealed to the CMA on the grounds that the regulation violated the due process clause of the Fifth Amendment because Congress lacked the general powers to legislate in the field of marriage under

Article I, section 8 of the U.S. Constitution. As had Nation and Jordan, Levinsky asserted that marriage was a natural right that no military regulation could supersede.

The Court of Military Appeals disagreed on the grounds that Private Levinsky "was not denied the right to marry the woman of his choice, he was only denied the right to marry *in the Philippines* without compliance with the commander's order." Because the rising rate of abandoned wives and children had "an adverse effect on relations between the Philippine and United States Governments," the military's high court upheld the constitutionality of the regulation as "reasonably necessary to safeguard and protect the morale, discipline and usefulness of the members of the command." Reiterating their fundamental rationale for upholding the constitutionality of regulations that granted commanders the power to prohibit international marriages, Judge Advocates Taylor, Brandenburg, and Griffin opined, "The lawfulness of such a prohibition to marry without permission will always depend, in part at least, on whether the procedures for obtaining permission are reasonably designed to insure that only those marriages are performed which are not liable to affect adversely the military effectiveness of the command."[54] The unions that undermined military effectiveness were, in effect, those in which service members abandoned their wives and children and compromised the international reputation of the United States during the Cold War.

By 1961 the courts utilized this logic to settle any remaining questions about the legality of the regulations. In the last court-martial of a service member for violating the marriage regulations between 1950 and 1975, U.S. Navy seaman Wheeler argued that the prerequisite of seeking marriage counseling from a military chaplain to obtain command permission to marry violated his right to religious freedom and expression. In the majority opinion, the CMA reaffirmed the legality of the regulations on the grounds that the required counseling by a Protestant chaplain did not impermissibly violate the sailor's right to freedom of religious belief or the free exercise of religious practices. As the majority expressed it, "However high or thick the wall of separation of church and state, the interview [with a chaplain] does not breach that wall. It does not force, influence, or encourage the applicant to profess any religious belief or disbelief." Echoing its stance in the *Nation* case, the majority ruled that "a military commander, may, at least in foreign areas, impose reasonable restrictions on the right of military personnel of his command to marry."[55]

CMA approval of the marriage regulation was far from unanimous, however. In a vigorous dissenting opinion, Judge Ferguson asserted service members had the right to choose when and with whom they married despite the strict immigration laws or the relative desirability of the intended spouse. Marriage, Ferguson reasoned, simply "cannot be regulated by requiring the consent of a superior officer" because the marital relationship was a profoundly personal choice regardless of its tangential influence on the morale, efficiency, or discipline of the service community.[56] As a result of the questionable constitutional grounds on which the services mandated premarital counseling by a military chaplain, subsequent revisions of the regulation encouraged rather than required service members to seek premarital counseling from a military chaplain before obtaining command approval to marry non-U.S. citizens.[57]

Coincidentally, the services implemented this revision immediately after the U.S. Supreme Court's revolutionary ruling in the 1967 case *Loving v. Virginia*, which asserted marriage is a fundamental right of all U.S. citizens.[58] In this case, the high court struck down the state of Virginia's long-established miscegenation law that criminalized the interracial marriages of white persons with nonwhite persons as felonies. Though originally implemented during Reconstruction to prevent newly freed black males from intermarrying with and impregnating white women, white supremacists eventually utilized state miscegenation laws as legal justifications to prevent the intermarriage of whites with other nonwhites including Asians, Native Americans, Chicanos and Latinos, Filipinos, and Puerto Ricans. These laws also threatened to void military marriages between American GIs and spouses of other nationalities. By overruling all state miscegenation laws on the grounds that marriage (and the right to choose when and with whom one should marry) is a fundamental right of all U.S. citizens, the Supreme Court curtailed the states' constitutional authority to restrict the right of citizens to marry "for less than compelling reasons." Thereafter, any governmental interference with a U.S. citizen's right to marry when and whom he or she desired would theoretically be subject to strict judicial scrutiny.

Loving had significant consequences for the military's future regulation of overseas marriages. Under the threat of heightened judicial scrutiny and accountability, commanding officers were forced to justify the continued presence of the regulations with a legitimate "compelling interest" that superseded the oft-cited reasons that troop efficiency, morale, and discipline necessitated command approval of overseas marriages. The new justification for continued command intervention in overseas marriages made its debut in the 1978 revision of the regulations in the name of "national security." Quoting verbatim the purpose of the 1953 regulation, the primary goal of the 1978 directive was to "protect aliens and U.S. citizens from the possible disastrous effects of an impetuous marriage entered into without appreciation of its implications and obligations." By making respective couples "aware of the rights and restrictions imposed by the immigration laws," commanders sought to prevent the "creation of U.S. military dependents [who were] not eligible for immigration to the United States." An American GI's alien spouse who was ineligible for a visa not only would "pose a logistical burden on . . . the U.S.

military service concerned" but could also become a "possible embarrassment to [the service]."[59]

To avoid these embarrassments and logistical burdens, the 1978 revision enhanced command authority to prevent international marriages by requiring applicants to undergo mandatory counseling by their unit commanders. The serious concerns the *Wheeler* case raised about the constitutionality of the regulations' mandatory counseling sessions with military chaplains (as a violation of servicemen's right to freedom of religious worship and expression) necessitated a revision to remove the religious overtones of these sessions by shifting counseling responsibilities from military chaplains to commanders. The purpose of this counseling session was to educate the serviceman about "the financial and moral obligations to provide a home and adequate support for the prospective spouse and dependents."[60] It is unclear whether the commanders who led these counseling sessions were trained using a specific curriculum to "educate" prospecive service husbands on the financial and moral obligations of being good providers, but the content of these sessions was undoubtedly colored by commanders' personal biases and beliefs about what constituted "moral obligations" and "adequate" support.

This session also enabled commanders to alert servicemen that they could face new career obstacles if they pursued their marriage plans. Calling attention to the "possible adverse effect upon a military member's career as a result of marriage to an alien," AR 600-240 authorized overseas commanders to revoke service members' secret and top-secret security clearances in the name of national security. In theory commanders typically revoked a security clearance when the military member seeking marriage approval occupied a "sensitive position requiring access to classified defense information and cryptographic matter." Though the regulation did not explain which alien groups posed potential national security threats or how such a marital union could threaten the national welfare, commanders could deny marriage requests for "security reasons" without having to "divulge the source of information or other data which would involve violation of security or jeopardize sources of information available in the conduct of these investigations." In such cases, the applicants received only a brief letter explaining in general terms that their proposed marital union posed a potential national security threat and was impermissible.[61]

Although commanders could deny service members the right to marry alien spouses who posed a possible national security threat to the United States, the official policy of the services held that "all active duty personnel have basically the same right to enter into marriage as any other citizens of the United States in the same locality."[62] According to AR 600-240 (1978), commanders were obligated to approve all applications where the couples in question complied with local regulations, the service members gave financial evidence that they would prevent their intended spouses from becoming a "public charge," and the intended alien spouses met all statutory physical, mental, and character standards required for admission into the United States. The regulation also stipulated that the denial of a marriage application was only acceptable when the prospective spouse would likely be ineligible for immigration and citizenship.[63] This disparity in the regulation regarding when and under what circumstances commanders could deny marriage requests therefore enhanced the commanders' authority to approve and deny marriage applications on an individual basis.

The 1978 court-martial of Seaman Parker exposed the futility of the claim that all service members enjoyed "basically the same right" to choose when and with whom they would marry in the last quarter of the twentieth century. In a familiar scenario, Parker was charged with violating command orders by marrying a Filipina without express command permission. Though

Parker challenged the legality of the regulation, given the Supreme Court's affirmation of marriage as a fundamental right in *Loving*, the U.S. Navy–Marine Corps Court of Military Review (NCMR) swiftly approved the navy regulation in the Philippines command on the grounds that constraints on such marital unions were a "lawful and reasonable exercise of command authority."[64] The CMA's subsequent denial of Parker's petition for a rehearing not only destroyed his hopes of escaping punishment and enjoying married life to a non-U.S. citizen but also reaffirmed the legal authority of overseas commanders, in the interests of national security, to deny American servicemen permission to enter into cross-cultural marriages.

Conclusion

Incorporating marriage and military wives into the U.S. military's mission became more complex with the country's emergence on the international stage in 1945 as the leader of the free world. Policing the borders of acceptable military marriage meant that military officials played a political game of exclusion, endorsing stereotypes of alien women as undesirables whom they deemed incapable of positively contributing to the U.S. military community. In the midst of the burgeoning civil rights movements of both racial and sexual minorities in the United States, the prospect of faltering racial borders and sexual promiscuity outside of marriage in international hot zones threatened the moral fiber of a nation whose democratic ideals were intimately tied to the wholesomeness of nuclear families. In the *Nation* case, if sharing the same race and nationality was reason enough for Nation's commander in the Philippines to waive the six-month waiting period regardless of the propriety of the prospective marriage, then the seemingly arbitrary cooling-off period was fundamentally designed to prevent American men from marrying Filipina women and guaranteeing U.S. citizenship to their interracial children. Likewise, the policy that restricted Reese from marrying the German mother of his son effectively prevented the marriage of American service members to German women who had children by multiple men, thus protecting the sexual purity of future service wives. By the time Seaman Wheeler challenged the services' marriage regulations in 1961, legal officials openly castigated the "undesirables," or those potential alien spouses who were the implicit targets of the marriage regulations. Even those alien wives who did marry American servicemen were strongly encouraged to participate in command-sponsored guidance classes, where military chaplains counseled them on Western moral values and the importance of maintaining "high standards of social conduct" in their new military communities.[65]

Perhaps more than any other family policy military officials created and enforced during the Cold War, the overseas marriage regulations reflected the critical importance of the marital institution to preserving democracy on a global scale. Because international marriages could have deleterious effects on both U.S. foreign relations and the fixed racial boundaries that justified the continued discrimination of nonwhite U.S. citizens, military courts maintained a guarded interest in structuring and preserving the military family as America's societal unit on a global scale. This guarded interest resulted in the Court of Military Appeals' stunning consistency in upholding the constitutionality of regulations granting commanders the authority both to prohibit international marriages and to punish violators via court-martial into the twenty-first century.[66] Ironically, these regulations made it more difficult for service members with good intentions to fulfill their obligations as fathers and husbands. Arbitrary designations indicating the servicemen's financial inability to support a wife and children often justified their commanders' denial of marriages that would legitimate the men's multiethnic children.

The services crafted justifications to fit every circumstance in which service members sought permission to marry noncitizens. These rationales ranged from preventing divorce, assuring troop efficiency, and maintaining the discipline and morale of the military community to proactively managing the logistical burdens, the potential embarrassments, and the national security threats that alien spouses potentially posed to the mission. This is not to say that commanders always—or even routinely—exercised their authority to deny marriage requests. The scant evidence available from overseas commands suggests that command denials of marriage were rare and highly contingent upon individual circumstances.[67] But the ever-present possibility of such denials served as a constant reminder to service members that their private decisions about whom to marry carried profoundly public (and political) consequences, which the services used to justify their continued use of the overseas marriage regulations. As chapter 3 suggests, the courts also policed servicemen's extramarital affairs with equal fervor because acts of infidelity threatened unit discipline, morale, and efficiency, as well as the family as the moral bedrock of U.S. democracy.

3

Enforcing Monogamy

On May 7, 1952, on a U.S. military post in Bad Aibling, Germany, army warrant officer B. O'Brien murdered his wife, D. O'Brien, by striking her in the head with a pickax in the presence of their two small children. He then loaded her mutilated body into his automobile and tried to kill himself by deliberately driving into a tree and wrecking the vehicle. Three German nationals testified as witnesses for the prosecution, stating that they had passed O'Brien on the autobahn, saw his wife leaning against the window and looking very pale, and witnessed the subsequent wreck that rendered D dead. Lt. William B. Bissell, assistant chief of the laboratory at the Ninety-Eighth General Hospital, performed the autopsy. He concluded D's death was caused by "a rather severe, presumably single blow on the head delivered directly so as to be received in . . . the right temporal region" and that "such a blow could cause death immediately."[1]

Though the evidence indicated that D was dead prior to the wreck, O'Brien first testified that the wreck was the unfortunate result after a truck forced his vehicle off the road and into a ditch as the couple drove home from a fishing expedition. The same day, O'Brien changed his story when Agent McNine (first name not given) of the Criminal Investigation Detachment interviewed him. Confessing that after arguing with D about his "going with other women," O'Brien "just got mad and walked back into the other room where [he] got a pick axe . . . and hit her on the side of the head." Before loading his wife's body into their vehicle, he hid the pickax under the bathtub and instructed his children that he was taking their sick mother to the dispensary and would bring them candy upon his return. After putting her body into his vehicle, he "drove the car over the bank and hit the tree," figuring that "maybe [he] would be killed in the crash." In Agent McNine's subsequent interviews, conducted to "clarify in his [O'Brien's] own mind just why he had killed his wife," O'Brien revealed a long history of marital discord that was rooted in their different views of sex.[2]

From the beginning of their marriage in 1946, O'Brien "had quite a bit of relation[s]" with D, "thought the world of her, and did all he could to make her happy." A few years into the marriage, however, he "started going with a few women because he did not get enough relations with his wife." According to O'Brien, "he was oversexed and she was undersexed." When D discovered her husband's adulterous activities, she began "nagging" and "teasing" him about his infidelity, further fueling his "running around" with other women. The nagging "was driving [him] crazy," and he considered killing D while they were stationed in the United States. Soon afterward, O'Brien was sent to Germany, while D remained in the States with their children. During the four months he was at Bad Aibling alone, he had illicit affairs with various women to "satisfy his sexual desires" and forged a serious relationship with Capt. H. E. King, a nurse with the Thirty-Second Mobile Army Surgical Hospital. He proposed marriage in the late fall of 1951 and continued his illicit relationship with King after D and the children arrived. Believing that O'Brien was a divorced single father and that D (whom O'Brien called "Miss Kibbe") was just a live-in nanny, King accepted O'Brien's marriage proposal in March 1952 and applied to the Rhine Military Post Headquarters for permission to marry. King's request for permission to marry was granted on May 7, 1952, the day of D's death.[3]

Meanwhile, after D and the children joined O'Brien in Germany, she and O'Brien "had a few relations," which she "just cut off" completely after she discovered O'Brien's continued infidelity with King. According to O'Brien, D's "refusals of relations lasted sometimes for maybe a month, maybe five weeks," until O'Brien had finally reached his breaking point. On the morning of her death, O'Brien "woke up and wanted to have relations with his wife but she refused and began arguing . . . telling [him] she wanted to make [him] suffer." He "started to get mad" and "went out of his head" when he grabbed the pickax. Though he did not make clear what he wanted to do with it, O'Brien claimed he "had no intention of killing his wife. He just wanted to make her suffer, that's all."

On cross-examination by the prosecution attorney, the following colloquy ensued regarding the last time O'Brien had sexual intercourse with D:

Q: When was the last time?
A: The last time was Monday before I did it.
Q: The Monday before you killed her?
A: Yes, sir.
    . . . .
Q: And you felt that the fact that your wife refused to have intercourse at 4:45 is justification for killing her?
A: We started arguing, sir.
Q: What about this argument that morning? Did you get mad?
A: Yes, sir, I did.
Q: Did she get mad?
A: Not that I know of, sir.
Q: She was not mad? You are the only one who was mad?
A: I was, yes, sir.
    . . .

Q: Is this argument what woke the children up?

A: No, sir.

Q: What woke the children, your blow on her head with the pick axe?

A: I imagine it did, yes, sir.[4]

In O'Brien's defense, his attorney argued that D's "continuous carping had driven him insane temporarily, with the result that he was incapable of entertaining a rational intent to kill."[5] Lt. Col. Raymond L. Hack, an expert neuropsychiatrist, negated the question of O'Brien's insanity, however, by concluding that O'Brien "was able to distinguish right from wrong and adhere to the right as to the acts charged."[6] Both the general court-martial and the Court of Military Appeals found O'Brien guilty of the premeditated murder of his wife resulting from his dissatisfaction with his wife's "reluctant attitude in the area of sexual relations."[7] Blaming the "infelicitous" and "wretched" nature of their relationship on the "continuous extra-marital adventures [of O'Brien] to secure that which his wife denied him," the CMA judges set a powerful precedent that protected spouses and children who became victims of their partners' and parents' infidelity.[8]

As if to remind married service members of the punishment awaiting those who murdered their partners over adulterous adventures, the *Stars and Stripes* ran a story on July 31, 1954, informing the U.S. military community overseas that O'Brien "will be hanged at the Kansas State Penitentiary at Lansing" the following day. After learning that President Dwight D. Eisenhower had approved his death sentence on July 9, O'Brien "declined his privilege of taking recourse through the Federal courts through habeas-corpus proceedings" and only requested that his body be donated to the University of Kansas Medical Center.[9] In an international hot zone where the rivalry between communist East Germany and democratic West Germany gained global attention and significance, O'Brien's death sentence for adultery-related spousal murder symbolized the military justice system's commitment to enforcing monogamy and justice and to protecting the wholesome influences of family at all costs.

Preserving marriage between one man and one woman was a critical aspect of the postwar U.S. military's strategy to control the morality and sexual intimacy of its service members. It was also, according to historian Nancy Cott, one of the primary means by which U.S. civil courts transmitted democratic values and constituted an ideal citizenry from the founding of the republic to the end of the twentieth century. Believing that marriage between one man and one woman was essential to the creation and maintenance of a republican government, America's founders grounded the structure of the democracy on the principle of monogamy. Through its promotion and enforcement of the heterosexual, monogamous model, the U.S. government reinforced gender, racial, and class hierarchies by reserving the privileges of "whiteness" and citizenship to couples who conformed to marital norms, effectively wielding marriage as an institutional tool of social control to exclude African Americans, Asians, interracial couples, and same-sex couples from the body politic. Not only were marriage laws and marital status embedded in public policies that controlled immigration, access to citizenship, military service, tax benefits, property ownership, welfare, sexuality, and reproduction but also the assumption of female economic dependency (based on the system of coverture) embedded in the structure of the marriage ideal contributed to women's economic and political subordination well into the twentieth century.[10]

The services idealized heterosexual, monogamous marriage as the means through which U.S. democratic values were transmitted, and legal officials utilized Articles 133 and 134 of the UCMJ to prosecute myriad forms of marital infidelity that threatened the singular devotion between husbands and wives. Criminalizing actions that the UCMJ vaguely defined as prejudicial to good order and discipline and as unbecoming an officer and a gentleman, Articles 133 and 134 functioned similarly to the elastic clause (Article I, section 8, clause 18) of the U.S. Constitution in that their application could be expanded and retracted to fit multiple and unforeseen circumstances. During the Cold War, legal officials and commanding officers harnessed the elasticity of these articles in a majority of cases to prosecute servicemen who committed sexually deviant crimes. Sodomy was the only exception. Its threat to heterosexuality was so great that the creators of the UCMJ assigned the crime its own punitive article, Article 125.[11]

Articles 133 and 134 were the two most important weapons with which legal officials enforced marital monogamy during the Cold War. They targeted bigamy, adultery, wrongful cohabitation (a lesser form of adultery where a man and woman lived as husband and wife without direct evidence of illicit sexual relations), and alienation of affections cases, where servicemen destroyed the marital bonds of others by attempting to divert the dependent wives' love for their soldier-husbands. As the O'Brien case illustrates, the courts also heard tragic cases of spousal murder rooted in adulterous liaisons. Though an untold story, the justice system's ongoing (and sometimes evasive) efforts to enforce monogamy in the post–World War II military community were central to constructing notions of criminality, justice, and gender and sexual deviance that defined the parameters of the military's social organization at the height of its global expansion.

Sanctifying Marriage in Military Law: The Husband-Wife Privilege

The military justice system played an integral role in incorporating marriage into the military's mission in the postwar world by endorsing marriage as a sacred institution worth preserving at all costs. One of the key ways the courts sanctified marriage was by codifying into law the sacred and confidential nature of the husband-wife relationship.[12] As noted previously, the husband-wife privilege held that any communication between spouses was protected from becoming evidence at trial where there was "confidential disclosure or communication the publication of which would betray conjugal confidence and trust or tend to produce family discord."[13] To sustain "the confidence which must exist in order to create and maintain mutual and happy relations and fulfill the purposes of marriage," military courts defended the husband-wife privilege as a "necessary [measure] to preserve . . . the relationship of husband and wife."[14]

The military's endorsement of the husband-wife evidentiary privilege originated in American common law, where civil court judges historically considered a wife to be an incompetent witness at trials either for or against her husband unless she sustained physical injuries from her husband. In the event that an injured wife petitioned a civil court seeking relief from her husband's maltreatment, she could not initiate the proceedings on her own; rather, a reputable man with whom she had a familial connection—usually a father, brother, or uncle who could vouch for the injured woman's credibility—had to represent her. Stemming from the age-old system of coverture, in which women's legal identities were literally "covered" by their fathers, husbands, brothers, or sons, the courts' endorsement of the legal incompetency of wives ultimately made marriage the primary means through which men attained legal and social control over women. The view that wives were incompetent to testify both for and against their husbands went unchallenged in U.S. legal history until 1933, more than a decade after women of Anglo-Saxon heritage in the United Kingdom achieved suffrage.[15]

The tide began to change for wives in the 1933 landmark case *Funk v. United States*, where the U.S. Supreme Court overturned the ancient common law rule that disqualified wives from testifying as competent witnesses in trials involving their husbands. Claiming the authority to make such a revolutionary legal change in the absence of congressional legislation that either modified the old rule or directed federal courts to follow state laws on the subject, the Supreme Court abandoned the disqualification as an "outworn and antiquated rule of the past."[16] Since the court's 1933 ruling, federal courts have consistently held that wives were competent to testify in support of their husbands because such testimony strengthened the marital bonds between husbands and wives. On the question of allowing wives to testify against their husbands, however, civil courts remained reluctant to give wives an unconditional legal voice of their own. Instead of leaving husbands legally vulnerable to their wives' uninhibited and usually damning testimony, civil courts placed restrictions on when wives' adversarial testimony against their husbands would be permissible.

Following the spirit of an 1887 congressional statute that permitted a wife's adversarial testimony only in cases of bigamy, polygamy, and wrongful cohabitation, civil courts in the era after the Supreme Court's landmark *Funk* ruling endorsed the practice of allowing wives to testify against their husbands only when the husbands' offenses involved infidelity, which was injurious to the spouse and to the sanctity of the marital union. In all other criminal cases, however, civil courts continued the historic pattern of silencing wives by deeming any communication between the spouses during the marriage as confidential and hence impermissible as evidence at trial. The Supreme Court supported the civil courts' stance on the benefits of the privilege (despite its 1933 ruling making wives competent witnesses at their husbands' trials) when it rejected a government plea to abandon the rule as inappropriate in criminal trials in *Hawkins v. United States* in 1958. The husband-wife privilege, the Supreme Court rationalized, was historically legitimate because it was based on the "persistent instincts of several centuries" during which public policy has favored the maintenance of the family relationship for the public welfare.[17] In upholding the constitutionality of the husband-wife privilege, the Supreme Court ultimately aimed to prevent the dissolution of the marital union that might result from the admission of adversarial testimony by one spouse against another.

The newly formed military justice system under the Uniform Code of Military Justice promulgated the Supreme Court's views on the sanctity of heterosexual, monogamous marriage by enforcing the husband-wife privilege among military couples to "foster and encourage the marital relationship as long as there [was] hope for reconciliation."[18] CMA chief judge Quinn held that the rule that a wife cannot testify against her husband was "one of the legal rules best known to the public [because it] is founded upon the venerable and ancient policy of the state to avoid possible destruction of the marital bond by pitting a wife against a husband, in a trial in which *his* liberty is at stake" (italics added).[19] The dual purpose of the military justice system's observance of the husband-wife privilege was not only to "foster private relationships between husband and wife, but also to advance the public interest."[20] In upholding the husband-wife privilege, military courts protected the confidential nature of husband-wife communication from public scrutiny at court-martial by preventing counsel from using the private communication between a husband and wife as evidence against either party.

Paragraph 148e of the *Manual for Courts-Martial* (MCM) designated specific sexual crimes that, when committed by one spouse against another, nullified the accused spouse's right to the privilege prohibiting the use of the injured spouse's testimony. Included among the crimes the MCM originally deemed injurious to the receiving spouse (usually the wife) and the marital relationship were assault and battery inflicted upon the wife by the husband, bigamy, polygamy, wrongful cohabitation, abandonment of wife and children or failure to support them, pandering or prostitution of the wife for profit, and forgery of the wife's signature. Mirroring the 1918 and 1929 civil cases in Iowa and Colorado in which judges added adultery to the list of spousal injury crimes, the Court of Military Appeals added adultery to the list of crimes deemed injurious to military spouses in the 1956 case *United States v. Leach*.[21] Sympathizing with the distress aggrieved spouses experienced from their partners' adulterous affairs, the CMA expanded the definition of *injury* beyond the physical injuries that wives sustained at the hands of their husbands' maltreatment to include the "mental suffering arising from violations of the marriage relationship."[22]

The MCM denied the right of accused husbands to invoke the privilege in all cases where, according to CMA judge Latimer, "the offender has, to all intents and purposes, largely destroyed the relationship he seeks so ardently to protect [by invoking his right to the husband-wife privilege that would ban his wife's testimony against him]. By [the] accused's own misbehavior, he has not only injured his wife, he has undermined the family unit which is one of the cornerstones of society. Not only does the wife have an interest in it being uninterrupted by his transgressions, each state and the country as a whole are directly concerned with its stability."

To "protect the marital relationship from being disrupted" and to prevent wives from becoming "the instrument[s] through which the[ir] husbands are condemned," military courts also granted witness-spouses the option of refusing to testify against their husbands.[23] Countless numbers of service wives invoked their right not to testify against their husbands at courts-martial during the Cold War, even in cases where the facts established indisputable evidence that the crimes their husbands were convicted of inflicted substantial physical and mental injuries on both them and their children.

Military courts consistently enforced the husband-wife privilege at courts-martial during the Cold War, often at the expense of punishing child sex offenders. In the 1958 case of U.S. Army sergeant W. Benn, for example, the board of review overturned his guilty conviction because the admission of his wife's testimony at the original trial violated Benn's right to assert the husband-wife privilege. Benn was found guilty of attempted carnal knowledge and indecent sexual acts with a minor female. In a devastating blow to Benn's wife, the convening authorities ruled that "however disgraceful, disgusting and degrading" the offenses of attempted carnal knowledge and of committing lewd and lascivious acts with a minor can be considered, these offenses "do not injure the wife in her marital relationship so as to permit her testimony against her husband at his trial for such offenses."[24]

In a similar case in 1963, the CMA overturned the ruling by the U.S. Air Force Board of Review (AFBR) that a father's sexual abuse of his biological child resulted in an injury to the wife. In this case, Staff Sgt. J. Massey was charged with two counts of carnal knowledge of his nine-year-old daughter and two additional counts of indecent liberties with her. Arguing that "the criminal violation of her minor child would cause as great, if not greater, mental suffering to the mother [Massey's wife] as would be caused by the infliction of a simple assault upon her own person," the AFBR challenged the logic of the *Benn* case, which held that the sexual molestation of a minor child neither injured the wife nor permitted her to testify against her husband at trial. In the review board's opinion, to determine that Massey's molestation of his natural daughter did not injure his wife "would give effective license to a degenerate father to wantonly abuse his minor child, even in the very presence of his wife, and then escape punishment in those cases where because of young age or insufficient understanding, the injured child could not testify as to the wrong inflicted upon it."[25]

On appeal to the CMA for relief from what Massey's counsel deemed a violation of his right to assert the husband-wife privilege, the presiding judges upheld Massey's right to the privilege on the grounds that his wife's testimony was inadmissible, for she was not directly injured by Massey's molestation of her natural daughter. The judges reasoned that incestuous carnal knowledge, or the rape of a minor female relative, did not constitute direct injury to the wife because the injury was not a "palpable invasion of, or injury to, the interests of [Massey's wife]." In seeking "something more than the reprehensibility of the accused's misconduct and the outraged sensibilities of his wife" to justify denying Massey his right to the husband-wife privilege, the CMA prioritized the protection of an accused child molester's right to the husband-wife privilege over the protection of a child victim of heinous sexual crimes.

The CMA did not reach the *Massey* decision unanimously, however. Chief Judge Quinn, in his dissenting opinion, castigated his judicial peers for their strict definition of what constituted "direct injury" to the witness-spouse in cases where the accused spouse sexually assaulted the natural child of the witness-spouse. The *Manual for Courts-Martial*, Quinn argued, "unmistakably contemplates that an injury perpetrated by the defendant-spouse upon a child of the marriage is an injury to the witness-spouse." Citing the U.S. Supreme Court's 1958 ruling in *Hawkins v. United States*, which established that the treatment of children formed a critical piece of the decision to deny the privilege to an accused spouse, Quinn unequivocally prioritized the swift prosecution of child sex offenders with the testimony of their injured spouses over asserting the privilege of confidential spousal communication in an attempt to "shield the marital union" and "foster family peace."[26]

Given that the military courts held the sexual molestation of a natural daughter did not sustain direct injury to the witness-spouse, then neither did the same offense against adopted children. U.S. Air Force master sergeant P. Nees's case illustrates where the military courts' exertion of the husband-wife privilege to attempt a marital reconciliation between warring spouses over adopted children failed to prevent divorce. After sixteen years of marriage, Mrs. Nees divorced her husband after initiating court-martial proceedings against him at the request of M, their adopted Japanese daughter, in 1968. M explained to her mother in sordid detail the numerous instances where Mr. Nees had "bothered" her.

After moving to Florida to separate herself and M from the situation, Mrs. Nees exchanged a few letters with her husband in which he admitted that he was "completely guilty of any and every charge . . . short of murder."[27] At the original trial, the presiding law officer admitted these letters into evidence as Nees's confession of his guilt. On appeal the CMA dismissed the charges against Nees and ordered a rehearing of his trial because it found the letters between Nees and his wife were confidential and thus inadmissible as evidence. Rather than convict a child sex offender who admitted his guilt, the CMA instead reiterated the general view held by military courts that the sacred and confidential nature of husband-wife communication would be protected at all costs—even at the expense of child victims of sexual abuse.

Children scarred by sexual abuse were not the only victims whose well-being went unprotected in military courts as they sought to advance the public interest by upholding the husband-wife privilege. In their efforts to protect the confidentiality and sanctity of marital communication, military courts also left military wives who were subjected to domestic violence without legal recourse. As one judge candidly explained:

> Certainly, not all husbands and wives are paragons of patience, restraint, and understanding; if they were, the rates of divorce and separation would not be as high as they are.

But love, especially in the marital relationship, contemplates a turn of the other cheek. Matthew 5: 39 [*sic*]. The will and the desire to continue the marriage, despite the infliction of some injury by one spouse upon the other, are not only for those who believe in the sacramental nature of matrimony. European psychologist, Ignace Lepp, has pointed out that marriage possesses a strong "sociological value."[28]

Because the sociological value of marriage as a tool of social control in the military community was so high, judges encouraged military wives to turn the other cheek. As referenced in Judge Quinn's opinion, "It is certainly much more desirable, especially if there are children involved, that she remain in a united household with her husband, in spite of any passing injury to her, if the husband otherwise fulfills his marital responsibilities and obligations."[29] The passing injury in the aforementioned case came from Airman 2nd Class J. Moore's repeated violent beatings of his pregnant wife. Preserving the husband-wife privilege in this case was more important than protecting Moore's wife from domestic violence, as the CMA made clear when it reversed Moore's guilty conviction for assault and battery. It did so on the grounds that his rights to a fair trial were violated when his wife was forced to testify against him, although her testimony clearly indicated that she was the injured recipient of her spouse's rage.

In an equally candid example of the military justice system's strict adherence to upholding the husband-wife privilege at the expense of injury to the wife, U.S. Army private H. Parker was court-martialed for committing homosexual sodomy with another man. On appeal the Court of Military Appeals dismissed the charges against Parker, arguing that his wife's testimony about the homosexual act should not have been admitted at the original trial despite the injury such infidelity inflicted upon her.[30] Ultimately, countless married servicemen escaped punishment for crimes of marital infidelity and child sexual abuse in the courts' herculean efforts to honor the husband-wife privilege. The military courts retained an avid and devoted interest in protecting the marital union between husbands and wives as the cornerstone of society and the bedrock of a democratic, free nation, even when evidence proved beyond a reasonable doubt that the accused husbands were guilty of the crimes for which they were charged.

Alienation of Affection Cases

Military courts enforced the sanctity of heterosexual, monogamous marriage not only by upholding the husband-wife privilege, which (theoretically) protected the intimacy of the marital relationship from outside interference, but also by punishing servicemen for inducing married women to be unfaithful to their service husbands. As one of two cases of this kind to come under the purview of the Uniform Code of Military Justice, U.S. Air Force captain R. Hanna was prosecuted in 1952 for conduct unbecoming an officer by "wrongfully seducing another service man's wife."[31] Hanna began his criminal course when he met S. Druian, wife of Captain Druian, in Great Falls, Montana, in 1950. Captain Hanna and Mrs. Druian forged a close relationship after her husband was sent on a remote tour to the Far East for roughly one year, after which Hanna's wife filed for and received an interlocutory decree of divorce. At trial Captain Druian presented fifteen love letters between Hanna and Mrs. Druian as evidence that Hanna tried to persuade Mrs. Druian to quit her marriage and be with him. One of the letters detailed a six-bedroom home that Hanna had purchased in Boise, Idaho, near Mountain Home Air Force Base in a successful effort to entice Mrs. Druian to leave Guam, where she then resided with her husband and four-year-old son. The U.S. Air Force Review Board dismissed the charge against Hanna, however, on the grounds that his rights to due process were violated during the trial.

Claims of seduction and enticement toward immorality in the case of *United States v. Hanna* were rooted in the ancient Roman legal precept that men who owned slaves and servants held property interests in their slaves' bodies and sexualities, thus allowing masters to sue someone who injured his slaves and servants for their loss of service. By the mid-eighteenth century, English common law had expanded the scope of men's propertied interests in seduction suits to include the sexual defilement of their wives and daughters.[32] Seduction suits (also known as alienation of affections, enticement, breach of promise to marry, and criminal conversation suits) became so commonplace in the United States by the mid-nineteenth century that the expansive body of case law dealing with the complex issues of enticement and seduction became popularly known as the "heart balm" statutes. Between 1866 and the end of the 1930s, every state except Louisiana had adopted similar statutes recognizing a man's legal right to protect his interests in the bodies and sexual activities of his wife and daughters. In the first military prosecution of its kind, the army court-martialed an officer named Sheridan for this crime in 1926.[33]

Both military and civilian proponents of the heart balm acts argued that their main goal was to protect the sanctity of marriage and the family by deterring immoral behavior and by shielding emotionally vulnerable women and children from the evil temptations of wayward men. Although the AFBR dismissed Hanna's charge due to procedural error, by hearing the case the board honored centuries of English and U.S. common law precedent that criminalized the action of seducing another man's wife. What is more, the *Hanna* precedent firmly established the military justice system's exclusive jurisdiction over future seduction cases that threatened the marital bond between servicemen and their wives, ironically at the dawn of an era that witnessed a drastic decline in state support of the heart balm acts.

The tide began to turn against civil seduction suits in mid-twentieth-century U.S. common law (and at the end of Captain Hanna's court-martial) when these claims had become such a common weapon of blackmail and extortion that fifteen states overturned the heart balm acts by 1952. Indeed, the majority of states that had initially passed the heart balm acts in the late nineteenth century overturned them by the end of the twentieth century for this reason. But despite the increasing danger that such a suit would be used for blackmail or extortion, a handful of states—as well as the newly revised military justice system under the UCMJ—reserved jurisdiction over seduction cases in a continued effort to protect the sanctity of the marital union and the nuclear family against the moral degradation accompanied by a wife's fall from grace.

In an unforgettable extortion case that went to court-martial in 1965, U.S. Air Force master sergeant L. Lyon was acquitted of extortion charges against the plaintiff, whom Lyon had caught having sex with his wife. Staff Sgt. J. Williams, the alleged victim who filed the charges against Lyon, forged an illicit relationship with Lyon's wife after meeting her at the base commissary. After giving Mrs. Lyon a diamond engagement ring and convincing her to leave her husband, Williams confronted Lyon and offered him a thousand dollars to cover the cost of obtaining a divorce from Mrs. Lyon so that he might marry her instead. Williams brought extortion charges against Lyon in the midst of this saga when, after supposedly giving Lyon the agreed-upon amount of money, Lyon refused to acknowledge the payment and continued to demand more money for damages. The general court-martial found Lyon guilty of extortion and sentenced him to a bad-conduct discharge, confinement at hard labor for eight months, and reduction to the grade of airman basic.

On appellate review, however, the CMA dismissed the charges against Lyon entirely, sympathizing with the unfortunate circumstances that led his wife astray. Judge Ferguson described the case as "strange," "perplexing," and one in which "the alleged 'victim' is painted as an adulterer, while the accused appears to have been an injured husband of previously impeccable reputation, whose long and honorable service in the United States Air Force has earned the merited praise of his superiors."[34] In spite of evidence strongly suggesting that Lyon was indeed guilty of extortion, Judges Ferguson, Quinn, and Kilday unanimously agreed that the real victim was Lyon, whose marital union was so irreparably damaged by Williams's successful attempts to alienate the affections of Mrs. Lyon that "causing him [Lyon] to suffer through the harassment of a rehearing is not justified."[35]

It is interesting to note here that the entire premise of alienation of affections cases was based on the courts' assumption that married women were passive victims of seduction who could not resist the advances of an illicit paramour. Mrs. Lyon and Mrs. Druian were similarly presented in the court transcripts as objects of affection between two men. Male judges, plaintiffs, and defendants talked about the women with a language of ownership and territoriality that neither afforded the women agency in choosing their sexual partners nor acknowledged the husbands' responsibility for contributing to their wives' estrangement. Reading these trial records against the grain (that is, putting ourselves in the women's shoes), however, offers a different perspective. Rather than becoming complacent in unhappy marriages, Mrs. Lyon and Mrs. Druian challenged the meek and faithful military wife ideal espoused by the guidebooks of the era and actively sought relationships that brought them sexual and probably emotional fulfillment.

Similar to the language used by the CMA in *Lyon*, civil courts in those states that maintained jurisdiction over seduction cases sympathized not with the victims of extortion but rather with the aggrieved husbands or fathers of the seduced women. In the

1999 case of *C.M. v. J.M.*, for instance, the New Jersey Superior Court justified its continued recognition of seduction claims by parents (mothers included) in an attempt to "recompense an aggrieved parent for the consequent degradation, mortification, and wounded feelings visited upon [the daughter] as well as upon her parents stemming from the child's loss of chastity."[36] As recently as 2000, the Utah Court of Appeals upheld a husband's right to damages incurred by the defendant when he successfully induced the plaintiff's wife "to surrender [her] chastity and virtue."[37] Reasoning that "the protection of love, society, companionship, and comfort form the foundation of a marriage and give rise to the unique bonding that occurs in a successful marriage," the Utah Court of Appeals echoed the paternalistic rationale of the Court of Military Appeals for retaining jurisdiction over seduction cases. That the military justice system retains its jurisdiction over alienation of affections cases into the twenty-first century (though these cases rarely occur), mirroring those jurisdictions that continue to recognize heart balm torts, suggests that the notion of wives as sexually protectable property continues to influence gender dynamics in the military community.

The rarity of alienation of affections cases in the military during the Cold War had no bearing on their importance. The courts' decisions in *Hanna* and *Lyon* left no doubt about the justice system's continued commitment to punish service members whose actions breached the sacred marital bond between spouses. Just as the husband-wife privilege aimed to preserve the sacred relationship between spouses, the courts' continued commitment to prosecuting alienation of affections cases sought to protect couples from outside interference. These outsiders, or "third parties" as the AFBR so aptly labeled them, had "no right to cut off the chance for reconciliation [between spouses]" by estranging wives from their husbands.[38] Policing third-party attempts to estrange wives from their soldier-husbands bolstered the legitimacy and sanctity of monogamous, heterosexual marriage in the military community while simultaneously granting the military justice system an unprecedented level of authority to regulate the intimate relationships of service members and their spouses.

Bigamy

Nothing threatened monogamous marriage more than the crime of bigamy. Because incidents of bigamy "undermined community standards of marriage" and challenged both "formality and ritual, so important in military culture," the courts punished these offenders more harshly than those service members found guilty of adultery or wrongful cohabitation.[39] The *Manual for Courts-Martial*'s table of maximum punishments assigned the crime of bigamy a maximum sentence of two years in contrast to that of one year for adultery and wrongful cohabitation.[40] Legal officials justified prosecutions for bigamy on the grounds that it was both service connected and service discrediting, though judges rarely agreed on a uniform definition of these terms. From the early 1950s until 1970, however, military courts consistently maintained that bigamy cases were service connected "by reason of [the] economic benefits which accrue to the wife of an active duty serviceman." According to the CMA judges, "It takes but little persipicacity [*sic*] to understand the plethora of ways in which the services are involved when one of its members acquires an illegal second set of dependents."[41]

Service members committing bigamy were "but the springboard from which" the accused service members proceeded "to illegally extract from the Government monies and benefits to which [the] bigamous partner[s were] not entitled." Thus, bigamy was a service-connected crime because it involved a "flouting of military authority" and "directly facilitated the obtaining of . . . unauthorized money, services, and other military benefits." In addition, it was considered a service-discrediting offense because it undermined the military community's cherished belief that a monogamous, lifelong, and heterosexual union between one man and one woman was the most effective means for transmitting democratic values to America's youth.[42]

To protect the economic interests of service communities, military courts exercised jurisdiction over cases where illegal wives and children received military housing and health-care benefits to which they were not entitled due to the fraudulent nature of the marriage contracts. But as the *Guidry* case in chapter 2 illustrates, often the service members, whom judges viewed as deceitful criminals who undermined the sanctity of monogamous marriage, perceived themselves as innocent.[43] Indeed, most service members prosecuted for bigamy in the postwar era claimed they did not commit bigamy intentionally but rather mistakenly assumed that their divorces were official.[44] It was not at all uncommon for a service member to initiate divorce proceedings while stationed in one location, then move to another geographic location, and remarry, all the while assuming that his first divorce was official. Take the case of U.S. Navy senior gunner's mate chief P. Grogen in 1963. Grogen first married L. La Duska in 1946, ten years after he joined the service at twenty-seven years old. Feeling responsible for the well-being of his unborn son, Grogen had married L. in New York when she was four months pregnant. One year later, Grogen petitioned for an absolute annulment, justifying his request by stating, "I do not love this woman."[45] After the New York State judge denied Grogen's request for annulment, he continued to support L. and their son until 1963, while she repeatedly refused to grant him a divorce.

When Grogen met Miss Marcos in Charleston, South Carolina, in 1962 and expressed an interest in marrying her, L. finally consented to a divorce and told Grogen she would initiate the proceedings in New York. Grogen married Miss Marcos on September 1, 1962, assuming that the final divorce papers would have arrived by then. Because Grogen was aware that L. would receive military benefits until the divorce was finalized, he initially refused to get his new wife a dependent ID card granting her access to base facilities and health care. Her dependency status would have raised a red flag to military officials, who could look up Grogen's record and see that he already had a dependent wife who was drawing benefits. Reaching his "ropes end [*sic*]" after his new wife's consistent pressure to receive a dependent ID card and seeking to appease her, Grogen obtained the dependency forms and forged the official's signature to obtain her ID card and to keep his marital situation a secret. When prodded by the military judge at court-martial about Grogen's knowledge of the bigamous marriage, Grogen replied, "There is no doubt in my mind that I thought that I had the final divorce papers coming or I would not have sacrificed over twenty-seven years in the U.S. Navy."[46] Ultimately the Navy–Marine Corps Board of Review dismissed Grogen's bigamy charge on the grounds that the trial judge committed a prejudicial error by allowing Grogen to plead guilty to multiple charges without a lawyer present to explain the ramifications of his plea.

Grogen's case illustrates the military justice system's key rationale for maintaining unquestioned jurisdiction over the bigamous unions of service members from the early 1950s until 1970—that is, the depletion of government resources by frauds.[47] The case was typical of most "mistake of fact" bigamy courts-martial in the postwar military in that the accused service member claimed he mistakenly believed his divorce was official before he married another woman. Exceptions to the "honest mistake" cases included those where married servicemen committed bigamy under the influence of alcohol without full knowledge of the act, where character evidence was so outstanding as to render the bigamy charge void, and (in one fascinating case) where an accused service member denied his right to counsel to manipulate the court-martial proceedings in his favor.[48]

The rationale that bigamous unions depleted valuable government resources became so pervasive in legal bigamy discourse that by 1960, when Sgt. V. Whitaker challenged the court to show evidence that his bigamous union was service discrediting and prejudicial to good order and discipline, the U.S. Army Board of Review overtly dismissed his challenge as "so patently without merit that discussion of it is unnecessary."[49] By the late 1960s military courts ruled that bigamy was inherently service connected when an active duty service member committed the crime regardless of where and with whom the crime was committed. For instance, in 1969 a U.S. Air Force Board of Review ruled at Staff Sgt. J. Burkhart's trial that bigamy not only was service connected but also threatened the good order and discipline that was central to fulfilling the mission because fraudulent dependents could undermine the military community's trust in the efficiency of the government.[50]

The CMA finally weighed in on the debate over what constituted a service-connected bigamy crime in 1970, when a U.S. Army Review Board sentenced Spc. M. Hadsell to a bad conduct discharge and confinement at hard labor for nine months in violation of Article 134. Hadsell's defense counsel challenged the general court-martial's jurisdiction of the case, arguing that Hadsell's bigamous offense was in no way service connected because he was not on duty, in uniform, or on post when he entered into the marriage contract. Additionally, the two women involved were civilians and bore no connection to the army. Since bigamy was a crime under the Texas statute, Hadsell's defense argued, military courts lacked jurisdiction over his case. Summarily, the CMA judges ruled in favor of Hadsell, dismissing his charge and reversing the doctrine that bigamy was automatically and inevitably service connected when service members committed the crime. In Hadsell's defense, they asserted, "the fact that a biga-mous marriage may lead to or facilitate the commission of other offenses which are service-connected does not render the bigamy service-connected."[51]

By 1970 bigamy prosecutions all but stopped as legal officials struggled to justify continued intervention after the CMA severely curtailed their jurisdiction over such cases. By limiting the courts' jurisdiction to service-connected bigamy cases (or cases where the service members were on duty, in uniform, or on post when enter-ing into the marriage contract), the CMA effectively reduced the military justice system's regulative capacity to police the marital lives of service members. This liberal shift carried over into other aspects of the courts' regulative authority to police the sexualities of service members when around the same time judges started to question the military's jurisdictional authority to criminalize con-sensual sodomy.[52] The irony of prosecuting bigamy in the services after World War II was that it was (and still is) an incredibly easy crime to commit in the military, as service members attempted to fit stable, married relationships into an unstable living framework that promoted transience rather than permanence.

Wrongful Cohabitation and Adultery

Alongside bigamy, wrongful cohabitation and adultery demor-alized the military community because, according to CMA judge George Latimer, they "offend against the canons of decency and . . . prejudicially affect the credit of the military service [involved]."[53] Defining wrongful cohabitation as a nonmarital living arrange-ment with sexual implications in which a serviceman resided with a woman who was "neither wife, nor sister, nor mother," and adultery as the commission of intercourse with a person other than a spouse, military courts unequivocally held that such illicit arrangements publicly discredited the armed forces by undermin-ing the marital values so central to the military's social order.[54]

Though legal censure and social stigma of marital infidelity in the military community likely dissuaded many potential wayward spouses from gratifying their criminal sexual desires, the looming threat of legal punishment hardly succeeded altogether in eliminating incidents of adultery and wrongful cohabitation.

Though legal officials agreed that wrongful cohabitation and adultery poisoned the moral order and should be punished, they disagreed over how severe the punishments for each should be. Because the table of maximum punishments made no specific provision for wrongful cohabitation, some legal officials categorized the offense as a general disorder deserving of a maximum punishment similar to that given for all other general disorders— confinement at hard labor for four months and forfeiture of two-thirds' pay for a like period. Other officials interpreted the table's silence on wrongful cohabitation as a license to use their discretion on a case-by-case basis, in effect granting them the authority to impose on wrongful cohabiters the harsher punishment of one year's confinement at hard labor that was normally given to adulterers.

This debate crystallized with the case *United States v. Bailey*, in which the army board of review held that the offense of a married serviceman's wrongful cohabitation with a woman not his wife "was so similar to the offense of adultery that it could be equated to that offense for purposes of punishment."[55] Reasoning that continuous cohabitation "raises a strong inference of habitual sexual intercourse" and that "the marriage of the offending party is the element that distinguishes the offense from a mere 'general disorder,'" the board concluded that the increased gravity of the offense appropriated a punishment mirroring that for adultery, or confinement at hard labor for one year. Twelve years later, another review board explicitly rejected the logic of the *Bailey* decision and limited the punishment for wrongful cohabitation to that imposable for a simple disorder.[56]

Because the crimes of wrongful cohabitation and adultery similarly disregarded cherished marital values, legal officials debated their relative effects on military discipline and morale into the late 1950s without reaching reconciliation. CMA judges Quinn, Latimer, and Ferguson epitomized this continued struggle to determine the relative severity of each crime by measuring its impact on military morale and discipline in the 1958 case of U.S. Army captain C. Melville. Court-martialed for a charge of wrongful cohabitation but receiving the punishment for adultery, Melville appealed his case to the CMA on the grounds that his sentence was excessive by the standards set forth for general disorders in the *Manual for Courts-Martial*'s table of maximum punishments. The original ABR reasoned that because the cohabitation of a married man with a woman not his wife was so "closely related to the offense of adultery," punishing Melville for a felony crime rather than a misdemeanor was permissible.[57]

Judge Ferguson, however, disagreed with the original ruling. He argued that wrongful cohabitation in Melville's case was "not so closely related to and destructive of military discipline that it should be punished as a felony in the absence of some specific provision contained on the Table of Maximum Punishments." To the contrary, Quinn and Ferguson identified concrete differences between the two crimes that forever after protected service members accused of wrongful cohabitation from receiving the heavier punishment for adultery. Significantly, this decision theoretically protected all service personnel accused of misdemeanors from being punished for felony crimes. Whereas in adultery prosecutions it was necessary to prove that one of the participants was married at the time the offense was committed, wrongful cohabitation cases required no such proof. Furthermore, where adultery trials required evidence of sexual intercourse for a sustainable conviction, wrongful cohabitation trials contained no such element although the sexual nature of the relationship was often implied. Upholding Melville's right to a fair trial whereby the punishment should fit the crime, Judges Quinn and Ferguson determined that it was "manifestly unfair . . . to permit [Melville] to be punished on the basis of the more serious of offense of adultery."[58]

This decision was not unanimous. In keeping with his famous dissenting opinions in courts-martial concerning homosexual sodomy (discussed in chapter 4), Judge Latimer argued in favor of punishing Melville for the crime of adultery even though he was charged with wrongful cohabitation because "even a cursory reading of . . . the transcript of testimony will disclose how closely similar the pleadings and facts of the case are to those necessary to allege and prove the crime of adultery."[59] It was impossible not to infer from the evidence, Latimer argued, that Melville's relationship with Mrs. Tipton, the accomplice to the charge, was sexual in nature given that Melville was a married man living "openly and notoriously with an enlisted man's wife" over a period of roughly sixteen months. Even without specific proof that sexual intercourse took place, Latimer concluded, Melville's conduct "so nearly equates to that of an adulterer that I see little difference in its impact on both the civilian and military societies. It offends against the canons of decency and so prejudicially affects the credit of the military service that to hold it to be no more than a mere disorder for punishment purposes is contrary to my concepts of proper military jurisprudence. Disorders are generally considered to be offenses which are petty, and I would not force a crime which demoralizes the military community into that class."[60]

Servicemen did not have to be married, like Captain Melville, to commit the crimes of wrongful cohabitation and adultery. In multiple instances unmarried servicemen were court-martialed for cohabiting with women who were either separated or married. U.S. Army first lieutenant B. Parker, for example, was court-martialed for living with Mrs. Pechenino in Fayetteville, North Carolina. Though Mrs. Pechenino was "separated but not divorced from her husband," she and Parker "held themselves out as man and wife" from February to June 1953. In conjunction with a charge of reckless driving, the ABR sentenced Parker to dismissal from the service for his incredulous conduct.[61] In a similar case involving 2nd Lt. D. Knight, a single serviceman court-martialed for living with a married woman at Camp Rucker, Alabama, the ABR actually reversed his guilty sentence on the grounds that the trial counsel prejudicially erred by "using his questions solely as a vehicle to prejudice the court against the accused."[62] Taken together, these cases (and countless other courts-martial of unmarried servicemen for engaging in extramarital sex with dependent wives) illustrate how legal officials held unmarried servicemen to the same standards of sexual restraint as their married comrades in arms.

Legal officials also prosecuted crimes against marriage overseas, though with less frequency than they did so for Stateside prosecutions. Hillman attributes the disparity in wrongful cohabitation and adultery prosecutions overseas and in the United States to the normalization of extramarital sex into the culture of military service abroad.[63] Certainly prospects of extramarital sex were greater when long distances separated husbands and wives for months and even years at a time—a struggle military couples know well— but to suggest that extramarital sex was normalized in overseas military service overlooks the military justice system's regulatory presence that followed American troops to the farthest reaches of the globe. In reality, the extent to which extramarital sex was prevalent in overseas military life depended to a large degree on the location and type of assignment a service member received. Unaccompanied tours to remote and potentially dangerous duty stations, such as Korea, typically had higher rates of illicit sexual relations altogether in comparison to locations where service members were accompanied by their families.

In fact, the military establishment's decision to send military families overseas beginning in 1946 was largely motivated by the need to crack down on sexual and other crimes servicemen were committing in occupied countries such as Germany and Japan that were critical U.S. allies in the global fight against communism.[64] The preservation of the U.S. military's international reputation necessitated that the military justice system enforce the heterosexual, monogamous marriage standard overseas. The armed forces received negative publicity on the international scene if service members violated moral codes of conduct in host territories without facing legal intervention; thus, commanding officers were compelled to take legal action against alleged adulterers and wrongful cohabiters as their deceitful behavior undermined the moral credibility of the United States and its top-notch armed forces.

In the U.S. Army's first overseas prosecution for wrongful cohabitation in 1952, for example, Capt. R. Hudson's openly public infidelity and his physical abuse of his wife threatened to tarnish the credibility of the military's mission of helping reconstruct war-torn Japan into a democratic, capitalist powerhouse. Hudson was convicted of an Article 128 violation for domestic violence against his wife, L. Hudson, and an Article 134 violation for unlawfully cohabiting with M. Kurihara, a Japanese woman, in Yokohama, Japan, from August to December 1951. Captain Hudson elected to remain silent at trial but made an out-of-court statement alleging that he had been living apart from his wife because he had been "placed in restriction" after beating her with his fists. According to Hudson, his wife "provoked him into striking her by smashing the windshield of his automobile, using an object which splashed filth on the accused and his front seat." In spite of her husband's violence and infidelity, Mrs. Hudson testified that she had forgiven him and wanted "him to come back to her."[65] The judge advocates sentenced Hudson to dismissal from the service and a monetary fine associated with an unrelated charge of fraud.

Hudson's case is important because it represents one of the few where a serviceman was found guilty of domestic violence. Prosecutions for spousal violence that did not result in death were rare at courts-martial because they undermined legal efforts to sanctify and protect marriage from outside interference. During the Cold War, if they appeared at all, domestic violence charges usually appeared in conjunction with other charges, as in Hudson's case with associated charges of wrongful cohabitation and fraud against the government. In addition, legal officials usually doled out mild sentences (in comparison to other misdemeanors) to service husbands convicted of spousal abuse. But Hudson's case reveals exceptions to this general rule existed and that, in rare instances, courts-martial protected wives of cheating and abusive husbands at the expense of preserving the marriages in question.[66] In a similar case occurring in Naples, Italy, the CMA affirmed U.S. Navy yeoman N. Smith's sentence to a bad conduct discharge, reduction in rank, and six months' confinement at hard labor after finding him guilty of cohabiting with M. Taylor while his lawful wife resided in Memphis, Tennessee. The discharge portion of the sentence was suspended for a year, however, providing that Smith could be remitted into the navy after the suspension ended.[67]

Infidelity Gone Awry: Adultery-Induced Homicide

Policing the borders of marital infidelity encompassed the most extreme cases of infelicitous marriage that the military witnessed during the Cold War—namely, adultery-induced homicide.[68] These alarming cases featured service husbands who murdered their own wives either out of revenge for their wives' extramarital affairs or in attempts to conceal their own adulterous liaisons. In all such cases to come under the purview of the courts during the Cold War, the perpetrators shared a notable characteristic: they were all active duty husbands. Recall the chapter's tragic opening

O'Brien case in which the warrant officer's premeditated murder of his wife in 1952 was a punishment for her sexual unresponsiveness upon discovering his ongoing affairs. As the first and most important case of adultery-induced spousal homicide to come under the jurisdiction of the UCMJ, *O'Brien* was significant because it set a precedent for how spousal homicide would be handled at courts-martial in the future. By finding O'Brien guilty and condemning him for the "infelicitous" and "wretched" nature of his relationship with his wife, the courts publicized their commitment to enforcing monogamy in military marriages in an effort to prevent the disastrous and costly consequences that could occur when married service members had extramarital affairs.

Five cases featuring husbands who murdered their wives resulted in premeditated murder convictions, but no defendants after the *O'Brien* case received the death sentence.[69] The other four husbands convicted of premeditated murder were more fortunate than O'Brien was and received sentences of life confinement at hard labor. For example, U.S. Air Force master sergeant M. Marymont was charged with the premeditated murder of his wife by arsenic poisoning on June 9, 1958, at Royal Air Force Station Sculthorpe, Norfolk, England, and was sentenced to life imprisonment at hard labor rather than death.[70] The courts convicted more than twenty service husbands of unpremeditated murder from 1952 to 1975 for killing their wives. Countless more cases reveal that unsuccessful attempts at killing their spouses landed other service husbands at court-martial. These numbers alone reveal that domestic violence in its most extreme form was rampant in the military during the Cold War. Although military justice officials often counseled turning the other cheek when confronted with evidence of milder forms of wife abuse, they had no choice but to step in when the abuse resulted in homicide.

Service husbands murdered not only their wives to conceal illicit sexual activities. In a singular case, a cheating service husband in Hoechst, Frankfurt am Main, Germany, murdered his adulterous lover when she threatened to inform his wife of their illicit relationship. U.S. Army sergeant W. Thomas was convicted of premeditated murder and robbery of J. Kuelbel on December 4, 1964. Although Thomas pleaded not guilty to all charges, the evidence proved beyond a reasonable doubt that fear of his wife finding about his adulterous intrigue compelled him to murder his lover by shooting her three times. The bullets penetrated her brain, cheek, and chest, killing her instantly. According to Thomas, J became scared when he showed her the pistol after she threatened to tell his wife about their affair. When J attempted to run away, Thomas claimed he pursued her with the gun "not with the intention of shooting her but only to hit her with the pistol and silence her screams." The CMA affirmed Thomas's sentence to life imprisonment at hard labor and a dishonorable discharge. Ironically, the actions Thomas took to prevent his wife from finding out about his affair led not only to her discovery of his infidelity but also to the painful reality that her husband's life imprisonment barred any chance she might have had to try and repair the marital damage his infidelity caused.[71]

Many service husbands who unsuccessfully attempted to murder their wives also appeared at court-martial. Tech. Sgt. V. Riska's case was typical of those service husbands who were court-martialed for attempting to murder their cheating wives. After suspecting his wife, I. Riska, of adultery with Airman H. Paul, Riska finally secured a separation on December 31, 1962. After peeking through I's window and seeing her with her illicit lover, Riska reached his boiling point and followed them to a store on Whiteman Air Force Base, Missouri. As his wife waited in the car while Paul entered the store, Riska secretly approached the car, entered on the driver's side despite I's attempts to lock the door, and said, "This time I'm going to kill you." He then proceeded to cut her throat and wrists with a knife. Upon hearing I's screams,

Paul ran outside and forced Riska out of the car long enough to escape and get I to the hospital. Though Mrs. Riska made a full physical recovery after the incident, the emotional trauma she endured was not as short lived. After this incident, Riska harassed Paul by breaking into his barracks room, stealing his television set, and replacing it with his own television set.

Upon being questioned at trial about his actions, Riska claimed his reason for taking Paul's television set and replacing it with his own was "to prevent his wife from 'hocking' his new set as she had 'hocked' so much of their personal property in the past." Regarding the violence toward his wife, Riska emphatically argued that he never intended to kill her. He used the knife "only for the purpose of scaring her . . . and to persuade his wife to come back to him."[72] The AFBR affirmed Riska's guilty conviction of assault with a dangerous weapon and larceny, sentencing him to a bad conduct discharge, confinement at hard labor for three months, forfeiture of forty-three dollars per month for three months, and reduction to airman basic.

The conclusion of Riska's case highlights the tension that injured spouses endured while serving in a postwar military culture that valued monogamy but condemned retaliatory behaviors. In a culture that idealized and enforced marital monogamy, the military justice system ironically made no excuses for injured spouses who violently acted out of jealousy or anger toward their adulterous partners. The same was true of cases featuring aggrieved husbands who assaulted or killed their wives' illicit lovers because, as Judge Ferguson aptly noted, "the day is gone . . . when the rude bark of the pistol could be substituted for the divorce courts or serve as an effective deterrent to the supposed adulterer."[73]

How did the courts respond to service husbands who sexually victimized their children to punish their adulterous wives? The case of *Mercer v. Dillon* provides insight into such a deplorable circumstance. In this sad case, army sergeant J. Mercer's stepdaughter became embroiled in her parents' marital difficulties at Schofield Barracks, Hawaii, in 1970, when her stepfather became jealous that her mother was going out with another man. Warning his wife that if she continued her unfaithful course of action "something was going to happen that night," Mercer followed through on his threat. Frustrated by his wife's conduct and seeking revenge, he drove his eight-year-old stepdaughter off base and raped her. When he returned home after committing the heinous crime, he had his stepdaughter call her mother to tell her "what he had done." Mrs. Mercer reported the incident to the military police and her husband's commanding officer. The ensuing general court-martial found Mercer guilty of rape, a violation of Article 120, and sentenced him to a dishonorable discharge, reduction in grade, and hard labor for life. The convening authority, upon determining that Mercer's sentence was excessive, reduced his sentence to ten years.[74]

After Mercer began serving his sentence at the U.S. Disciplinary Barracks at Fort Leavenworth, Kansas, he petitioned the CMA in 1970 for a rehearing in light of the Supreme Court's recent decision in *O'Callahan v. Parker*, which severely limited the military justice system's jurisdiction over cases that were not service connected. *O'Callahan* held that a crime was not service connected if it occurred outside the bounds of a military installation and if it was punishable by civil courts. Because Mercer raped his stepdaughter outside the boundaries of Schofield Barracks, he assumed the CMA would side in his favor and apply *O'Callahan* retroactively. To Mercer's disappointment, the CMA avoided a dangerous precedent when the judges unanimously ruled that *O'Callahan* could not be applied retroactively to any courts-martial, regardless of the crime or punishment inflicted. Making *O'Callahan* retroactive in Mercer's case would literally have opened the floodgates for thousands of convicted service members to seek redress under *O'Callahan*.[75]

Along with the standard adultery and bigamy cases, adultery-induced homicide cases constitute a critical component of the postwar military justice system's regulatory apparatus. Being married in the postwar military meant ceding rights to sexual privacy, as the intimate details of couples' sex lives became public at courts-martial. These highly publicized cases also served as a regulatory medium by reinforcing the standard of monogamy to which all military members were held. But they also raised disturbing questions about the limits of enforcing monogamy and the instability that the breakdown of these relationships had on the children who were caught in the middle. Tragically, as with the O'Brien children, the children who endured these circumstances had to live the rest of their lives without both parents—their deceased mothers and their incarcerated, or deceased if given the death sentence, fathers.

Confronting the Constitutional Limits of Enforcing Monogamy

Though the courts' authority to prosecute adulterous servicemen expanded exponentially in the fledgling years of the UCMJ's existence, it was short lived. As convicted service members began to raise questions about the constitutional limits of prosecuting adultery and other sexual crimes in the late 1950s, a U.S. Army Review Board established a precedent that dealt a damning blow to the courts' historic commitment to enforcing monogamy. The context for these questions of constitutionality emerged from the courts' customary practice of convicting servicemen of adultery in instances where they faced convictions for more serious sexual offense such as rape, indecent liberties with a minor, or sodomy. In theory, legal officials reasoned that men who committed such heinous sexual crimes should be punished both for the commission of the crime itself and for the damage the crime inflicted on the perpetrators' wives and families (hence the added charge of adultery). But this practice was nearly universally discontinued in 1959 after the controversial and precedent-setting ruling that punishing defendants twice for the same crime was a violation of the one of the cardinal rules of U.S. law—namely, protection from double jeopardy.

In the first of such cases in which the courts convicted a married serviceman of statutory rape and adultery arising from the same offense, Capt. V. Francis was court-martialed at Keesler Air Force Base, Biloxi, Mississippi, in 1953 for raping his stepdaughter. The evidence established that Captain and Mrs. Francis married on June 15, 1947, after which Mrs. Francis's fourteen-year-old daughter from another marriage moved into their home and lived with them until the trial date. From January 1950 through September 1952, Captain Francis raped his stepdaughter at least once a week. These continuous sexual encounters usually occurred early in the morning when Mrs. Francis was still asleep. On one particular occasion, which resulted in charges of cruelty toward his stepdaughter, the captain entered his stepdaughter's room at 4:30 a.m. on November 29, 1952; awakened her; and gave her an ultimatum: either engage in sexual intercourse with him or pack her belongings and leave his home indefinitely. Refusing to engage in the illicit act, Miss Francis called herself a cab apparently without alerting her sleeping mother to the circumstances. Shortly before her departure, the captain struck her on the face with his hand.

The infliction of physical abuse on members of his household was not limited to Miss Francis alone. At trial Mrs. Francis provided evidence revealing the captain's physically abusive tendencies, and that resulted in assault charges. She also confirmed she was aware of the captain's repeated rapes of her daughter (though her silence on her husband's repeated molestation of her daughter is shocking), establishing evidence that Captain Francis had engaged in extramarital intercourse for longer than two years. His defense counsel appealed the original court-martial's sentence of dismissal from the air force, total forfeiture of pay and allowances, and confinement at hard labor for twenty years, citing numerous accounts of prejudicial error throughout the trial. The AFBR confirmed the captain's guilt as to the charges of raping his stepdaughter, adultery, and assault against both his wife and stepdaughter over a two-year period. But the presiding judge advocate dismissed the cruelty charge on the grounds that lacking corroborating testimony to confirm the stepdaughter's facts surrounding the alleged cruelty incident, the commission of the offense was not established beyond reasonable doubt. Consequently, the AFBR reduced the term of confinement from twenty to ten years. The CMA denied Captain Francis's petition for appellate review.[76]

One year later, Airman B. Farrell was court-martialed at Stead Air Force Base in Reno, Nevada, in 1954. Farrell, who was single, was charged with committing sodomy with a married woman, T. Steininger, resulting in adulterous relations. As the sole witness for the prosecution, Steininger's testimony was problematic, because according to the AFBR, "her evasive failure to state that the acts actually occurred leaves the evidence uncertain and subject to doubt." Because the dual sexual offenses stemmed from the commission of a single sexual act, as in the *Francis* case, the presiding law officer refused to indict Farrell on either charge because the uncorroborated testimony of the sole witness to the crime was legally insufficient to sustain a guilty conviction.[77]

The court-martial of army private Norris marked a turning point in the courts' practice of convicting servicemen of two separate offenses arising from the same incident. In the precedent-setting case *United States v. Norris*, an ABR convicted Norris of statutory rape and adultery arising from the commission of a single act of supposed sexual intercourse with a minor girl.[78] The case immediately raised questions about the legality of punishing an accused service member twice for the same offense. The board reasoned that the crimes of statutory rape, which required evidence that the victim was younger than the age of sixteen, and adultery were separate offenses and could arise from the single act because each offense required proof of an element not required to prove the other. The age of the victim/accomplice was unnecessary to prove adultery since adultery simply required proof that one of the participants in the act of extramarital intercourse was married. Relying on the table of maximum punishments, which authorized a maximum punishment for "two or more separate offenses arising out of the same act or transaction" so long as "each offense requires proof of an element not required to prove the other," the ABR sentenced Norris to a dishonorable discharge and eighteen months of hard labor confinement.[79]

But the convening authority reversed Norris's sentence on the grounds that a review board's authorization of the maximum punishment for two or more separate offenses arising out of the same act was unconstitutional if it violated "the cardinal principle of law that a person may not be twice punished for the same crime."[80] In a stunning reversal of a legal trend, the convening authority established a hard line against punishing service members for adulterous connections that arose from the commission of other sexual crimes. The message this new precedent sent legal officials was clear: future cases of this kind would be subjected to strict scrutiny to ensure that the postwar military justice system did not trample the servicemen's basic constitutional rights as U.S. citizens. The consequences of this precedent undermined the courts' efforts to preserve monogamy as the marital gold standard by limiting the circumstances in which legal officials could sustain an adultery conviction—that is, when the act occurred between two consenting adults (at least one of whom was married at the time the offense was committed) in the absence of any other sexual offenses. After the *Norris* decision raised the standard of scrutiny with which future courts would review dual conviction cases, the frequency of courts-martial for the crime of adultery steadily declined in the 1960s and all but stopped in the early 1970s, mirroring patterns of bigamy courts-martial almost identically.

Conclusion

As outlined in the mandatory character education programs taught to service members, the strength of both the nation and the military depended on the wholesomeness of military families. In the postwar military and civilian culture in the United States, wholesome family values were transmitted and enforced through prescribed gender roles contained within the nuclear family, the foundation of which was the marital union between one man and one woman. Thus, sex and marital vows in the postwar military community meant a great deal to those legal officials whose job was to enforce standards of marital fidelity and monogamy at courts-martial. So central was marriage to the military during the Cold War that one judge advocate reiterated it in a written opinion: "Marriage is not an exclusively personal relationship; it represents a status in which the Sovereign has an interest."[81] When private behaviors—from wife seduction, bigamy, and adultery to wrongful cohabitation and adultery-related violence and homicide—threatened the sanctity of marital monogamy and fidelity, then the intimate lives of service members and their spouses became public domain. Even though military courts used punitive measures to enforce standards of marital fidelity and monogamy, however, likely many more instances of infidelity and infidelity-related crimes occurred beyond the scope of the military justice system's radar.

Overall, the pattern of prosecution for bigamy, wrongful cohabitation, and adultery was similar, peaking in the 1950s and steadily declining to historic lows in the early 1970s. The cost of convening courts-martial played a large role in the declining number of adultery and bigamy prosecutions as all service branches leaned toward the cheaper and less time-consuming alternative of the administrative discharge. The political climate also influenced the declining rates of adultery and bigamy courts-martial as the combination of the antiwar sentiment and civil rights movements for women, gays and lesbians, and African Americans censured a seemingly antiquated military justice system that enforced archaic standards of sexual conduct that most civilian courts had abandoned. Within the military community, crimes of infidelity such as the *O'Brien* case stirred up controversy because the decision to prosecute generated negative publicity to a critical public that diminished the status associated with military service.

The devastating blow the U.S. Supreme Court delivered to the military courts' jurisdiction over service members in the *O'Callahan* decision all but sealed the fate of the military justice system's retreat from enforcing monogamy. Yet despite the general retreat from monitoring the marital and sexual lives of service members in the 1960s and early 1970s, the courts' struggle to retain jurisdiction over the intimate was far from finished.[82] As chapter 4 illustrates, the military justice system's dogged pursuit of suspected sodomites and homosexuals in the interest of normalizing heterosexism and "natural" sexual relations opened the floodgates for some of the most revolutionary legal and social changes in U.S. military history.

4

Normalizing Heterosexism and "Natural" Sex

In 1955 while stationed with the U.S. Navy on Guam, Fireman W. Adkins was found guilty of consensual sodomy with another man and was originally sentenced to a bad conduct discharge, total forfeiture of pay and allowances, and hard labor confinement for eighteen months despite numerous recommendations testifying that Adkins was a "truthful person and one of good morals." The prosecuting witness who brought the charges against Adkins, a man named Sandoval, was a "confirmed homosexual" who supposedly consented to the act of sodomy at Adkins's request.[1] The prosecution presented the testimony of a naval intelligence agent named Kinniry, whose claim to have investigated roughly four hundred homosexuality cases over a decade made him a supposed "expert" on homosexuals. Kinniry made a number of general remarks that cast Adkins in a guilty light: it was his experience that "birds of a feather flock together"; in all the cases he investigated, he had "never known a confirmed homosexual to intentionally name and falsely accuse the wrong person and stick to it"; homosexuals were "products of broken homes"; and "homosexuals typically came from large families where three to four children slept together in one bed."[2]

Fireman Adkins appealed his case to the Court of Military Appeals on the grounds that his right to a fair and impartial trial was compromised when the residing law officer admitted Kinniry's testimony as "expert" testimony. The CMA reviewed Adkins's case and reversed his guilty sentence, finding that his right to an impartial trial was in fact violated because Kinniry "lacked any sort of medical or other scientific training in psychiatric disorders." The judges also questioned Kinniry's credibility by highlighting that he did not have verifiable concrete evidence for his assertion that active homosexuals were always truthful about the persons with whom they had sex. Such concrete evidence was impossible to provide, in the judges' estimation, because consensual sodomy was "not customarily performed under conditions of publicity" since it was a felony in both civil and military law.[3]

The elements of Adkins's case were common among courts-martial for same-sex sodomy during the Cold War. Alleged sodomites were often subject to irrational and incriminating speculation about the nature and veracity of homosexuals because service regulations provided unclear definitions of what constituted homosexual behavior. Such speculation, though indicative of a larger culture of homophobia, often benefited the accused defendants, however, because the Court of Military Appeals consistently stepped in to protect their UCMJ-mandated rights to fair and impartial trials.

Discharging alleged homosexual soldiers from the U.S. military during the Cold War, whether administratively or by court-martial, was just one aspect of the military's broader, service-wide assault on all forms of sexual deviance from the heterosexual, monogamous norm. Homosexuals were criminalized by a military legal system that not only interpreted their sexual radicalism as the ultimate threat to national security, heterosexual marriage, and the nuclear family but also viewed their consensual sexual acts with as much abhorrence as they held the violent rapes and homicides committed by heterosexual service members. Despite an abundance of evidence illustrating the talents and dedication that homosexual soldiers brought to service missions, official policies created an intolerant atmosphere for gay and lesbian service members whose sexual "otherness" many legal officials deemed both a perversity of nature and a liability to the military's mission.

The military's criminalization and increasing surveillance of homosexuality in the 1950s were part of what historian David K. Johnson termed the "lavender scare," or the federal government's wholesale attempts to purge homosexuals from its ranks in the name of national security. The government's prevailing logic, whereby the alleged moral laxity and weakness of homosexuals made them susceptible to communist infiltration and blackmail, was almost identical to the military's exclusionary logic that resulted in thousands of administrative discharges and hundreds of courts-martial for suspected homosexual servicemen and women.[4]

But the military justice system's efforts to enforce heterosexism and natural, procreative sexual relations were largely unsuccessful because official policies pertaining to the disposition of homosexuals were rife with contradictions. Official and unofficial evidence repeatedly proved that sexual orientation had no bearing on job performance, while the vague language of the services' regulations established confusing and contradictory definitions of what constituted "confirmed" homosexuals. As historian Elizabeth Hillman addresses in her pathbreaking work on the Cold War courts-martial, the UCMJ—in one of the notable paradoxes of military law—itself criminalized consensual sodomy while upholding homosexuals' legal right to due process.[5] Similarly, military courts struggled to purge sexual deviants from the Cold War landscape without violating their rights to privacy, constitutional searches and seizures, impartial trials, and freedom from entrapment, "command control"—the age-old habit of commanders and high-ranking officers wielding their rank to their own benefit—and double jeopardy. In this tenuous environment, service members arraigned on charges of same-sex sodomy often successfully challenged their criminality by utilizing the appeals process to contest unfair sentences and trial proceedings. Their steady stream of appeals increased the length and cost of prosecution by courts-martial and contributed to a decreased prosecution rate for same-sex sodomy as the Cold War progressed. Just as the federal government's homosexual witch hunts during the lavender scare rallied victims against gross violations of their civil liberties and planted the seeds for an emerging gay rights movement, the military justice system's prosecutions of suspected homosexuals at courts-martial united service members in their efforts to challenge exclusion policies.[6]

Ultimately, gay service members in the 1950s and 1960s played a critical role in establishing their own legal protections in military courts, though scholars typically identify the mid-1970s as the turning point when homosexual soldiers such as Tech. Sgt. Leonard Matlovich of the U.S. Air Force openly challenged the military's exclusionary regulations. In a typical example of this trend in historiography, G. D. Sinclair asserted that until the 1970s "the legality of the military's anti-homosexual policy was challenged by Leonard Matlovich and others . . . with little success."[7] Matlovich's courageous stand certainly opened the floodgates for other gay service members to challenge publicly the exclusionary policies the military endorsed.[8] But he stood on the shoulders of dozens of soldiers whose resistance to the military's attempts to control their sexual lives established legal precedents that protected their rights as citizen soldiers within the purview of the UCMJ.

Service members' victories at courts-martial for same-sex sodomy were not widely publicized because the precedents they established challenged the military's exclusionary logic by acknowledging that sexual preferences had no bearing on their job performance or on troop morale. These precedent-setting cases of the early Cold War planted the seed for the acceptance of homosexual service members both within and beyond the sphere of military justice that was embodied in the later repeal of the "don't ask, don't tell" (DADT) policy. By acknowledging that homosexuals were worthy of the same legal safeguards that heterosexuals enjoyed from the early 1950s onward, the CMA enabled service members such as Leonard Matlovich to challenge openly the military's exclusion policies into the twenty-first century with the confidence that the service members would receive fair treatment at courts-martial.

The tendency to overgeneralize about who supported the military's exclusion policy and how it was enforced oversimplifies historical reality by presenting an American fighting force that was ideologically monolithic in its prejudicial stance toward homosexual service members. This misrepresentation denies agency to service members who were prosecuted for homosexuality by assuming that all courts-martial for homosexual activity would inevitably end in a guilty conviction, and it equates policy with practice without examining the complex process by which the gay ban was enforced and challenged. In reality, neither punishments nor protections were applied universally to alleged homosexual service members during the Cold War. Instead, courts-martial records detail a rich and complex history of activism on behalf of troops who utilized the appeals process to challenge violations of their constitutional and UCMJ rights to protection from double jeopardy, unfair searches and seizures, unfair and biased trials, command control, and entrapment.[9]

The History of Anti-Sodomy Efforts, Pre-UCMJ

The military legally criminalized sodomy (both consensual and forcible) as a felony in a 1919 revision of the Articles of War. Drawing on the official lexicon created by centuries of religious and medical associations between homosexuality and unnaturalness, moral depravity, and sexual perversion, military officials legally defined homosexuals as those who committed (or attempted to commit) sodomy, which was considered an unnatural act and crime against nature because the sexual organs were used for non-procreative purposes.[10] The military's criminalization of sodomy was part of a tumultuous history of anti-sodomy legislation in U.S. history.[11] By World War II, the fledgling field of psychiatry diagnosed homosexuality as a mental illness that could be "cured." Consequently, "gay" characteristics such as effeminacy in men or excessive masculinity in women became legitimate grounds for investigations.

The first regulations instructing military psychiatrists to identify "persons habitually or occasionally engaged in homosexual or other perverse sexual practices" were instituted in 1942, and those recruits deemed sexually deviant (or, by the military's definition, those who engaged in non-procreative sex for pleasure) were "unsuitable for military service."[12] By 1943 homosexuals were officially banned from all branches of military service, though as historian Allan Berube illustrates, homosexual life flourished among servicemen and women paradoxically because military service brought homosexuals together en masse for the first time in U.S. history.[13] According to Francine D'Amico, the language of these wartime regulations "blurred the distinction between identity and conduct and allowed greater command discretion to determine whether soldiers identified as gay would be retained or discharged."[14]

Defining Sodomy under Article 125

The Uniform Code of Military Justice, instituted in 1951, streamlined the diverse policies and procedures of the service branches for criminalizing and punishing sexual deviance. Article 125 criminalized both consensual and forcible sodomy, and it penalized consenting adults with a maximum punishment of five years' confinement at hard labor, total forfeiture of pay and allowances, and dishonorable discharge. Defining sodomy as "unnatural carnal copulation, either with another person of the same or opposite sex, or with an animal," the *Manual for Courts-Martial* did not linguistically discriminate between homosexuals and heterosexuals.[15] Since military courts interpreted Article 125 to include "oral or anal sexual penetration, regardless of either consent or the sex of the persons involved," heterosexuals who deviated from "natural" copulation were also court-martialed though at a drastically reduced rate compared to prosecutions of homosexual sodomy.[16] As one judge quoting the Bible candidly explained the crime, "A charge of sodomy, like the virtue of charity, covers a multitude of sins" including common law sodomy, fellatio, and cunnilingus, although military courts recognized that "in medical phraseology, the term 'cunnilingus' does not necessarily involve penetration of the female sexual organ."[17]

Criminalizing both homosexual and heterosexual sodomy as "the infamous crime against nature," the UCMJ established heterosexual marital sex as the normative standard against which deviant sexuality was measured. Sodomy was regarded as "a degradation of the virile organ" and the most "vicious insult to manhood" that should elicit no less than feelings of "outrage" and "revulsion" among heterosexual male victims.[18] Sodomites were supposedly the most dangerous variants of sexual deviates because their unnatural sexual behavior violated both religious and secular tenets of moral decency. But although Article 125 criminalized both heterosexual and homosexual consensual sodomy equally, the Cold War courts-martial overwhelmingly targeted alleged homosexuals, in effect homosexualizing sodomy.[19] Article 125 did not specify, however, how convicted sodomites should be prosecuted and discharged from the services.

Legal authorities could also convict suspected sodomites of an additional Article 133 or Article 134 violation because sodomy constituted conduct that was both unbecoming an officer and a gentleman and prejudicial to good order and discipline in the armed forces. As noted previously, the vague language of Articles 133 and 134 made them extremely elastic; thus, they could be applicable in many cases where homosexuality was suspected but could not be proven.[20]

Policies of Exclusion and the Classification of the Homosexual Service Member

The navy established the first exclusionary regulations pertaining to homosexuals on December 10, 1949. Secretary of the navy (SECNAV) directive 1620.1 stated that "homosexuals were liabilities to the service, and must be discharged."[21] The army followed suit with AR 635-443 on January 12, 1950, and the air force implemented U.S. Air Force Regulation (AFR) 35-66 on January 12, 1951.[22] Similar in content and form, these regulations dictated the process by which homosexuals were to be investigated and discharged under Article 125.

These policies applied to females and males alike, though in practice the vagueness of SECNAV 1620.1 and its subsequent revisions regarding what constituted homosexuality subjected servicewomen to harrowing investigations that amounted to what historian Margot Canaday calls "psychological rape."[23] Canaday argues that policing homosexuality among women was not as "clear-cut" as it was for men. Whereas investigations of homosexual servicemen usually revolved around the commission of the act of sodomy, with testimonies from corroborating witnesses to "prove" the act occurred, investigations of suspected lesbians more often focused on scrutinizing women's female networks because authorities assumed women would not commit homosexual acts in public. The *Adkins* case at the beginning of this chapter is one of many examples in same-sex sodomy courts-martial where judges did *not* believe that men were more likely to commit sodomy in public than women. Given the judges' logic that concrete evidence of consensual sodomy was very difficult to provide because, as a felony crime, it was "not customarily performed under conditions of publicity," these cases suggest that investigations into alleged acts of same-sex sodomy for servicemen were not as unambiguous as they might seem. The majority of male same-sex sodomy courts-martial from 1950 to 1975 featured defendants who supposedly committed sodomy in private. Given that women tended to commit sodomy in private, according to Canaday, investigators relied heavily on evidence of women's gendered performance of "mannishness," their affiliations with "mannish" women, their habitual recreational activities, and their close relationships with other women to help authorities identify servicewomen with homosexual tendencies.

To determine the type of discharge and punishment appropriate for convicted sodomites, the services' exclusionary regulations created a classification system that defined different levels of homosexuals into military law.[24] Class I homosexuals were considered the most dangerous because their behavior involved assaulting or coercing unwilling victims, even minor children younger than the age of sixteen, into homosexual acts.[25] Class II homosexuals included "overt, confirmed" homosexuals who had engaged in "one or more provable homosexual acts not within the purview of Class I." Defining homosexual acts as "overt acts, active and passive in nature, and proposals, solicitations, or attempts to perform any homosexual act even though no overt act is committed," the regulation dictated that no distinction be made "in the administrative handling of cases of alleged participation in homosexual acts because of the active or passive nature of the participation in such acts by the Army personnel involved." Class III homosexuals included cases of "overt, confirmed" homosexuals who had not engaged in any homosexual acts "since entry into military service" and "individuals who possess homosexual tendencies to such a degree as to render them unsuitable for military service."[26] The vagueness of the term "homosexual tendencies" subjected servicemen and women to increasing state surveillance.[27]

The process for discharge differed according to the legal class military officials assigned to alleged homosexuals. Deemed deserving of punishment for having "uncontrollable, perverse tendencies," troops categorized as Class I homosexuals were automatically prosecuted by courts-martial and, if found guilty, imprisoned and discharged.[28] Class II and III homosexuals could elect to bypass courts-martial trials and accept undesirable administrative discharges to decrease the length and cost of the legal prosecution mounted against them. Demanding trial by courts-martial in lieu of accepting a dishonorable discharge was apparently common practice, however, among servicewomen investigated for homosexuality in the 1950s.[29]

Personnel could refuse the board hearing and voluntarily agree to accept an administrative discharge, but the officer exercising general court-martial jurisdiction over the accused ultimately determined and recommended to the personnel council whether administrative discharge or disciplinary action was warranted.[30] Even if the record disclosed that the accused committed a punishable offense, the officer could still recommend administrative discharge without punishment. The secretary of the air force, for example, retained ultimate authority to approve the sentence upon the personnel council's recommendation.[31] Accused personnel who refused to accept either a board hearing or separation from the services under dishonorable conditions were court-martialed to establish the facts of their cases and to determine both their guilt or innocence and their usefulness to the services.[32] This process was similar in the army, navy, and marine corps.

Service members charged with the sexual abuse of minors were usually ranked as Class I homosexuals because their preying on innocent children meant that their sexual perversion was uncontrollable. Cases of Class I homosexuals abound in the *Court-Martial Reports* between 1950 and 1975. The publicity these cases received in military news media made homosexuality synonymous with perversion and pedophilia, stereotypes that proved exceedingly difficult (though not impossible) for convicted soldiers to overcome at courts-martial. Class I was the least ambiguous tier of the classification system, however, because it involved only cases of nonconsensual coercion.

Classes II and III generated extensive debate among legal officials over what behaviors and mannerisms counted as evidence of homosexuality because the regulations neither defined the behaviors that constituted "homosexual tendencies" nor explained which tendencies (and to what degree a person exhibited these tendencies) rendered individuals "unsuitable for military service." For example, the regulations dictated that individuals who possessed "homosexual tendencies to such a degree as to render them unsuitable for military service" should be court-martialed, but they conversely determined that "individuals who profess homosexual tendencies should normally be retained in service."[33] Without any instruction on how to determine an individual's degree of homosexual tendencies, legal officials were ill equipped to enforce the exclusion regulations consistently in same-sex sodomy courts-martial.

If the ambiguous language of the classification regulations left room for multiple interpretations of what constituted homosexual behavior, then contradictions complicated the linguistic imprecision of the regulations. Accused service members who had engaged in "provable" consensual homosexual acts were categorized as Class II homosexuals, for instance, but the same regulation defined Class II homosexual acts as "overt acts, active and passive in nature, and proposals, solicitations, or attempts to perform any homosexual act *even though no overt act is commit-*

ted" (author's emphasis).[34] Thus, Class II homosexuals could be accused based on acts and attempts to act that could be "provable." Without criteria for what constituted provable behavior, however, legal officials were often at odds over what counted as "proof" because the testimonies of the facts from witnesses were almost always at odds. At sodomy trials especially, often what was provable depended on whom legal officials chose to believe since such intimate encounters rarely occurred in the presence of an audience whose testimony could tip the scales toward guilt or innocence.

Linguistic Imprecision Leads to Debate

Airman 3rd Class N. Smith's case offers an excellent illustration of how confusion over proving a person's homosexuality led to disagreement and debate among judicial officials at courts-martial. Smith was charged with committing sodomy against a fellow airman at Nouasseur Air Base's military stockade in Morocco in 1959. The staff judge advocate presiding over Airman Smith's court-martial hearing initially recommended Smith for clemency, enabling him to be rehabilitated and to remain in the air force. But the staff judge advocate later withdrew his clemency recommendation "partly because accused [Smith] had a falsetto voice and an effeminate manner."[35] Unsure about how to pinpoint Smith's sexual orientation, the staff judge advocate altered his recommendation for restoration in the service based largely upon Smith's effeminate characteristics.

The review board reversed Smith's guilty sentence on the grounds that the staff judge advocate's withdrawal of his clemency recommendation for rehabilitation was "hasty, ill-advised, and almost injudicious because it was based on no more than flimsy information pertaining to physical characteristics of the accused which were deemed to lend substance to the report that he had committed a homosexual act."[36] Protecting Smith's right to a fair trial—in his case, a trial free from prejudicial error—the officers sitting on the review board condemned the indictment of an alleged homosexual based on physical characteristics alone. Though Smith's case provided some clarity on the confusing issue of how to prove a person's sexual orientation, legal officials continued to struggle with the ill-defined classifications of the service disposition regulations into the 1970s.

Categorizing service members into Class III of the homosexuality tier was an equally contentious task because the regulations did not dictate how an individual's sexual orientation should be confirmed. If Class III homosexuals were persons who had not engaged in homosexual activities since entering the service, then on what basis—if not sexual activity—was sexual orientation confirmed? Class III was especially controversial because the logic suggested that a person's gender-coded mannerisms or character traits, rather than specific sexual behaviors, indicated his or her sexual orientation. But if mannerisms such as an effeminate gate and a falsetto voice equated to homosexual tendencies, nowhere did the UCMJ specifically authorize legal authorities to punish service members for such traits. Article 125 criminalized the act of sodomy but not mannerisms or sexual orientation. However, commanders could, and often did, prosecute suspected homosexuals with violations of Articles 133 and 134, because their linguistic imprecision allowed commanders the leeway to criminalize any action or mannerism that threatened the heterosexual, masculine normative behavioral standard that ordered the social conduct of Cold War service members.

Army v. Air Force Dispute over Homosexual Exclusion Policies

The case of Pvt. E. Goins illustrates the confusion that the vague language of disposition regulations such as AR 635-89 created. Court-martialed for two charges of homosexual sodomy with other enlisted army men at Fort Knox, Kentucky, in 1956, Goins pleaded guilty and received the maximum sentence of dishonorable discharge, total forfeiture of pay and allowances, and confinement at hard labor for five years.[37] Prior to sentencing, however, military psychiatrist major M. Finn examined Goins and testified that since he fell under Class II as a "confirmed homosexual," he should be "administratively separated from the service under appropriate army regulations."[38] AR 635-89 stated that "Disposition in Class II cases will normally be accomplished by administrative separation . . . unless the individual resists separation from the service . . . in which case he will be recommended for trial by court-martial or board action if trial is not feasible."[39] Goins did not resist his discharge because he was not given the opportunity to do so. Thus, the U.S. Army Review Board reversed Goins's sentence on the grounds that his rights were substantially prejudiced when he did not receive the opportunity afforded under AR 635-89 to accept an undesirable discharge in lieu of trial by court-martial.

The issue at hand was whether AR 635-89 constituted a mandate that all Class II homosexuals should be afforded the opportunity to accept an undesirable discharge in lieu of trial by court-martial or whether the regulation gave the accused's commander the discretion to withhold this opportunity. In a surprising assertion of Class II homosexuals' right to choose how they would be separated from the services, army officials on the ABR interpreted AR 635-89 as a mandate that granted Class II homosexuals the opportunity to accept an administrative discharge to avoid court-martial "as a matter of right."[40] Only by resisting administrative discharge, the board interpreted, should Class II homosexuals be tried by court-martial. The irony of Goins's case was that the very regulation that defined him as a criminal also established his right as a soldier to choose the method of his own discharge. Certainly AR 635-89 was designed to entice "confirmed homosexuals" to choose the cheaper and quicker administrative discharge, but Class II homosexuals often resisted discharge because courts-martial offered the possibility of being found innocent, of clemency, and of the chance to continue serving their country.

A U.S. Air Force Review Board flatly disagreed with the ABR's interpretation of the regulation as a mandate of the accused's rights in the *Goins* case. In 1960 Tech. Sgt. W. Sheehan appealed his sodomy conviction on the grounds that he, like Goins, was not given the choice of administrative separation before his trial by court-martial. The AFBR interpreted AFR 35-36, however, not as a mandate asserting alleged homosexuals' rights to choose the method of their discharge but as a procedure "for the administrative elimination of homosexual persons if resort to this method (administrative discharge), is determined to be the preferred action by those empowered to make such decision." Because the *Goins* decision divested commanders of their decision-making powers, air force officials ruled that "such holding [referring to *Goins*] is not followed in the Air Force." To the contrary, air force officials argued that "while a declaration of policy by a service may influence the manner in which an officer exercises his discretion, it cannot place him in a mental straight jacket which denies him any freedom of choice."[41] Thus, where the army interpreted the regulation as a mandate of rights of the accused, the air force interpreted the regulation as mere guidance for an officer if he chose the route of administrative discharge over trial by court-martial. Since AFR 35-36 was interpreted as a procedural guideline for officers rather than a mandate of Sheehan's right to choose his method of discharge, Sheehan was sentenced to dishonorable discharge, total forfeiture of pay and allowances, confinement at hard labor for one year, and reduction to the grade of airman basic.

In addition to debating the nature of the regulations as mandates of rights or procedural guidelines, judicial personnel questioned the legality of AR 635-89, AFR 35-36, and SECNAV 1620.1.

Army private first class V. Green's case illustrates this trend. Green pleaded not guilty to one charge of sodomy and was found guilty of the lesser offense of a violation of Article 134, or of committing an "indecent, lewd, and lascivious act with another." He was sentenced to a dishonorable discharge, total forfeiture of pay and allowances, and confinement at hard labor for three years, and the convening authority reduced Green's sentence to two years but otherwise approved the sentence. Green's attorney, however, argued that AR 635-89 improperly influenced Green's commanding officers and those presiding over the trial. The staff judge advocate wrote a letter to Green's commander, Colonel Dawson, explaining that the wording of AR 635-89 "directly tends to control the judicial processes."[42] Feeling that AR 635-89 was a directive of "doubtful legality," the staff judge advocate returned Green's file to Colonel Dawson "for reconsideration and appropriate actions as to disposition of this offense, *disregarding the directive provisions of paragraph 6b(1)(b), AR 635-89*" (emphasis in the original).[43]

After reviewing the staff judge advocate's request for reconsideration, Colonel Dawson recommended to the convening authority that the charges against Private Green be dropped completely and that he simply be reassigned to a different command. To justify his change of heart, Dawson argued that Green was not a "confirmed homosexual, and did not possess strong homosexual tendencies," because there "was no evidence of actual penetration." According to paragraph 2 of AR 635-89, "Individuals who cannot be regarded as true and confirmed homosexuals, but who have been involved in a single act as a result of . . . intoxication, when the psychiatric evaluation concludes that they are not confirmed homosexuals and do not possess strong homosexual tendencies, should normally be retained in service."[44] The convening authority, despite Dawson's recommendation for Green's charges to be dropped, referred the charges to a general court-martial for trial.

Private Green turned down the offer of an administrative discharge and opted instead for trial by court-martial, but Captain Pilon, Green's immediate commander who filed the charges against him in the first place, testified in an out-of-court hearing that "he did not feel that a general court-martial was warranted, and that the only reason he recommended such was the mentioned regulation." Green's attorney argued that Captain Pilon was "subjected to command influence from Department of the Army level by the mentioned regulations, and was thus prevented from freely exercising his discretion as provided by the Code and the *Manual*."[45] The ABR disagreed, however, and maintained Green's guilt with a reduced confinement period of six months.

In Green's case, as in those of Goins and Sheehan, court officials debated the intentions of the service regulations that codified homosexuals into military law. Army officials in *Green* and *Goins* debated AR 635-89 as both a mandate of the accused's rights and as a directive of "doubtful legality," while air force officials debated AFR 35-36 as a procedural outline that did not prevent officers from freely exercising their professional discretion in homosexual sodomy cases. SECNAV 1620.1 was no less controversial in navy courts-martial, especially after it released the Crittenden Report in 1957. The commissioned report showed that no evidence supported the argument that homosexuals were service liabilities, but the navy hid the report for more than two decades.[46]

Challenging the Logic: Policy Contradictions

Legal officials debated not only the nature and intentions of the exclusion policy but also the parameters of sexually perverse behavior. Air force major L. Yeast's case offers a prime example of the military courts' struggle to enforce vague standards of morality as his association with a reputed homosexual and his sexual solicitations of a young airman pushed the boundaries of decency and conduct appropriate for an officer and a gentleman. Yeast was charged with a violation of Article 133, or conduct unbecoming of an officer and a gentleman, at Lockbourne Air Force Base, Ohio, in 1965, when a young airman testified that Yeast had invited him to spend the night in an apartment, asked him to pose for nude photographs, and caressed his thigh.[47] Yeast had taken Airmen Jackson and Tompson to the Kismet and Kiri Cafés, public gathering places widely reputed to be homosexual havens. The apartment to which Airman Tompson was invited was owned by one Mr. Rawson, a self-proclaimed homosexual and good friend of Yeast's, and Yeast knew the apartment was "the repository of a large quantity of photographs of nude and seminude males and homosexual type literature."[48] Agents with the Office of Special Investigations searched the apartment with Rawson's consent and discovered homosexual literature and photographs that would "tend to debauch and corrupt the morals of an immature, inexperienced airman."[49] The review board admitted these photos into evidence as "criminal intent" during Yeast's court-martial.

Yeast appealed his case on the grounds that the search of Rawson's apartment and the seizure of photographs were unconstitutional, that he did not violate an order by escorting airmen to reputed homosexual gathering places, and that he associated with Rawson without being aware of his homosexual tendencies. Yeast also challenged the testimony of a witness, Lieutenant Colonel Booth, whose claim that Rawson was "effeminate in his movements and ways" and probably "queer" was prejudicial.[50] The review board ruled that the search and seizure was, indeed, legal because Rawson had permitted the officers to enter his apartment and examine the obscene materials in public view on the mantelpiece. The board also dismissed Yeast's claim that he was unaware of Rawson's homosexual orientation with evidence that Yeast received mail at Rawson's apartment and, further, that even after Yeast became aware of Rawson's "deviate proclivities," he went to Rawson's hotel suite to stay overnight with him.[51] Regarding the testimony of Colonel Booth, however, the review board acknowledged that Booth "did not possess any expert knowledge concerning homosexuality or the identification of sexual deviates" and thus "strayed beyond his area of competence" when calling Rawson a "queer."[52]

Although Booth's testimony was inadmissible, the board ruled that it did not prejudice Yeast's rights to an impartial trial because, even without Booth's testimony, "the record contains a quantity of credible and persuasive evidence that Rawson was, and was reputed to be, a homosexual."[53] The board dismissed the charge that Yeast violated a lawful order by frequenting a place with a homosexual reputation, however, with evidence that the order was not in force when Yeast actually visited the Kismet and Kiri Cafés. Yeast ultimately received a sentence reduction not only because the charge of violating a lawful order was dismissed but also because of his "impressive combat record, his over twenty years' active military service, the high regard in which he has been held by his military associates, and his parental record" (though to what this parental record referred is unknown).[54] The review board upheld his dismissal from service and total forfeiture of pay and allowances but reduced his period of confinement at hard labor from one year to six months. The Court of Military Appeals denied Yeast's petition for a rehearing on the basis that the review board's decision did not violate his rights to due process.

Yeast's case exemplifies many courts-martial for "indecency" during the Cold War when military courts struggled to reconcile sexual deviates with their outstanding job performance records. Given the high regard that Yeast's military associates had for him and his impressive combat record, Yeast's homosexual associations and behaviors appeared to have no negative impact on his job performance. What is more, Yeast's excellent parental record and his twenty-year-plus commitment to the service earned him kudos with the judges, who reduced his sentence as a compensation for his responsibility and commitment. Because the military's logic of liability left no room for homosexual service members to be decent individuals—that is, good parents or good soldiers capable of possessing qualities of commitment and responsibility—the presence of troops such as Yeast exposed the fault lines in the services' flawed logic of homosexual exclusion by showing that a person's sexual orientation did not dictate his or her character, intelligence, or work ethic. Class II and Class III homosexuals, like Yeast, were legal impossibilities in the military justice system during the Cold War because military law excluded the possibility that consensual homosexuals could be hardworking, responsible citizens. The courts responded to these legal impossibilities by reducing or reversing their sentences altogether.

Contradictions in the disposition regulations such as SECNAV 1620.1 mirrored the contradictions between official policies and reports. The navy's Crittenden Report of 1957 challenged the exclusionary logic of SECNAV 1620.1 by arguing that homosexuals showed no difference in job performance or ability from that of heterosexuals.[55] If homosexual troops posed no substantial national security risk in terms of their susceptibility to extortion, then how did homosexual personnel pose liabilities to the services according to SECNAV 1620.1? The report's findings startled military officials and created an atmosphere of apprehension and denial. To quell any potential uprisings within the ranks over the irrationality of the service-wide exclusion policy, the navy hid the report for thirty-two years until a federal court, under the Freedom of Information Act, ordered its release to the public in 1989. The report's revolutionary potential was not specific to the navy. Since the army and air force had adopted the same exclusionary logic and classification system for defining homosexuals that the navy did in SECNAV 1620.1, courts-martial for homosexual sodomy in the army and air force had an equally revolutionary potential to challenge traditional notions of military masculinity.

But even before rumors of the Crittenden Report caused a firestorm of controversy within the services over the exclusion policy in 1957, military officials at courts-martial were questioning the validity of the military's stance that homosexuals were security threats. Positive character recommendations from high-ranking officers, for example, challenged the logic of the job liability issue by offering evidence of defendants' exemplary job performance. Take the army's case against 1st Lt. H. Davisson, for example. Charged with two counts of sodomy with enlisted men at Fort Benning, Georgia, in 1952, Davisson pleaded guilty and was sentenced to dismissal. Attempting to explain his "unnatural urge" to have sexual relations with men, Davisson testified that he first experienced an attraction to men in 1938, but at the time he became engaged to a Red Cross nurse. After consulting a psychiatrist for eighteen months and feeling "cured," he lived a normal heterosexual life even after the tragic death of his fiancée in 1944. Since his engagement to another woman, Davisson admitted that "in the past couple of years, this urge again has come upon me." With searing honesty, Davisson went on to explain that he felt his situation "must be corrected because of society's attitude toward it" and that he planned on seeing physicians and psychiatrists "with the idea of overcoming whatever it is that makes me do this." The chief of the neuropsychiatric section at Fort Benning's hospital evaluated Davisson and concluded that even though he was "mildly effeminate in appearance . . . there is no definite psychiatric evidence at this time to indicate that he is a sexual deviate."[56]

Two colonels testified on Davisson's behalf, offering evidence of his outstanding job performance in spite of his admission of homosexual sodomy. Lt. Col. S. J. Codner of the Adjutant General's Corps described Davisson's job performance as being "marked by outstanding efficiency and devotion to duty" and stated that "since being implicated in these present difficulties it has made no difference in the performance of his duty." Colonel Codner added that Davisson's "conduct in an official capacity has been all that would be desired. I know of no officer in the Adjutant General's Corps in his grade that I would desire more for duty in his specialized sphere of activities than Lieutenant Davisson."[57] Codner assured court members that his superior, Colonel Shugart, the adjutant general of the Infantry Center, shared his sentiments about Davisson's stellar work ethic.

Davisson's own admission of his homosexual urges and actions did not influence the professional testimony in support of his retention. To the contrary, the chief psychiatrist's conclusion that Davisson was not a sexual deviate directly negated Davisson's testimony, while Colonel Codner's glowing praise of Davisson's job performance did not waver the least after hearing Davisson admit to having homosexual urges and actions. By arguing for Davisson's retention in the service in spite of his homosexuality, Colonel Codner—and by extension his commander, Colonel Shugart—exposed the flawed logic of the military's policy that "homosexuals were liabilities and must be eliminated from the services."[58] Far from being a liability, Davisson's job performance was so stellar that two colonels risked their professional reputations on supporting the young officer, whose admission of homosexual sodomy defied the military's normative moral standards. The psychiatrist's conclusion that Davisson "is of value to the military," despite the evidence indicating his homosexuality, also opposed the exclusionary logic by suggesting that homosexuals could be valuable assets to the services.

As Davisson's case suggests, military officials struggled to confirm the sexual orientations of service members in the context of competing evaluations that sometimes contradicted the defendants' personal testimonies. As early as 1952, high-ranking military officials challenged the military's exclusionary logic by arguing that a soldier's private sexual encounters had no bearing on his public duties. Ultimately, the absence of a universal standard to determine the degree to which homosexual tendencies made personnel unsuitable for military service created a legal climate for alleged homosexuals to challenge their sentences. In this tenuous environment of vague and contradictory definitions, accused soldiers often successfully challenged their criminality by utilizing the appeals process to contest unfair sentences or trial proceedings and to receive sentence reductions, reversals, and rehearings. Their steady stream of appeals increased the length and cost of prosecution by courts-martial and contributed to the falling rate of courts-martial for homosexuality as the Cold War progressed. As the court-martial's popularity receded given the choice of the quicker and quieter administrative discharge (and with the gay rights' movement), military courts lost much of their authority in the quest to regulate both heterosexual and homosexual service members' sexual lives.

Establishing Legal Protections for Homosexual Service Members

Alongside the thoroughly documented legal persecution of homosexual soldiers ran a parallel, but less visible, pattern of legal protection that preceded the civilian gay rights movement. The creation of the Uniform Code of Military Justice after World War II and the Court of Military Appeals in 1951 made the postwar military justice system ripe for legal reform because the UCMJ streamlined the services' various policies by which criminals were prosecuted and guaranteed all soldiers the right to due process regardless of their crimes. The CMA, in turn, was vested with supreme authority to interpret the provisions of the UCMJ in a manner that respected the rights of all service members to due process in the military justice system. Accused service members often contested unfair trial proceedings and sentences by appealing to the CMA, which had the power to reverse, reduce, or dismiss court-martial sentences.[59] Ruling on a series of homosexual sodomy cases that began in 1952 and continued into the 1970s, the CMA and a handful of military review boards reversed nearly as many guilty sentences as they upheld, setting a powerful legal precedent of protecting the basic constitutional rights of service members regardless of their sexual orientations and their alleged criminality. These legal victories challenged the legitimacy of the military's exclusionary logic by recognizing homosexuals as legitimate citizens whose private sexual lives had no bearing on their job performance or troop morale. However, because no one systematically studied these cases, their collective implications often went unnoticed to both the general public and the military community.

Navy chief engineman E. Knudson was the first of many alleged homosexual soldiers to achieve the justice commonly afforded to heterosexual service members. Charged with and convicted of sodomy in violation of Article 125, the general court-martial sentenced him to a dishonorable discharge, total forfeiture of all pay and allowances, reduction to the grade of fireman recruit, and confinement at hard labor for one year. Knudson contested being tried by court-martial and petitioned the secretary of the navy for relief on the grounds "that he was tried and acquitted in a California state court on 4 April 1952 for the identical offense involved in the present trial." Navy policy generally dictated that "a person in the naval service should not be tried a second time for the same act for which he was once punished as a result of a conviction in a civil court."[60] The review board denied Knudson's petition for relief of trial by court-martial on the grounds that the Navy Department's policy protecting soldiers from double jeopardy did not apply to alleged homosexuals. SECNAV directive 49-882, dated December 10, 1949, waived homosexual service members' rights to protection from double jeopardy in an effort to discharge as many homosexuals as possible.

Knudson also challenged the prejudicial nature of the court-martial proceedings by arguing that the presiding law officer permitted the trial counsel to "make inflammatory remarks without directing the court to disregard them."[61] Knudson felt the sum of these inflammatory remarks adversely impacted his right to an impartial jury. The review board agreed with Knudson that the "trial counsel's questions and remarks concerning an alleged attempt by the accused to exert political pressure to forestall trial by court-martial were improper," but it concluded that such "misconduct" on the trial counsel's part "did not result in substantial prejudice to the accused" since "the record established beyond reasonable doubt that the offense of sodomy was committed."[62] In other words, the NBR reasoned that the jury would have found Knudson guilty even without the inflammatory remarks because his guilt was obvious from the evidence alone.

The CMA heard the case in 1954 and reversed Knudson's guilty conviction on the grounds that the convening authority's action of interfering with the law officer's decision to grant Knudson's request for a continuance was illegal and "prejudiced the accused in a substantial right."[63] Knudson's case was ultimately the first to protect alleged homosexuals from double jeopardy despite regulations exempting them from such protection. As one of the first cases of homosexual sodomy to reach the newly created CMA, Knudson's legal victory during the McCarthy era's lavender scare set the tone for the legal victories to follow.

PROTECTIONS FROM UNFAIRLY PREJUDICIAL EVIDENCE AND TESTIMONY

In addition to protection from double jeopardy, the CMA enforced alleged homosexuals' right to a fair trial without prejudicial evidence or testimony, as revealed by U.S. Navy lieutenant R. Warren's court-martial. In 1955 Warren was charged with two offenses of sodomy and two offenses of taking indecent liberties. His trouble began in March 1952 when he was a university-based Reserve Officers' Training Corps (ROTC) instructor for the navy. An ROTC student of Warren's named Durant filed a sexual assault charge against him, claiming that Warren made "improper advances" toward him after a night of drinking that "ultimately resulted in the completed act of sodomy." Before Durant's trial took place, a seaman named Swailes filed similar charges against Warren a year later, claiming that on January 2, 1953, he and Warren "occupied the same bed" at the South Caroline home of "Kip and Jerry," where sodomy and other "immoral acts" occurred.[64] At the court-martial hearing, a prosecution witness named Cisa attested that he knew Kip and Jerry had lived together in numerous apartments and that he had seen Warren frequent those various places. On one occasion in 1949 or 1950, Cisa had observed Warren impersonating a woman and claimed that Warren "cracked a few jokes and did a little jig of some sort and embraced, took a peck or a kiss as you call it" with "Kip and Jerry." Another prosecution witness, one Hoblitzell, testified that he had met Warren in Charleston in 1949, and on an automobile ride Warren had "fondled his person." Hoblitzell "was drunk at the time," but he "presume[d] it went on further, on into the act of homosexuality."[65]

Warren testified on his own behalf, corroborating many of the facts stated by Cisa and Hoblitzell but denying all facts of an incriminating nature. He challenged the general court-martial's ruling of guilty on the grounds that the law officer presiding over the court-martial admitted prejudicial evidence against him that negatively influenced the trial outcome. The CMA heard Warren's appeal in 1955 and ruled that "the damning nature of the evidence could not help but prejudice the accused in the minds of the court-martial members" since it undermined his credibility. Judge George Latimer concluded, "We are sure that when [Warren] was tarred with the possible commission of two despicable crimes, his credibility was impaired."[66]

The evidence the law officer admitted against Warren was prejudicial because the acts of sexual misconduct described by Swaines and Cisa were completely unrelated to Durant's charge. In the case of Cisa's testimony, Judge Latimer reasoned that "it is difficult for us to ascertain how a prior unrelated act of misconduct by the accused with a third party has a tendency to establish an illicit relationship with either of the present participants." Whether Warren impersonated a woman and embraced a man or not was irrelevant to the charges of sodomy committed with Durant because an accused "does not bare his soul to all of his previous sexual habits and he can hardly be expected to defend against one or many other separate lewd and lascivious transactions which are uncharged and unrelated to the one in issue."[67]

Regarding Hoblitzell's testimony, Latimer reasoned that "his inability to fix dates and places with any degree of certainty magnifies the unfairness to an accused in admitting testimony of this kind" because "the more remote the prior conduct, the more difficult it becomes to refute the charge."[68] The CMA protected Warren from prejudicial testimony by ruling that evidence in sexual perversion cases was only admissible if it proved that acts of prior sexual misconduct were between the accused and the victim in the present case. In ruling that testimony of past homosexual tendencies did not presume Warren's guilt in the present charges of sodomy, the judges clarified the blurry distinction that the service regulations confused between homosexual *acts* and homosexual *tendencies*. The CMA ultimately reversed Warren's original sentence to dismissal, total forfeiture of pay and allowances, and confinement at hard labor for one year, and it ordered a rehearing of the entire case. By banning all third-party testimony unrelated to the incident between Durant and Warren, the high court sent a strong message to legal officials: the past intimate relationships of alleged homosexuals that were unrelated to the present court-martial were not open to legal interrogation and interpretation.

Accusatory questions and suggestive innuendos also posed formidable barriers to homosexuals' rights to a fair trial. In Sgt. 1st Class R. Bird's case, the U.S. Army Review Board reversed the court-martial and the convening authority's finding of guilty and ordered a rehearing of the case to protect Bird from accusatory questioning and innuendos. Tried by general court-martial in Stuttgart-Möhringen, Germany, in 1957, the court found Bird guilty of attempted sodomy with two privates, Greene and Murphy. Bird denied the charges and offered good character evidence from one colonel, Kunzig, but the accused was subjected to a lengthy interrogation. The prosecuting attorney asked Bird, among other questions: "Back in 1954, did you ever fondle anybody's legs—male legs? . . . Have you ever given anybody in your company, Headquarters Company, any reason to feel that you were queer? . . . Do you have a bad character when it comes to homosexual tendencies?"[69]

The review board ruled that these questions were prejudicial because they insinuated Bird's guilt and deprived him of a fair trial by jeopardizing his credibility in the eyes of the court members. Reasoning that the prosecuting attorney "may not, through the use of accusatory questions and other tactics suggest the existence of offenses of the accused which he cannot otherwise prove," Judge Advocates Lancefield and Howell protected Bird's right to impartial interrogations and established a precedent of enforcing alleged homosexuals' rights to a fair trial in future sodomy cases.[70]

Bird's case illustrates a noteworthy trend in military justice during the Cold War—that is, the CMA was not the only court that protected alleged homosexuals from injustice. At intermediate levels within the military justice system, review boards often upheld alleged homosexuals' rights to due process.

Prejudicial evidence and accusatory questioning were not the only ways service members' rights to a fair trial were jeopardized. The bias of court members on the issue of homosexuality and improper punishment also threatened service members' rights to a fair hearing and sentencing, especially when the court members were high-ranking officers or commanders who used their superior rank to sway the actions and opinions of lower-ranking court members. Both the CMA and military review boards asserted alleged homosexuals' rights to trials free of such command control. Trials for sodomy and homosexuality during the Cold War were especially vulnerable to command influence because homosexuality evoked extremely strong opinions from service personnel about morality and religion. Court members ranged in rank from the lowest to the highest grades, and officers often presided over trials as presidents, giving them wide-ranging authority to dictate the circumstances of the trials. Presiding officials often wielded the power of their ranks to influence other court members' decisions about a defendant's guilt or innocence.

Consider the 1956 sodomy case of U.S. Army private C. Lackey. Pleading guilty to the charge, he received a dishonorable discharge, total forfeiture of pay and allowances, and confinement at hard labor for two years. While the convening authority reduced the length of his confinement to one year, the review board ultimately dismissed the charges after it found the president of the court had abused his rank and deprived Lackey of his right to an impartial trial, which Article 61 of the UCMJ guaranteed to all soldiers regardless of sexual orientation. On voir dire examination by the defense counsel (who was a first lieutenant), the president of the court, Colonel Hollis, expressed dissatisfaction with the declining severity in punishments for guilty soldiers.[71] Colonel Hollis recalled, "It was rather simple when I started because I was told that my duty was to find a man guilty or not guilty and when found guilty I was to sentence him very strong, usually giving him the maximum and let the convening authority cut it down."[72]

Hollis's statement indicated that he felt courts should impose severe sentences since higher authorities could reduce extreme punishments. When Lackey's attorney challenged Hollis on the grounds that his beliefs prevented him from fairly and impartially considering the issue of appropriate punishment, Hollis interpreted the defense council's challenge as a personal attack on his professional competence. Emphasizing his seniority over the defense council, Hollis stated, "I've had twenty years service and I've set [sic] on a lot of courts. If I am incompetent to sit on this court," he continued, "then frankly I consider myself incompetent to continue wearing this uniform."[73] The defense council responded by withdrawing his challenge of Hollis's impartiality.

The judge advocates reasoned that Colonel Hollis intimidated the defense council with his superiority when he stated, "I would think that you were not doing your duty if you felt that I was sitting up here prejudicing." Arguing that "the argumentative remarks of the president of the court . . . objecting to his challenge and making it a personal issue possibly may have overawed the latter and deterred counsel from pressing the challenge for cause," the judges asserted Lackey's right to an attorney who felt free to perform his duties fully. Reprimanding Hollis on his embarrassing display, "whereby he draws around himself the mantle of the military uniform, and utilizes his superior rank and longer service to discredit a counsel who is properly endeavoring to perform his duty in representing an accused," Judge Advocates Lancefield and Ayars asserted Lackey's right to have impartial court members.[74]

The CMA faced a similar case in 1957 that "must be catalogued with those which are a discredit to military law," and it moved swiftly to protect the accused's right to impartiality of the court members. In what the judges termed an "unparalleled situation," a law officer had persuaded the staff judge advocate and the convening authority "to use their influence to compel a conviction of the accused."[75] The accused, U.S. Army private J. Kennedy, was found guilty of assault with intent to commit sodomy and given the maximum punishment of five years' confinement at hard labor, total forfeiture of pay and allowances, and a dishonorable discharge despite the "victim" of Kennedy's assault's refusal to acknowledge that Kennedy had attacked him. In an extremely rare circumstance, the convening authority approved the maximum punishment (normally convening authorities reduced sentences), though the majority of service members found guilty of homosexual sodomy received much more lenient sentences.

Kennedy appealed to the CMA on the grounds that he was denied a fair and impartial trial "by improper influence of the law officer and authorities not detailed as court personnel." In an effort to "bring home to all law officers the necessity of remaining neutral," the judges dismissed Kennedy's case entirely. They reasoned that "to affirm a finding of guilty nurtured in that sort of climate would resurrect all the evils of command control and leave the court processes in the hands of those who should be outsiders to the courtroom drama."[76] Had Kennedy not appealed to the appellate court, he would have spent five years in military prison and the remainder of his life struggling to overcome the stigma of a dishonorable discharge for a crime that the prosecution could not prove. By protecting Kennedy's right to an impartial trial by court-martial—a right granted to all soldiers by Article 61 of the UCMJ—the CMA refused to allow military courts to trample soldiers' rights to due process regardless of their criminality or sexual orientation. The cases of Lackey and Kennedy were monumental legal victories for homosexual service members because they established that alleged homosexuals would not be excluded from Article 61's protection.

In addition to protection from double jeopardy, prejudicial evidence, and biased court members, the CMA asserted homosexuals' rights to immunity and protection from government entrapment in the case *United States v. Haynes*. In 1957 Airman 1st Class C. Haynes was tried by general court-martial for charges of sodomy, attempted sodomy, and extortion. Agents with the Air Force Office of Special Investigations (AFOSI) brought the charges against Airman 1st Class Haynes after he made questionable admissions of homosexual tendencies. The record established that Haynes underwent extensive questioning and polygraph testing by various AFOSI agents in order to receive a security clearance. The agents told him that the sole purpose of the testing was to ensure that he was qualified to receive a top-secret security clearance and that he had "complete immunity as to any revelations he might make and that everything he said would remain secret and confidential."[77] Despite the agents' assurances, they used his answers as evidence of his homosexual acts. The review board dismissed Haynes's claim that he was unfairly denied a grant of immunity by ruling that the AFOSI agents did not have the power to grant such immunity in the first place. The review board also denied the defense's challenge for cause after the voir dire examination revealed that one of the court members had participated in the administrative disposition of homosexual service members and was biased in his determination of Haynes's guilt or innocence.

Airman Haynes appealed to the CMA on the grounds that the AFOSI agents did not uphold their grant of immunity and that he had been entrapped in a direct violation of his constitutional and UCMJ rights. The high court reversed Haynes's guilty sentence in 1958 on numerous grounds, including that of inadmissible evidence. Ruling that the prosecution's evidence was inadmissible because it was obtained deceitfully—that is, under the promise of confidentiality—the judges upheld Haynes's right to protection from "entrapment." Mirroring the logic of a similar case in civil court, the CMA refused "to convict an entrapped defendant, not because his conduct falls outside the proscription of the statute, but because, even if his guilt be admitted, the methods employed on behalf of the Government to bring about conviction cannot be countenanced."[78]

Though the conviction was dismissed by the review board, Haynes's attorney claimed he could prove that his client's experience "was not an isolated incident" but an "improper and illegal scheme on the part of the testing agency to which not only the accused, but others, fell victim."[79] Recognizing the likelihood that the AFOSI employed similar deceitful tactics to weed out other alleged homosexual service members, the CMA wielded its appellate authority to prevent AFOSI agents from trampling alleged homosexuals' rights to immunity and protection from entrapment.

PROTECTIONS FROM UNREASONABLE SEARCHES

Service members suspected of homosexuality often had their rights to privacy violated when investigators, attempting to prove sexual perversion, sought evidence in the service members' private quarters. Navy radarman C. Hillan became the poster boy for this issue in 1957 when he was court-martialed for homosexual sodomy. The evidence that prosecution witnesses offered as the basis for Hillan's homosexuality was obtained illegally. A shore patrol officer at a YMCA in Norfolk, Virginia, entered Hillan's room without a warrant after hearing his bedsprings creaking. The officer caught Hillan and another man engaged in anal sodomy.

The prosecution justified Hillan's guilt based on what the patrol officer saw after he entered the room unannounced, but the military review board invalidated it because the patrol officer's entry without a warrant, regardless of what he saw after he entered the room, violated Hillan's Fourth Amendment right to privacy. Condemning the patrol officer's unannounced entry into Hillan's room on the grounds that no reasonable cause existed to support the officer's action, the review board dismissed the prosecution's circular logic by reasoning that "if the noise incident to a YMCA bed be sufficient to establish 'unusual circumstances,' then every squeaking bed in every hostelry would be grounds for search."[80] In a striking admission that service members, regardless of sexual orientation, were citizens first and service members second, Judge Tyson remarked:

> It is only these rights and privileges, that make up the Bill of Rights, which stand between the citizens of this great country and the Police State—a phenomenon not unknown to today's world. The greatest, most impressive and solemn duty of the courts is to zealously guard and preserve these rights. In guarding these rights courts are not concerned with the guilt or innocence of a particular accused, for our system of justice—the system that has given this country strength, courage, and preserved independence—provides that no man may be convicted except by due process of law.[81]

The CMA echoed the review board's protection of Hillan's rights to privacy in the 1963 court-martial of C. Battista, a U.S. Navy officer and dentist who was charged with sodomy and inducing seamen who were under the influence of drugs to pose for nude photographs. As in Hillan's case, the prosecution's evidence was obtained in violation of Battista's Fourth Amendment right to privacy and against searches without probable cause. After a dental patient complained to the Office of Naval Investigations agents that Battista had engaged in an act of sodomy with him while he was semiconscious from drugs purportedly administered for medical purposes, the agents searched Battista's office "to see if they could uncover something that would suggest homosexuality."[82] They found photographs to which the victim had also alluded; however, the appellate court ruled these photographs were inadmissible evidence in Battista's trial because the agents' reasons for the search were "purely intuitive." Although the photographs proved Battista's guilt, since the search was "exploratory and general and made solely to find evidence" of Battista's guilt, the CMA ruled that it was unconstitutional and that the photos were thus inadmissible.[83]

In a similar case in 1968 involving army captain J. Woodard, the CMA again upheld service members' Fourth Amendment rights to privacy and searches based strictly on probable cause. In Woodard's case, the prosecution used a book of photographs, described as "homosexual literature," as evidence of Woodard's motive to commit homosexual sodomy. With cutthroat logic, the judges countered, reasoning that the mere "possession of a book of photographs of famous paintings is not evidence that the possessor is a lover of art."[84] By ruling that the book was not evidence of Woodard's commission of the act of sodomy, the CMA reiterated the distinction between homosexual tendencies and homosexual acts, again protecting alleged homosexuals from the dangers of blurring such distinctions.

By 1972 military judges were questioning the UCMJ's criminalization of homosexuality altogether. In the only case where military courts prosecuted a female soldier for same-sex sodomy between 1950 and 1975, legal officials debated the limits of regulating adults' sexual lives. Pvt. C. Ortega of the U.S. Army Women's Air Corps (WAC) was convicted of committing an "indecent, lewd, and lascivious act" against another female WAC, Miss Meehan, in violation of Article 134. The general court-martial found Ortega guilty, but the CMA dismissed the charge on the grounds that the presiding legal official erred when he recommended polygraph testing to ensure Ortega's honesty *after* he declared Ortega's guilty sentence. Protecting Ortega's rights to a fair trial—in this case a trial at which the presiding law officer did not adhere to an appropriate sequence of events to verify the evidence beyond a reasonable doubt—two judges argued that the UCMJ's criminalization of consensual private sexual acts perhaps went too far when it violated the adults' rights to privacy.[85]

Judge Vinet dissented from the majority opinion that Ortega's charges should be dismissed and argued that Ortega's sexual orientation led to sexual acts that, although consensual and private, were antithetical to good order and discipline in the armed forces. Lesbianism, in Vinet's opinion, was tantamount to sexual promiscuity because two members of the same sex could not be legally married. Vinet considered any sexual relationship outside of marriage to be the moral taboo of fornication, but lesbianism, in his opinion, was a particularly degrading form of fornication. He wrote that the sexual promiscuity that inevitably resulted from same-sex relationships "frequently leads to assault or more grievous crime as a result of jealousy, or to extortion based on well-established societal norms."[86] Notably, the courts increasingly adopted Vinet's mind-set in the last quarter of the twentieth century when prosecutions for same-sex sodomy reached an all-time high.

Conclusion

Alongside the legal persecution of homosexual soldiers in the U.S. military during the Cold War ran a parallel pattern of legal protection that laid the groundwork for the eventual repeal of the military's controversial don't ask, don't tell policy. Seizing upon the tenuous environment created by ambiguous definitions of what constituted homosexual acts and tendencies, many alleged homosexuals challenged their criminality by appealing guilty sentences to the CMA on the grounds that their rights to protection from double jeopardy, unfair trials with prejudicial questioning and evidence, command control, entrapment, and unfair searches and seizures were violated. In a stunning admission that homosexuals were worthy of legal protections from tyranny in the military justice system, the CMA and select review boards overturned or reduced roughly half of the guilty sentences for alleged homosexuals between the Korean and Vietnam Wars.[87] This is not to suggest that the CMA was entirely immune to homophobic stereotyping, however. As Judge Vinet noted in his dissenting opinion in Private Ortega's case, after the review board overturned her guilty sentence for homosexuality at court-martial: "The seduction of our young men in the service by the homosexual is a singularly detestable and reprehensible crime. It is apparently a growing evil, or else it is more noticeable now than ever before. The evil corrupts; it can destroy those it touches. It should be wiped out. But it must be wiped out in a manner consistent with the protection of our Constitution."[88]

Despite the reprehensibility of what Vinet believed was the homosexual's inevitable tendency to seduce young heterosexual men, he admitted that the court's primary role was to protect the due process rights of even the most perverse sexual deviants.[89] Though suspected homosexual soldiers were discharged via court-martial more than they were retained in the services, their legal victories complicate the misconception that the Cold War witnessed the intensification of discrimination against all homosexual service members.

That the declining prosecution rates for same-sex sodomy mirrored those of adultery and bigamy was no coincidence. The financial cost and time investment required for courts-martial in the face of manpower and money restrictions certainly contributed to commanding officers' decisions to handle crimes of sexual deviance administratively. Administrative discharges were a cheaper and more efficient means of ridding the services of alleged sexual deviants. But the changing political climate between the Korean and Vietnam Wars also contributed to the declining courts-martial rate. During the McCarthy era of the 1950s, in the midst of the federal government's relentless witch hunt to oust purported homosexual government employees from their jobs, the services' rates of prosecuting alleged homosexual service members by courts-martial were at an all-time high. As lesbian, gay, bisexual, transsexual, and queer (LGBTQ) people began to organize into a publicly cohesive movement after the Stonewall riots in 1968, the gay rights movement began to target the military's homosexual exclusion policy specifially.[90]

After the highly publicized Stonewall riots carved out a legitimate public space for voices of LGBTQ people to criticize discriminatory homophobic policies, the services increasingly bypassed prosecutions by courts-martial to minimize public criticism that the gay exclusion policy received (especially at the height of the U.S. military's involvement in Vietnam). The number of same-sex sodomy courts-martial dwindled to an all-time low immediately after the Supreme Court's ruling in *O'Callahan*, which limited the military courts' jurisdictional authority to crimes that were strictly service connected. But as chapter 6 illustrates, this record low was only temporary. The rise of the New Right and the momentum of President Ronald Reagan's conservative revolution in the 1980s steadily drowned out public criticism of the military's gay ban with a call for a return to traditional family values (and their accompanying notions of masculinity and femininity).

Ultimately, same-sex sodomy victories (and the legal debates from which they stemmed) posed a considerable challenge to the courts' simultaneous efforts to enforce a standard legal definition of military masculinity that was avowedly heterosexual. More than courts-martial for extramarital sexual relations or moral misdemeanors such as consuming and sharing pornographic material, prostitution, exhibitionism, and voyeurism (as discussed in chapter 5), same-sex sodomy courts-martial had the powerful and, for some, dangerous potential to redefine the parameters of the military's social relationships by proving that service members did not have to be heterosexual to be outstanding troops, providers, or protectors. These cases also illustrate the messy, fluid, and highly contested nature of the military justice system's efforts to define and enforce gender and sexual classifications that, though treated in such a manner, were not necessarily biologically "fixed" and unchangeable categories. As a result of this haphazard process of translating exclusionary policies into practice at sodomy courts-martial, alleged homosexuals were not universally discharged from the services. Though an unintended consequence of Article 125 and of the courts' commitment to enforcing it, the very policies that discriminated against alleged homosexual service members generated legal avenues through which gays and lesbians could exercise their due process rights as both service members and U.S. citizens.

5

Protecting the
Public Morals

On February 9, 1951, Lt. Col. H. Jewson, commander of the army's 235th Field Artillery Observation Battalion at Camp McCoy, Wisconsin, permitted the showing of an obscene film. Titled *Mamie and Her Box*, it featured "a naked woman lying on a bed facing the camera . . . slowly caressing her genital area and then fondling her naked breasts and body."[1] Prior to the party, Jewson had granted Pvt. R. Levy a three-day pass to travel to Columbus, Ohio, and obtain "dirty" films for use at the battalion party. Meanwhile, men in Jewson's command procured a motion picture projector and set it up in an indiscreet room, where "tarpaulins were draped over the windows" to ensure secrecy of the operation.[2] When the battalion was assembled, Jewson turned off the lights and started the film, only to be interrupted moments later by Colonel Bullard, the post commander, who had learned of the battalion's plans for the stag party days prior.[3]

Colonel Bullard crashed the party, immediately relieved Jewson of his duties, and appointed Maj. F. Stewart, the executive officer of the battalion who was visiting his home on a three-day pass, to assume temporary command. Colonel Bullard directed Captain Rehfuss, the battalion adjutant, to call Stewart and inform him of the incident. Stewart commanded Rehfuss to "hold the officers there" until he arrived on post so he could speak with them about the incident. Once on post and out of earshot of Colonel

Bullard, Stewart told the men that "nobody was to know where these films came from" and that he would see to it that Private Levy, the procurer of the films, would remain silent so that no one would get in trouble. According to Levy's testimony at trial, Stewart summoned him from his quarters and ordered him both to deny any knowledge of the films and to lie about the reason for his three-day pass to Columbus, pressing him to "have a darn good reason for going home."[4] Levy's determination to tell the truth to investigators after initially denying any knowledge of the films led to Stewart's being tried jointly with Jewson.

Colonel Bullard brought charges against Jewson and Stewart for conduct unbecoming of officers and prejudicial to good order and discipline. Jewson was charged with making false official statements to investigators about his role in the incident and with wrongfully and knowingly permitting and assisting in the exhibition of a lewd and obscene motion picture to a mixed group of officers and enlisted men under his command. He unequivocally denied the charges, arguing instead that he thought the film was "based on the technical manual relating to a happy marriage."[5] Stewart similarly denied his guilt on multiple charges of "wrongfully and corruptly attempting to influence prospective witnesses . . . with intent to impede an official investigation."[6] To indict Jewson on the charges, the U.S. Army Board of Review had to establish a uniform definition of the interchangeable terms "obscene" and "lewd." Relying on the *Webster's New International Dictionary* for its interpretation, the review board adopted a working definition of *obscene*: "offensive to taste; foul; loathsome; disgusting; offensive to chastity of mind or to modesty; expressing or presenting to the mind or view something that delicacy, purity, and decency forbid to be exposed."[7]

In the ABR's unanimous opinion, the film *Mamie and Her Box* met all of the requirements necessary to be ranked as obscene and lewd because "in any community," the members reasoned, "a motion picture portraying such actions would be considered vulgar, repulsive to good taste and offensive to common decency and morals."[8] What made the incident even more repulsive to the board was that Jewson, as acting commander, abused his responsibilities as a commander, husband, and father in public to the detriment of his family, his career, and the army. His leadership role in showing such a film to the men in his command, the board concluded, "unquestionably compromised his position as an officer[,] . . . disgraced him as an individual[,] . . . and [was] of a nature to bring discredit upon the military service."[9] To add insult to injury, showing the pornographic film violated a Wisconsin statute making it illegal for a person to possess obscene moving pictures for the purpose of exhibition. The board found Stewart's dishonest and manipulative conduct, in attempting to use his rank to influence the witnesses at trial, no less disturbing. The court's unanimous decision to dismiss Jewson and Stewart from the army foregrounded the authorities' intentions to protect the decency and morality of the service community by punishing its members' forays into the underworld of perversity and obscenity.

Though adultery, bigamy, and sodomy occupied most of the courts' attention when policing service members' intimate relationships, they did not encompass the entire scope of the legal system's sexual surveillance apparatus. Where marital infidelity and sodomy were, by nature, private crimes that offenders typically committed out of public view, military courts defined other crimes of sexual deviance in relation to the public spectacle and disturbance they created. These offenses included possession and distribution of pornography, exhibitionism and voyeurism (more commonly known as indecent exposure and window peeping), and engagement in prostitution and pandering. Though some of these crimes did not directly threaten the sanctity or stability of the marital unit, the nuclear family, or even human life (with the exception of prostitution), the married servicemen—and they were all men in the time frame studied—who committed such offenses usually lost their families as a result of separation and divorce. Moreover, they did something legal officials believed was just as dangerous: they exposed the general public to immoral ideas and actions that, if left unregulated, would slowly corrode the communal standards of social responsibility, self-discipline, and integrity that many believed were the moral bedrocks of democracy.

Wielding the vague and elastic power of Articles 133 and 134, legal officials defined these moral misdemeanors as conduct that was "offensive to common propriety, offending against modesty or delicacy, grossly vulgar, lewd, or obscene."[10] For officers, such ungentlemanly conduct included but was not limited to "public association with notorious prostitutes" and crimes of "moral turpitude."[11] Additionally, such conduct generally "must offend so seriously against law, justice, morality or decorum as to expose to disgrace, socially or as a man, the offender, and at the same time must be of such a nature or committed under such circumstances as to bring dishonor or disrepute upon the military profession which he represents."[12] But the *Manual for Courts-Martial* did not specify which actions constituted crimes of moral turpitude, leaving such determinations to the discretion of individual judge advocates.

Similar to the problems arising out of Article 133's vague definition of moral turpitude were uncertainties with Article 134 about the extent to which indecent conduct was prejudicial to good order or disreputable to the military. Though the MCM advised that conduct was prejudicial to good order and discipline or disreputable to the military when the prejudice or disrepute was "reasonably direct and palpable," what was reasonably direct and palpable to one judge advocate was often unreasonably direct and impalpable to another.[13]

Legal officials' efforts to protect public morals often contradicted the basic tenets of masculine military culture that condoned (even encouraged) overt, public forms of sexual expression and conquest. Public displays of sexual virility functioned as key ways in which servicemen validated their own heterosexuality and earned each other's respect. Fraternal consumption and exchange of pornographic material, indecent exposure, and window peeping, for example, provided outlets for servicemen to prove their heterosexuality, daring, and manliness to each other and themselves. Violence often accompanied both public and private acts of sexual conquest, however. One need only look to the thousands of court-martial transcripts featuring prosecutions for group rapes of women and children on a global scale to see an unseemly side of a culture of masculinity rooted in a deadly combination of violence and sexual conquest. For this main reason, many commanders of overseas U.S. military installations turned a blind eye on their troops' sexual engagements with prostitutes.[14]

As a result, legal officials struggled to reconcile public displays of military masculinity with their responsibility to protect public morals from the obscene, indecent, and perverse. Interpreting crimes of moral turpitude in terms of marriage and the nuclear family, the courts prosecuted obscene conduct that undermined the attitudes about loyalty and morality that the UCMJ dictated servicemen should exhibit in their relationships with women and children in public. The significantly smaller numbers of courts-martial for these crimes (as compared to those for adultery, bigamy, and sodomy) suggest not that servicemen committed these acts less frequently but that commanders often resorted to other means besides the courts to punish such conduct. The incidents that did warrant trial by court-martial were typically so overtly public in nature and damaging to the military's reputation that legal action was the only viable means of counteracting the negative stigma associated with such crimes.

Pornographic Consumption

The extent to which the military justice system regulated service members' possession and distribution of obscene and pornographic matter served as a litmus test for determining how far into service members' private lives legal officials would venture to enforce standards of sexual decency. One main challenge was reconciling a practice that seemed deeply ingrained in military culture with a revised legal code that condemned service members' engagement with the realm of the obscene. Another challenge was establishing a universally agreed-upon definition of what actions, materials, and circumstances constituted "obscene," "pornographic," and "indecent." As one judge candidly explained, "Like obscenity, indecency is a word that eludes a clear, simple definition conveying a generally accepted meaning. Although we have difficulty in defining what indecency is, we believe we know what it is not."[15] The crime of pornographic consumption evoked considerable debate among legal officials not only about how to define indecency but also about how far the military's jurisdiction extended into the private homes of prosecuted service members. These debates also mirrored the issues facing obscenity regulation in civil law at the same time.[16]

Pornography was threatening to the military's status quo on a number of levels. Not only did it promote the idea that sex could be used for pleasure rather than strictly for procreation but it also challenged traditional gender roles by revealing women pleasuring themselves or each other independently of male participants. Most important, material that featured "unnatural" sexual encounters, such as anal and oral sodomy between both same-sex and heterosexual couples, violated biblical and legal norms of appropriate sexual expression. The military courts struggled with the following questions: When did pornographic consumption become indecent, and what exactly was indecent about it?

Was it the public spectacle of sex for pleasure that made fraternal viewing of pornographic film indecent, or was it the nature of the material itself—threatening as it was to the military's notions of loyalty to family, traditional gender roles, and sex within marriage for procreation—that made its consumption indecent even in the privacy of service members' own homes?

As the military took legal action against suspected homosexual service members, the fraternal viewing of films featuring homoerotic encounters complicated the issue by exposing an uncalculated number of troops to ideas about the potentially pleasurable experiences they might have with other men. In response, legal officials established a zero tolerance policy toward the consumption of any pornography that aimed to "excite the animal passions, and to corrupt and debauch the mind."[17] Between 1951 and 1966, legal officials utilized a series of pornography cases to establish exclusive jurisdiction over this moral misdemeanor, which threatened to undermine cherished values about what constituted decent sexual behavior, both on public military installations and in service members' private residences. Though slight in number in the 1950s and 1960s, the stunning persistency with which justice officials dismissed or discharged from the service a handful of officers and enlisted personnel for viewing pornography exemplified the gravity of the offense and the swift punishment other service members would receive if they trod the same path. No other crimes of sexual deviance elicited such a uniform and unanimous display of legal censure from the courts.

From its inception in 1951, the Court of Military Appeals formulated an official stance on the circulation and consumption of pornographic material in the military community. The 1951 joint trial of army officers Jewson and Stewart, whose organization and exhibition of a series of pornographic films at a battalion party earned them a permanent spot in the military justice system's hall of shame, established a precedent for all pornography cases that followed. In 1953 an army review board dismissed three officers in Georgia for committing identical offenses to those committed by Jewson and Stewart even though character evidence pointed to the three officers' continuous attendance at church, their high moral standards, and their prior combat service in World War II and Korea.[18] Because the officers failed to uphold the standards of moral conduct deemed essential to officers and gentlemen by "wrongfully and willfully debauch[ing] the minds and morals of subordinate military personnel, including minors, by exhibiting . . . an obscene, lewd and filthy motion film," the ABR unanimously agreed to their dismissal, while the CMA refused to hear their appeal.[19] Thirteen years later, a U.S. Air Force Review Board discharged an enlisted airman stationed in France for showing a pornographic film to a group of his comrades, thereby extending the responsibility for lapses in moral conduct to enlisted personnel as well as officers.[20] By 1966 service members of all ranks and stations around the world were expected to refrain from public, fraternal consumption of pornographic material.

Military courts did not limit their jurisdictional scope solely to fraternal viewings of pornographic material. To the contrary, legal officials aggressively regulated service members' consumption and transfer of pornographic material in their private residences and through the mail. In the first court-martial to address the transfer of obscene matter, an army convening authority defined *transfer* in a way that protected service members' right to travel with and possess pornography on federal military installations so long as they used it individually (rather than sharing it or viewing it communally) and did not give it to anyone else. In this case, U.S. Army private C. Schneider was court-martialed for (in addition to numerous instances of illegal drug abuse) bringing obscene photographs in his luggage from Fort Dix, New Jersey, onto Fort Jackson, South Carolina. The photographs were discovered in Schneider's coat pocket during a routine luggage check.

The original review board sentenced Schneider to a dishonorable discharge, total forfeiture of pay and allowances, and one year in hard labor confinement on the grounds that (in addition to being convicted of drug possession) his possession of pornography violated Title 18, section 1462 of the U.S. Code. The convening authority dismissed the pornography-related charge on the grounds that the ABR misapplied the federal statute in question. Rather than prohibiting "pornography and smut in Federal enclaves within the United States," the purpose of the statute was to "close the channels of foreign commerce to the importation of [obscene materials] and to assist the states by prohibiting the shipment in interstate commerce of such materials."[21] According to the convening authority, the evidence at Schneider's trial was insufficient to establish his participation in the interstate commerce of obscene materials because he was simply transporting the photographs as private possessions among his other personal belongings. By preventing the ABR's misapplication of the federal obscenity statute, the convening authority established (for the first and only time in the appellate record from 1951 to 2000) a precedent of protection for service members' rights to possess and use pornography in private on an individual basis.

The right of service members to consume pornography alone and in private stopped short of allowing personnel to exhibit obscene matter to others within the confines of their personal residences. This issue was resolved in the 1961 landmark case *United States v. Ford*, where an army review board charged Capt. R. Ford with conduct prejudicial to good order and military discipline after he mailed several obscene letters and exhibited and loaned a lewd book to a fellow officer within his private residence on a weekend afternoon.[22] Had Ford kept the lewd book in question to himself for his personal pleasure, he would have faced no criminal liability. In the confines of a private residence when the possession of obscene matter morphed into the exhibition of the material to an audience, the owner and exhibitor violated the high standards of moral conduct by which officers were expected to abide. Characteristic of the sodomy cases that involved legal officials' surveillance over the most intimate aspects of service members' lives, the *Ford* case set a precedent that granted the military justice system unlimited access to service members' private residences to monitor their use and transfer of pornographic materials.

Exhibitionism and Indecent Exposure

The fervor with which military courts carried out their moral mission to stamp out fraternal pornographic consumption carried over into prosecutions for public nudity, which was commonly referred to as exhibitionism or indecent exposure. Legal officials viewed the exhibition of one's private parts to public view as a crime of moral turpitude that, as one judge aptly summarized, "falls in that category of cases which are offensive to the decency, propriety, and morality of the community."[23] Public masturbation also fell under the category of indecent exposure because it undermined cherished beliefs about the sanctity of sexual fulfillment through heterosexual, monogamous marriage.

Part of what made the sexual pleasure associated with marriage so sacred was that (when performed appropriately and naturally and excluding sodomy) it occurred in private between one man and one woman and had procreative potential. This shared experience of private fulfillment theoretically strengthened the marital bond between heterosexual partners by cultivating desire, affection, and trust, which military courts protected from outside, public interference. Of what use was enforcing heterosexual, monogamous marriage and natural procreative sex if a man could get his sexual pleasure by watching other people having sex in public or by watching pornography in private? The courts found the same was true of pandering and participation in prostitution:

both acts undermined the sanctity of the marital institution by selling that which (at least legally and theoretically) should only be obtained through heterosexual, monogamous marriage.

Among the myriad crimes of moral turpitude that were prosecuted between 1950 and 1975, indecent exposure was the most frequently pursued. In the early 1950s when military courts were establishing precedents under the newly adopted UCMJ, service members who pleaded not guilty to committing crimes of indecent exposure were rarely given the benefit of the doubt, even when the accused had unblemished moral reputations and stellar service records. Similar to the statistics for pornography-related courts-martial, conviction rates for indecent exposure nearly equaled prosecution rates in the 1950s because the Court of Military Appeals consistently denied service members' petitions for rehearings. As this chapter illustrates, when the CMA finally reviewed an indecent exposure case in 1958, its decision to overturn hundreds of years of legal precedent ushered in an era in which convictions for indecent exposure became rare.

POLICING INDECENT EXPOSURE

After the UCMJ's inception, military courts wasted little time establishing precedents that enhanced their jurisdictional authority to prosecute active duty exhibitionists. The most important issues initially confronting the courts pertained to the sufficiency of related evidence and the nature of intent. In one of the first indecent exposure cases where the race of an accused service member became entangled in the trial proceedings (the race of an accused was explicitly noted in the trial record only in cases involving "Negro" service members), an army review board ruled that evidence of public masturbation was sufficient to sustain a conviction of willful and wrongful indecent exposure. In May 1951 Capt. J. Royston, an African American, was court-martialed at Camp Edwards, Massachusetts, for "willfully and wrongfully exposing in an indecent manner to public view his penis" in violation of Article of War 96.[24] The prosecution's sole witness, Miss Wallace, testified that on May 10, 1951, the man whom she later identified as Royston drove up and parked near her while she was sunbathing at Old Silver Beach in Falmouth, Massachusetts. Upon exiting the car, Royston meandered along the beach with his shirt off and pant legs rolled up until the two girls seated near Wallace left. When she arose to look for her dog, Wallace next noticed the man sitting on a log about fifteen feet in front of her was completely nude and "masturbating himself." She immediately left the beach and reported the incident to the military police (MP), offering the officers details about the man's car to assist in the criminal investigation. At a lineup shortly thereafter, Wallace unhesitatingly identified Royston as the man she had previously seen at the beach.

Royston knew nothing of the investigation until he was ordered to appear in a lineup with three other African American soldiers who, according to Criminal Investigations Detachment (CID) agent A. Culver, were "much darker" complexioned than the accused. After learning of the charges against him, Royston obtained Wallace's name and phone number and called to inquire whether she was certain that she had not mistaken him for another light-complexioned soldier. According to Royston's testimony, Miss Wallace informed him over the phone that she was unsure whether Royston was the man about whom she complained and that the accused's automobile was similar to the one she saw at the beach. At trial Royston testified that he did not go to Old Silver Beach on the day in question. Not only did his duties require him to be on post all day but also his wife had the vehicle from the time she dropped him off at work that morning until she picked him up that evening. Numerous witnesses testified on Royston's behalf that they had seen him in the office around the time Miss Wallace claimed he was at the beach committing his criminal act, though they could not say with certainty it was at the precise time in question.

In the face of competing testimony, the review board chose to believe Miss Wallace because the details she gave the CID agent about Royston's car—that it was black, had New York license plates, and had a sticker with the number 162 on the windshield—matched his registration information on file at the provost marshal's office. In defense of their decision to affirm the original ABR's conviction, Judge Advocates Barkin, Ruby, and Wolf argued that Miss Wallace's "forthright testimony" was more believable than the "conflicting" and "uncertain" witness testimony corroborating Royston's whereabouts. More problematic, the defense's evidence "intended to show not that the incident had not occurred but that the accused could not have been the perpetrator because he was elsewhere at the time Miss Wallace stated the offense was committed."[25] Though the original review board sentenced Royston to dismissal from the service, forfeiture of all pay and allowances, and confinement at hard labor for six months, the convening authority reduced his sentence to dismissal in light of his impressive educational and service record.[26] The CMA denied Royston's petition requesting an appellate review of his case.

The CMA's denial of Royston's petition for appeal is surprising given the seemingly blatant prejudicial error and racial discrimination that occurred before and during the trial. The participants in the lineup at which Miss Wallace unhesitatingly identified Royston as the perpetrator arguably set Royston up for a guilty conviction by giving Miss Wallace no other conceivable choice besides Royston. At the time the criminal act occurred, it is highly unlikely that Miss Wallace's quick glimpse at the man sitting fifteen feet away yielded a detailed memory of his physical characteristics. To the contrary, in such hurried and uncomfortable circumstances, Miss Wallace noted only general characteristics of the perpetrator—most notably, his "light" skin complexion.

Without other more specific physical features by which to identify the perpetrator, a lineup consisting of more than one light-complexioned African American man likely would have yielded different results.

That both Miss Wallace and the CID agent voluntarily noted the stark contrast in complexion between Royston and the lineup's other three men suggests that the difference was so pronounced that it caught their attention. How the review boards concluded that Miss Wallace's unhesitating identification of Royston under these circumstances contributed to the "forthrightness" of her testimony is inconceivable. While the review board found the choice of lineup members did not constitute prejudicial error or racial discrimination against Royston by precluding any possibility of his innocence, then its decision to believe Miss Wallace over a handful of army witnesses who corroborated Royston's testimony on the grounds that the witness testimony was "uncertain" surely violated Royston's right to a fair and unbiased trial. The convening authority extended this same irrational logic when it criticized Royston for providing evidence to prove that he was not the perpetrator. Rather than accepting reasonable evidence that Royston was innocent because he was not in the location at the time the crime was committed, the convening authority castigated him for not proving "that the incident had not occurred."[27]

But how was Royston to prove that the incident had not occurred if he was not at the crime scene? The convening authority's failure to see the correlation between Royston's absence from the crime scene and his innocence resulted in a gross violation of his due process rights to a fair and unbiased trial. Whether the ABR and the convening authority's refusal to evaluate Royston's case logically was motivated by racist inclinations is uncertain without other comparable indecent exposure cases featuring African American defendants. A preliminary comparison of Royston's case with the other indecent exposure courts-martial featuring white defendants, however, suggests that Royston's racial heritage had some bearing on the outcome. Whether intentional or out of a lack of common sense, stacking the lineup with men whose skin complexion differed so drastically from Royston's as to make Royston the obvious choice created the preconditions for finding him guilty. It is hard to imagine that any of the white servicemen charged with the same crime would have endured such unfair lineups if their skin complexion, like that of Royston, was a determining factor in their guilt.

Further, that Miss Wallace was a white woman diminished Royston's chances of walking free. In an era when miscegenation laws forbidding interracial marriages were still on the books in a last-ditch legal effort to protect white women's fictional "purity" and "chastity" from the alleged sexual predation of African American men, it is impossible to suppose that the review board was *not* influenced by the historic legacy of race relations in the United States. Royston's case suggests that judge advocates sometimes selectively ignored the cardinal rules regarding standards of evidence ("beyond a reasonable doubt") and the presumption of innocence when doing so reaffirmed their racial stereotypes. Certainly the CMA's subsequent refusal to review Royston's case in the face of such blatant violations of his due process rights enhanced the lower service courts' jurisdictional authority to determine both the scope of indecent exposure and the definitions of what constituted reasonable and sufficient evidence relatively free from appellate intervention.[28]

While *Royston* established (among other things) the precedent that willful and intentional exposure constituted indecent exposure, questions over the criminality of negligent exposure of one's private parts to public view enabled the courts to enlarge the scope of the crime. An army review board first ruled on the issue of negligent exposure in 1952 at the court-martial of Capt. W. Anderson, who was convicted of violating Articles 133 and

134 in Frankfurt, Germany. According to the trial record, two MPs apprehended Anderson in the Funfstube Café after a German waitress requested their assistance with a captain who had refused to pay his bill. Upon entering the café, the MPs found Anderson seated at a table in a drunken stupor with one shoe off, his trousers open, and his penis exposed and visible to the other patrons. His pants were wet, and there was a puddle on the floor and in the chair where he was seated. At the military police headquarters, Anderson testified that he had blacked out in the restaurant and remembered nothing except that he had gone to the café to have a beer earlier that day. At issue was whether Anderson should be convicted of indecent exposure since the evidence proved that he did not commit the act intentionally.[29]

After weighing the evidence, the review board unanimously convicted Anderson of "wrongfully exposing in an indecent manner his penis to public view" in violation of Article 134, as well as being drunk and disorderly in uniform in a public place to the disgrace of the armed forces in violation of Article 133.[30] To justify its decision, the ABR argued that it followed the precedents established in common law where indecent exposure could be committed whether it was intentional or negligent. The members also acknowledged that "the specification in question does not allege nor does the evidence reveal that the accused *willfully* exposed his penis to public view in an indecent manner." Regardless of Anderson's intent, they reasoned that his exposure was wrongful and constituted a violation of the UCMJ. Despite Anderson's combat record as a World War II and Korean War veteran, his sentence to dismissal and the CMA's subsequent denial of his petition for appellate review sent a powerful message to the global service community that war heroism would not excuse veterans from abiding by the military's ban on public nudity in any form.

Two years after *Anderson* expanded the definition of indecent exposure to include negligent instances of public nudity, an air force review board further expanded the scope of the crime when it ruled that indecent exposure could be committed against consensual adult partners of the same or opposite sex in private vehicles. In this strange case, Staff Sgt. L. Fletcher apparently picked up German national Herbert Berger in his car in Munich, Germany, and drove to the English Garden, where he parked in a secluded, dimly lit place. After exposing his penis to Berger, the two men climbed into the back of the car, where Berger committed an act of oral sodomy on Fletcher. H. Schedel, a German policeman who had been following Fletcher to give him a ticket for reckless driving, approached the car during this act and immediately called the MPs to retrieve Fletcher. At trial Berger testified that although he had consented to the act, Fletcher had indecently exposed himself to initiate the sexual relations. In response, Fletcher claimed that although his alcohol consumption had impaired his reasoning, he had not *willfully* exposed himself to Berger (author's emphasis added).[31]

In a puzzling decision, the review board convicted Fletcher of indecent exposure in violation of Article 134 rather than consensual sodomy, which was an Article 125 violation. Though Fletcher challenged the charge on the grounds that his exposure was not indecent because it occurred in his private vehicle with a consenting adult, the appellate review board affirmed his sentence of a bad conduct discharge and six months' confinement at hard labor. The judges rationalized that "the exposure occurred at a public place, albeit somewhat secluded, and that the occurrence of the act in a private automobile did not alter its 'public' nature." Although no one was present to witness Fletcher's exposure besides Berger, that "the indecency was capable of being seen by the public and . . . was observed only by a person who consented to it does not affect its criminal character."[32] Echoing the logic by which military courts prosecuted consensual sodomy, *Fletcher* established that public exposure of one's private parts precluded both the location and the nature (consensual or nonconsensual) of the crime. Combined with the precedent established in *Anderson*, by the end of 1954 the exposure of one's private parts was a criminal offense regardless of the perpetrator's intent, the victim's consent and/or biological sex, and the disposition (whether bustling with people or abandoned) of the public location.

The military courts' continuous expansion of what constituted exhibitionism came to a screeching halt when the CMA reviewed the case of Staff Sgt. L. Manos in 1958.[33] Manos petitioned the CMA for relief after a review board and convening authority ruled that he had committed indecent exposure in his private residence on Bergstrom Air Force Base in Austin, Texas, by getting dressed near his bedroom window. According to the AFBR, the actual commission of the crime occurred when, unbeknownst to Manos, a female neighbor saw him in the nude while peering through his window at midnight. Manos appealed the ruling on the grounds that he was the victim of his neighbor's criminal act of window peeping rather than the perpetrator of an indecent exposure crime. Ironically, Manos was also charged with window peeping, having been accused by the same neighbor who claimed to be the victim of his indecent exposure.[34]

The absurdity of Manos's conviction exposed the flawed logic underpinning the 1952 *Anderson* ruling. If negligent exposure was a crime in one's own private residence, practically anyone in the service community who showered or changed clothes in the vicinity of a window ran the risk of committing indecent exposure. Absurd as this logic seemed, however, the CMA judges readily acknowledged that European and U.S. common law criminalized negligent exposure, though not universally.[35] Even military courts had criminalized negligent exposure since 1944, or eight years prior to the *Anderson* ruling. The difference was that *Anderson* was the first case in which negligent exposure was held to be a criminal offense after the Uniform Code of Military Justice went into effect.

In a reversal of legal precedent, the presiding CMA judges unanimously overturned the *Anderson* ruling by decriminalizing negligent exposure. Dismissing the charge against Manos on the grounds that negligent exposure was not punishable as a violation of the UCMJ, the judges argued that intent was crucial for establishing the act's criminality. In keeping with the military justice system's universal precedent of intent, which required evidence of a purposeful motive for sustaining convictions and sentencing purposes, Chief Judge Ferguson asserted Manos was innocent because "an act resulting from simple negligence does not give rise to criminal liability." Adopting the logic of an Iowa case that held that exposure was a crime only when the perpetrator, as a "reasonable person," indulged in the behavior in the likely view of others, Judge Latimer reasoned that the circumstances of Manos's case proved that the exposure was hardly the act of an unreasonable man:

> If [Manos] had exposed himself during the daytime from a street window or where, as a reasonable man, he could expect women and their children to notice his performance, my result would be different. But here it was near midnight, the window had a rear exposure, the adjoining homes were clothed in darkness, and there was no indication of life. Those who viewed the performance were not members of a captive audience but willing observers who concealed their presence. Under those circumstances, the exposure could hardly be termed the act of an unreasonable man, for there was really no cause for [Manos] to suspect that he would be seen. . . . Merely because he did not exhibit the highest degree of care does not charge him with being negligent.[36]

In the aftermath of *Manos*, the CMA played an active role in reversing the guilty convictions doled out by lower courts for the crime of indecent exposure.[37] In the 1964 case of U.S. Air Force lieutenant colonel H. Conrad, for example, the CMA twice overturned the review boards' guilty convictions on the grounds that prejudicial error occurred and that the evidence presented at trial was insufficient to establish beyond a reasonable doubt that Conrad had publicly masturbated in his automobile.[38] Included among the evidence were outstanding character reports from multiple officers, efficiency reports characterizing Conrad as an "excellent officer seldom equaled," and testimony from Conrad's wife that she had no reason to believe her husband would commit such a crime because of the "great amount of moral degradation which [was] involved." Three years later, the CMA also overturned an AFBR's conviction of willful indecent exposure when the evidence established that the accused's conduct was negligent but, in light of *Manos*, did not constitute a criminal offense.[39]

By 1972 the CMA's reconceptualization of public nudity as an acceptable form of exposure when it occurred around members of the same sex solidified the liberalizing trend of the courts in the post-*Manos* era. It also illustrates the CMA's tendency to interpret policies through a heteronormative lens by assuming that sexual arousal could only occur when members of the opposite sex were in the nude together. Ironically, condoning same-sex exhibitionism ran counter to the courts' condemnation of "homosexual tendencies" in the service community. This reconceptualization of the association between public nudity and decency arose when Spc. 4th Class N. Caune defiantly removed all his clothes after the MPs ordered him to put his hands against a wall and spread his legs so they could search him for weapons. Though the original army review board convicted Caune of indecent exposure and insubordination, the CMA dropped the indecent exposure charge on the grounds that Caune's action did not constitute indecent exposure because it occurred in the presence of other males. According to the judges, "Nudity alone is not indecent, and there is nothing lewd or morally offensive in the presence of an unclothed male among others of the same sex."[40]

Though tempting to interpret this decision as evidence of relaxing attitudes about sex and nudity among military justice personnel in the mist of the women's and LGBTQ rights movements, the presiding judges more likely made it out of necessity. The realities of military service required personnel to live and work closely with each other, even sharing communal showers and commodes in army barracks and aboard navy vessels. If the CMA upheld the logic that nudity was a crime of moral turpitude among members of the same sex, then "members of the armed forces . . . would be vulnerable to charges as a result of their necessarily sharing sanitary facilities."[41] *Caune* had complex and far-reaching implications for the future enforcement of gender roles. By ruling that nudity among people of the same sex was not criminal, the CMA condoned the living and working conditions that, according to some, encouraged homosexual relations between servicemen—especially in remote locations where dependents were prohibited. Gendering the crime of indecent exposure also reinforced heterosexuality as the normative standard against which gender orientations and masculinities were judged. In an era during which accusations of homosexuality could ruin a service member's career and reputation, the best defense was to fulfill the heterosexual prototype by providing for and protecting one's spouse and children.

Voyeurism

Though rarely prosecuted in the history of military justice, military courts interpreted voyeurism (window peeping) as a crime of moral turpitude that violated community standards of decency, morality, and privacy. The voyeur was commonly labeled a "Peeping Tom," or one "who habitually sneaks up to windows and peeps in for the purpose of seeing the women of the household in the nude." Because of the indecency of fulfilling one's sexual desires by watching others in various states of undress without their knowledge, legal officials characterized voyeurism as "one of various sexual perversions . . . which tend to disturb the peace, endanger public morals, or . . . outrage public decency."[42] What made the crime especially indecent was the voyeur's blatant violation of the victim's (and the victim's family) right to privacy within the confines of a private residence. The victims of the voyeur's gaze were usually the dependent wives of active duty servicemen, and these actions presented a clear violation of the military's sexual code of ethics, which required brothers-in-arms to respect each other's privacy and sexual property (so to speak). Like adultery, a voyeur's violation of this unwritten sexual code of ethics often resulted in disorder, violence, and, in the worst cases, death. Consequently, the crime was both discrediting to the armed forces and prejudicial to good order and discipline in the military community.

The first voyeurism case to come under the purview of the UCMJ occurred in the 1956 court-martial of Airman 3rd Class D. Clark. The evidence established that Clark, under the cover of darkness, periodically watched two service wives through the window of a trailer without the women's knowledge or consent. Drawing on the only preceding voyeurism case that the army ever published, where the ABR ruled that window peeping was "contrary to ordinary standards of decency," Clark's review board sentenced him to a dishonorable discharge, forfeiture of all pay and allowances, and six months in hard labor confinement.[43] On appeal Clark challenged the charge on the grounds that his conduct was neither disorderly nor service discrediting because the victims of his gaze were the wives of servicemen "who were not such an integral part of the military service." By affirming Clark's conviction, the convening authority established the military courts' responsibility to protect not only service members from being the victims of the voyeuristic gaze but also their spouses and children who, according to the sexual code of ethics, were supposed to be protected from the sexual objectification of other servicemen. In denying Clark's petition, the CMA validated the convening authority's logic that the military justice system's duty was to "protect . . . the public from being involuntary subjects of the voyeur's curiosity."[44]

But not all suspected voyeurs committed the criminal act willfully. In the air force's 1963 court-martial of Lt. D. Merrill, for instance, the accused admitted his guilt to three charges of window peeping and to a prior history of voyeurism, but the convening authority reversed his conviction on the grounds that the law officer's instructions to the court regarding Merrill's mental responsibility amounted to prejudicial error. In a stirring testimony about his struggle to resist the overpowering impulse to peep into windows, Merrill testified that what began as his occasional engagement in window peeping in 1961 quickly morphed into a nightly routine that eventually garnered the attention of his supervisors and members of the housing community. While stationed at Hickam Air Force Base in Honolulu, Hawaii, Merrill admitted that "he had window peeped into approximately one-half of the homes there." Although knowing the behavior was wrong, Merrill explained that he had no control over his compulsion: "One minute I would be in the house; the next minute, I would find myself out in the lane. . . . I knew I was going out; I didn't have black-out periods or anything like that. I would think of my boy and my wife and tell myself 'Don't go,' and maybe even pick up a book or turn on the television, but in a few minutes I was out there."[45]

In Merrill's defense, a psychiatrist testified that Merrill suffered from "psycho-neurotic reaction or . . . a compulsive type of neurosis" that severely impaired his ability to control his strange urge. Similar to the behavioral patterns exhibited by addicts, Merrill's overriding impulse to window peep caused him so much anxiety that obtaining relief by indulging in the behavior overpowered his sense of guilt and responsibility to his family. Because Merrill's addiction to voyeurism compromised his ability to adhere to acceptable moral behavior, the convening authority ordered a rehearing of his case to ensure that he was not convicted for a crime over which he had no control.

Three years later, the CMA reversed army private J. Schoenberg's window peeping conviction on the grounds that the evidence proving his guilt was "scanty" and did not sufficiently corroborate the testimonials given by witnesses at trial even though the accused had confessed his guilt in a pretrial statement.[46] Unlike Merrill, whose voyeuristic impulses were not motivated by sexual desire, Schoenberg engaged in window peeping for the sole purpose of his sexual predation of a little girl. Though his window peeping charge was dropped, the CMA affirmed his conviction for the sexual assault of a minor.

Though scarce, voyeurism courts-martial were no less significant than those of pornography or indecent exposure for carving out the courts' jurisdictional authority to construct and enforce legal definitions of obscenity. They also complicated legal conceptions of sexual perversion by revealing that not all voyeurs willfully committed their crimes or did so to fulfill a sexual need. Notably, though classic window peeping cases largely faded from the case law in the 1970s, they reemerged in the last two decades of the twentieth century in a new, technologically advanced form. As chapter 6 illustrates, to keep up with the internet age, the military justice system adapted its means of "protecting the public morals" by redefining voyeurism to include surreptitiously using video cameras and web cameras (webcams) to watch others in various states of undress. As a result, legal officials entered the new millennium more committed than ever to preventing sexual perverts from corroding communal standards of decency.

Prostitution-Related Crimes

Nowhere was the tension between enforcing moral values and tolerating masculine military culture more readily apparent than at men's courts-martial for prostitution-related crimes. More than any other crime of moral turpitude, prostitution and pandering undermined the sanctity of the marital institution by buying and receiving for money that which theoretically and legally should have been attainable only through heterosexual, monogamous marriage. Yet, as numerous scholars have revealed, many overseas commanders seemed to tolerate, and even encourage, servicemen's interactions with prostitutes in foreign locales. Katherine S. Moon, for instance, argues that the Cold War alliance of the United States and the Republic of Korea (ROK) depended heavily on the illicit sex trade that flourished around the U.S. military's ROK installations from the 1950s through the 1980s. Both governments, she contends, promoted prostitution as a means of recreation for American servicemen, but they did so for different reasons. Whereas U.S. military commanders encouraged the trade to channel their troops' sexual needs into nonviolent and healthy outlets, ROK officials utilized the trade to make the alliance with their country more desirable to those military officials. The irony, of course, was that prostitution provided the context for countless crimes of sexual violence and homicide and for the rampant spread of venereal disease (although military brothels were often designed to prevent disease by subjecting the women to frequent gynecologic exams), and these consequences further strained the U.S.-ROK partnership.[47] Other scholars have uncovered similar trends in Hawaii; in occupied France, Germany, and Japan during and after World War II; and around U.S. military installations in Okinawa, the Philippines, and Puerto Rico.[48]

The U.S. military justice system contributed significantly to command responses to prostitution in overseas locales *and* the continental United States, though most scholars have focused solely on overseas locales.[49] Protecting the public morals meant that the courts cast a wide prosecutorial net over numerous activities that strengthened the illicit sex economy for servicemen including consuming and producing sexual favors for profit, publicly associating with notorious prostitutes, pandering, and maintaining or assisting in the maintenance of brothels. Of these criminal activities, military courts prosecuted service members the least for publicly associating with and purchasing sexual favors from prostitutes. Ironically, an "association with notorious prostitutes" was the only crime of moral turpitude that the *Manual for Courts-Martial* actually specified as an Article 133 violation. The frequency and leniency with which the courts prosecuted servicemen for such associations certainly contributed to the persistence of the illicit sex trade around U.S. military installations.

In the only case from 1950 to 1975 featuring a service member charged with the crime of publicly associating with a notorious prostitute, the appellate review board dismissed the charge because the original board erred by omitting the word "notorious" from the written trial record. The word "notorious" was an essential element of the offense because it "restates a time honored proposition of military law . . . that the discredit to the military service resulting from [such a public association] arises from the unfavorable reaction upon those observers of the association who are aware of the unsavory character and reputation of the accused's companion."[50] In essence, the military courts set a precedent early on by exempting public associations with prostitutes as a criminal offense punishable by the UCMJ. The lack of convictions for this crime was the direct result of this precedent: service members could legally associate with any prostitutes in public so long as the prostitutes did not have a "notorious" reputation.

Court-martialing service members for frequenting prostitution houses in violation of command orders was also rare in the U.S. military after World War II. Though the case law abounds with examples of American servicemen committing acts of violence in and around prostitution houses overseas, only three were actually charged with the crime of frequenting "houses of ill fame." The first, Pvt. 1st Class R. Moss of the Sixty-Seventh Technical Reconnaissance Group, was convicted of violating the provisions of a regulation from the Forty-Ninth Fighter-Bomber Wing headquarters by entering a house of prostitution in the vicinity of K-2 Air Base in Taegu, Korea, on July 5, 1951. The provision in question dictated that "all houses or buildings in the Taegu City-Taegu Air Base Area where prostitution is practised [*sic*] in any degree" were off-limits. Additionally, the provision designated a curfew of 9:00 p.m. for service members in Taegu City and within a ten-mile radius of Taegu. The evidence established that around three o'clock on the night in question, a military vice squad raided a house located a mile north of the base and discovered Private Moss lying on a mat in his underwear with a Korean woman while accompanied by two other airmen and four Korean girls.[51]

Though the evidence was indisputable—Moss was outside the limits of the air base after hours and in a state of undress with a Korean woman—the U.S. Air Force Review Board reversed the charge on the grounds that the evidence did not prove beyond a reasonable doubt that the house in which Moss was discovered was one in which prostitution was "practised in any degree." While it did sufficiently establish that the Korean woman had engaged in or at least contemplated illicit sexual intercourse with Moss, the board contended that "illicit sexual intercourse with one man does not constitute prostitution" and that the presence of other airmen and Korean women in the house did not support the prosecution's claim that the house in question was one where prostitution was practiced. The board also rejected the logic on which Moss's charge of violating curfew was founded because neither the regulation in question nor the *Dictionary of United States Military Terms for Joint Usage* (1948) contained a specific "military definition" of the word "curfew." Without such a definition, the board determined that Moss had not violated curfew based on the "commonly accepted definition" set forth in *Webster's New International Dictionary*: "A regulation directing that fires be covered or extinguished at a fixed hour in the evening, when a bell was rung, in force in Europe in the Middle Ages; also the ringing of the bell, the time of its being rung, or the bell itself; hence the ringing of a bell in the evening as a signal, as for retirement of persons, now usually juveniles, from the streets."[52] Unable to find a requirement in this definition that imposed a duty upon service members to return to the air base at the designated hour of curfew, the board of review dismissed the charges against Moss entirely. Though preliminary, the decision signaled the lenient attitude with which the courts would treat similar cases in the future.

To sidestep future complications arising from the use of outdated definitions of words such as "curfew" in command directives that targeted prostitution, the U.S. Army designated entire areas as off-limits to soldiers in Korea. The Seventh Infantry Division, for example, created circular number 36, which forbade all United Nations personnel from frequenting houses of prostitution, indigenous eating and drinking establishments, and private homes of Koreans. Capt. A. Rice was subsequently court-martialed in 1953 for violating circular number 36 by visiting a house of prostitution with an enlisted soldier in the off-limits village of Uijongbu, Korea. Though Rice contended that the house in which the MPs apprehended him was not one of prostitution and that he did not know the village was off-limits, the review board affirmed his guilty conviction on the grounds that the estimated thirty to fifty off-limits signs posted at every approach route were too obvious for Rice to overlook.

That the house in question was located in an area known for prostitution activities and was occupied by three women, one of whom Rice witnessed having sexual intercourse with his enlisted companion, reaffirmed the board's suspicions that Rice willfully violated circular number 36 to "get a little dicking."[53] Though the maximum permissible punishment for violating a lawful general order was dismissal, total forfeiture of all pay and allowances, and confinement at hard labor for two years, the board generously sentenced Rice to dismissal and a fine of three hundred dollars for his lapse in moral judgment and leadership in the presence of lower-ranking personnel. This punishment was a further indication of the court's lenient attitude toward servicemen's associations with prostitutes.[54]

If the court's intent was to make an example out of Rice and discourage other officers who contemplated pursuing sexual pleasures in off-limits areas, the ruling had the opposite effect. Rather than viewing it as a warning, some service members interpreted Rice's lenient sentence as an invitation to participate in the illicit sex trade around military installations in overseas commands. U.S. Army first lieutenant F. Plummer, for instance, was charged with wrongfully frequenting a house of prostitution in an off-limits area "while wearing the uniform of a noncommissioned officer."[55] For his lapse in moral judgment, however, Plummer received an even more generous sentence than what Rice had faced. Urging that the charges against Plummer were multiplicitous for sentencing purposes, the Court of Military Appeals dropped one of the two charges and remanded the case to the convening authority for a reconsideration of his sentence based on the single charge of willfully entering a house of prostitution.

What broader conclusions can be drawn from this handful of cases in which service members were prosecuted for frequenting prostitution houses in overseas commands? From the standpoint of the court-martial, these cases suggest that the military justice system played a significant, albeit inadvertent, role in encouraging servicemen's forays into houses of ill-fame in overseas commands when the courts responded in a manner that made the crimes of publicly associating with notorious prostitutes and frequenting brothels much more forgivable than other felonies and misdemeanors. By dismissing the *Mallory* and *Moss* cases, the courts made the act of publicly associating with notorious prostitutes nearly impossible to prosecute and undermined the legitimacy of any curfews that commanders subsequently instated. Neither of the court transcripts after *Moss*, for example, references any violations of curfews. Captain Rice's lenient sentence and the CMA's subsequent dismissal of one of the two charges against Lieutenant Plummer strengthened this trend.

Without the courts' support, the only other means overseas commanders had to control servicemen's engagement with prostitutes was to utilize informal punitive measures; otherwise, they had to ignore the behavior altogether. Within the larger context of the Korean and Cold Wars, a commander's choice to turn a blind eye when servicemen frequented prostitution houses (unless they engaged in extreme acts of violence) was probably more cost-effective and less time consuming than channeling precious manpower and resources toward managing the troops' sexual morals. Such a rationale expands the possible explanations for command responses to the problem beyond what many scholars have interpreted as the commanders' support for the illicit sex trade.

Pandering

Pandering, maintaining brothels, and selling sexual favors for profit were no less serious in their threats to the marital union than associating with prostitutes. These crimes occurred on and around military installations both abroad and in the continental United States, thus challenging the misconception that military prostitution was solely an overseas pastime. In both domestic and overseas commands, the military justice system played a leading role in detecting and punishing "commercialized vice" and minimizing its impact on the surrounding communities' perceptions of the U.S. military's moral standards of conduct.

Legal officials prosecuted the crime of pandering, or enticing others to engage in acts of prostitution, most frequently between 1950 and 1975. The military justice system initially confronted the crime in the 1951 case of Cpl. J. Barcomb of the 356th Medical Group. While stationed at James Connally Air Force Base in Waco, Texas, he was convicted of unlawfully procuring a prostitute named P. Jones who engaged in illicit sexual intercourse with five other airmen for profit in violation of Article of War 96. The court duly sentenced Barcomb to a bad conduct discharge, total forfeiture of all pay and allowances, and confinement at hard labor for one year.[56] The Court of Military Appeals reversed the charges and remanded the case to the judge advocate general of the air force for a rehearing on the grounds that the law officer committed prejudicial error. Among a number of reasons, the CMA cited the judge's decision to admit into evidence the deposition of P. Jones, whom the defense argued was an incompetent witness because she exhibited extreme emotional instability.[57]

Though the CMA stepped in to ensure Barcomb received his rights to due process, the real importance of *Barcomb* lay in the definition the case established for the word "prostitute" and its legal implications for women at courts-martial. Defining *prostitute* as "a woman who indiscriminately offers her body for sexual intercourse for hire, but includes as well a woman who submits to indiscriminate sexual intercourse which she invites or solicits by word or act or any device," the board (and the CMA, which accepted the definition without challenge) endorsed an ideal of femininity that linked respectability with sexual prudence. By labeling any woman who had sex outside of marriage (whether by force or by choice) as a prostitute, the board constructed a legal barrier that all women who participated at courts-martial in the postwar world had to overcome. Because the military justice system's accepted definition of the word "prostitute" made it legally impossible for men to be considered sexually promiscuous (though the sodomy courts-martial unraveled this convenient myth), the burden of proof was on women to prove beyond a reasonable doubt that their actions, whether intentionally or unintentionally, did not solicit the sexual advances of servicemen.

In subsequent pandering cases, military courts refined their definitions of pandering to justify their continued commitment to the zero-tolerance policy.[58] In the 1957 case of Spc. C. Brown, for instance, the accused appealed his guilty conviction to the Court of Military Appeals on the grounds that the original U.S. Army Review Board's definition of "enticement" was vague. Brown was convicted of "wrongfully and unlawfully enticing other [servicemen] to engage in intercourse with prostitutes" at Fort Knox. The evidence established that on the evening of May 31, 1956, Brown and two other sergeants were having drinks in downtown Louisville when three women approached them and requested a ride back to Fort Knox. Claiming that he was unaware of the women's profession, Brown and his companions transported them onto the military installation. Parking in an unlit area across from the post chapel and close to the soldiers' barracks, Brown and his companions left the women alone in the car while they went into the barracks to alert the other trainees (the barracks housed trainees serving under the Reserve Forces Act of 1955) to the presence of "the three Louisville prostitutes."[59]

After "word spread like proverbial wildfire that the women in the car were prostitutes desirous of transacting business," two other cars joined Brown's and became the base of operations for the illicit activities. At the height of these business transactions, between fifteen and twenty trainees were congregated around the cars "in much the same manner," Judge Ferguson wryly explained in his opinion, "as moths hovering around a flame." Despite both Brown's claims that he had no idea what the "Louisville prostitutes" were doing in his car and the "acute case of memory failure" that made the prosecution witnesses who participated in the incident "extremely reluctant to testify," the presiding judges determined the evidence against Brown was enough to justify his conviction.

Justifying their unanimous affirmation of the original review board's guilty sentence, Judge Ferguson explained that he and his "brothers" were extremely "unimpressed with the narrow limitations [Brown] place[d] upon the word 'entice.'"[60] In light of a recent ruling in *Gentry*, Brown claimed that his conviction was unfair because his actions fell far short of enticing the other trainees to have sex with the Louisville prostitutes, but Judge Ferguson countered that he and his brothers interpreted the word "entice" in much broader fashion to mean "to wrongfully solicit, persuade, procure, allure, attract, draw by blandishment, coax or seduce . . . to lure, induce, tempt, incite, or persuade a personal to do a thing."[61] Brown's conduct of "bringing three eager prostitutes on a military reservation and placing them in close proximity to a barracks housing young and immature trainees of 17 and 18 years of age, and then aiding in the dissemination of news concerning their presence" was, according to Ferguson, "conduct well-calculated to entice, encourage, and invite one to engage in sexual intercourse with the prostitutes."[62]

In a change of course, the CMA reversed two pandering convictions in 1969 against army sergeants F. Adams and P. Wysingle even though the evidence in both cases plainly indicated that the soldiers were involved in "commercialized vice." Though the circumstances were identical to those involved in Brown's court-martial, the defense counsel for both sergeants successfully challenged the charges that the soldiers "enticed the servicemen to offer their bodies to promiscuous or indiscriminate sexual intercourse" by proving that the trainees whom Adams and Wysingle supposedly enticed did not hire out their own bodies for profit.[63]

The person who drafted the charges apparently inadvertently inserted the trainees' names in the space provided for the names of the female prostitutes, resulting in a specification alleging that the trainees—or the customers of the female prostitutes—were the actual prostitutes for whom Adams and Wysingle had acted as procurers. Consequently, the defense counsel for Adams and Wysingle argued that the specifications were legally defective because, "by common understanding, a prostitute is a female, and pandering involves enticement of a female, not a male, to engage in prostitution."[64] Ultimately, the matter of the wording cost the courts two successful prosecutions against pandering. As Chief Judge Quinn explained, "There is no doubt the draftsman of the specifications intended to allege that the servicemen did not hire out their bodies, the prostitute did, but the words he chose state exactly the opposite."[65]

Though the CMA reversed the charges because the evidence did not establish that the trainees were the ones whom Adams and Wysingle enticed to hire out their bodies for profit, the judges unanimously rejected the logic that the label "prostitute" should only apply to females, especially in the context of the "dramatic and drastic changes in overt sexual expression that have taken place in society in the decade following our decision in *Brown*." Expanding on the changes in sexual expression, Quinn continued:

> The theater, the movies, and the novel currently portray sexual intercourse with such specificity, and with such apparent public approval, as to suggest that the pandect of morals of the preceding centuries may perhaps need further gloss to measure aberrant sexual conduct under Article 134. We are

willing to assume that public indifference to the individual doing his "own thing" in the area of sexual relations is increasing, but we are not aware of . . . any evidence indicating a groundswell of public acceptance of commercialized copulation or intercourse so indiscriminate as to constitute prostitution.

In this context of relaxing attitudes about nonmarital sex and public nudity, Quinn observed that "a male as well as a female can lend his body for indiscriminate intercourse or intercourse for hire." No matter how accepting societal attitudes about "illicit sex" become, Quinn explained, "no cogent reason . . . justifies overturning precedent to hold, as a matter of law, that prostitution by a serviceman is not conduct to the discredit of the armed forces or conduct to the prejudice of good order and discipline."[66] In keeping with this legal precedent and despite the defendant's "commendable work performance," a U.S. Air Force Court of Military Review sentenced Staff Sgt. J. Wright to a bad conduct discharge in 1974 because his four counts of pandering were "so serious and so destructive of military order and discipline" that they warranted his removal from the service.[67]

Keeping Houses of Ill Fame in Government Quarters

Not all servicemen participating in the sex trade received sexual favors or earned money by arranging the illicit sexual exploits of others. Some personnel, such as U.S. Army private R. Butler, partnered with their wives and made extra income by converting their government quarters into "bawdy houses." Butler was stationed in Frankfurt in 1952 when he and his wife decided to capitalize on the typically high demand for prostitutes from servicemen stationed overseas for long periods. Assigned to dependents' quarters from November 1952 to February 1953, the Butlers rented out their extra rooms to American soldiers and female

German nationals to "engage in illicit sexual intercourse." At trial Private Butler testified that his wife had started the illicit business without his knowledge by requiring their German maid, E. Hacioglu, to pay a fee before taking male companions to her room. In addition to converting their government quarters into a "haven to engage in illicit sexual intercourse" for profit, the Butlers allegedly participated in "sundry, lewd and obscene acts of sexual perversion" with various clients who frequented their house of ill fame on a regular basis.[68]

At court-martial the Butlers were tried jointly and found guilty of operating a house of prostitution and of misusing government quarters by utilizing the rooms therein for immoral purposes; both of which were Article 134 violations.[69] Because the case was the first of its kind to appear before the military justice system, legal officials confronted the challenge of how to define the crime in a way that would yield a fair sentence to the accused. The U.S. Army Review Board agreed that the terms "house of prostitution," "bawdy house," "brothel," and "house of ill fame" were synonymous. The *Manual for Courts-Martial*, however, made a key distinction between the offense of "keeping a bawdy or disorderly house" and that of "running a home of prostitution": the difference was one of profit motive. Whereas "keeping a bawdy or disorderly house" referred to the act of using a private residence for immoral purposes without a profit motive, "running a house of prostitution" implied that the owner of the establishment was making money by hosting the illicit encounter.

The MCM dictated that keeping a bawdy or disorderly house was punishable according to the precepts of the Code of the District of Columbia (section 22-2722), which prescribed a maximum punishment of a fine not exceeding five hundred dollars or imprisonment not exceeding one year. For the offense of running a house of prostitution for profit, however, the code's section 22-2712 authorized imprisonment for not more than five years and a fine of not more than a thousand dollars. The MCM's table of maximum punishments classified the misuse of government quarters for immoral purposes as disorderly conduct, which warranted a sentence of confinement at hard labor for four months and forfeiture of two-thirds' pay per month for a similar period.[70] Because the Butlers' actions of running a house of prostitution undermined the U.S. military's international reputation as the morally righteous leader of the free world, they both received the maximum punishment of five years' imprisonment and a monetary fine ascribed by the Code of the District of Columbia.

The Court of Military Appeals entered the debate over how to punish the crime in 1956 at Fort Hood, Texas, in a nearly identical case to that of the Butlers at court-martial. In this case, army sergeant H. Mardis was convicted of an Article 134 violation when the evidence established that both he and his wife knowingly and willingly allowed their government quarters to be used as a base of operations for two prostitutes, Miss Sally B. and Miss Shirley W., from June until December 1954. The record also indicated that Mrs. Mardis worked alongside Sally and Shirley "from time to time" with her husband's approval. Apparently the heavy amount of "traffic" the underground business generated attracted the unfavorable attention of their neighbors, who alerted the MPs to the situation.

Under interrogation by the military police, Sergeant Mardis voluntarily confessed that he willfully had agreed to rent a room to the prostitutes to serve as a base of operations for their business ventures, and in exchange he received a portion of the proceeds. At trial, however, Mardis testified that his pretrial confession was false and that he did not know the activities were happening in his home during the time in question. When asked to explain why he had lied during the interrogation, Mardis said that he uttered the false statement "in the hope that his wife would come forward and tell the truth concerning her activities, rather than have him bear the mantle of keeper of a bawdy house."[71] Despite Mardis's having changed his story, the ABR found him guilty of disorderly conduct.

On appeal the CMA affirmed Sergeant Mardis's guilty conviction on the grounds that his claim of having given a false voluntary confession was "incredible, inherently improbable," and ultimately "unworthy of belief."[72] The activities were "so flagrant and notorious," Judge Quinn argued, that Mardis could not have been ignorant of the illicit purposes for which his house was being used. Because the offense of abusing government quarters for illicit purposes "has a measurable impact on good public order and morality," Quinn concluded, the CMA's decision to uphold Mardis's original conviction was neither "unnecessarily narrow" nor "harsh." Warning that "a man may not safely close his eyes to what is done within the four walls of his own establishment," the CMA ultimately set a high standard of accountability for servicemen (whom the judges viewed as being the heads of their households) residing in government quarters.[73] After the *Mardis* case, the military asserted that servicemen residing in government quarters were legally responsible for ensuring that their residences were not used to promote sex outside of marriage for profit or pleasure.

The judicial warning that a service member should not ignore the conduct occurring within his own residence also applied to the homes and establishments of others whom service members chose to visit. This precedent was established in the army's case against Capt. C. Boswell, who was court-martialed in 1963 on several charges: assisting another person in keeping a house of prostitution, wrongful cohabitation, and adultery. Boswell's trouble started in May and June of 1963 when he began pursuing an "intimate friendship" with Frau Gloeckner, a German divorcée who managed a small hotel in Kaiserslautern. Most of the chambermaids and waitresses at the hotel were prostitutes who "plied their trade at night" with a steady clientele of American servicemen. Captain Boswell, who was accompanied by his wife and children on his overseas tour of duty, frequented the hotel three to five nights per week and usually stayed until two o'clock in the morning to assist Frau Gloeckner in her private apartment with managerial duties. During this time, Boswell interacted with the prostitutes and their clientele and was fully aware of the nature of the disorderly establishment.[74]

The U.S. Army Review Board dismissed the charges of wrongful cohabitation and adultery because the evidence was insufficient to prove that illicit sexual relations occurred between Boswell and Frau Gloeckner; however, legal officials affirmed his guilty conviction for assisting in the maintenance of a disorderly house. For enlisted service members, the crime was punishable by no more than a partial forfeiture of pay and confinement at hard labor for four months. In a surprising modification of Boswell's sentence, the appellate review board replaced his original punishment of a dishonorable discharge with a fine of a hundred dollars on the grounds that assisting in the keeping of a disorderly house was no more serious an offense than "habitually participating in the disorderly practices of the house." A fine of one hundred dollars for an officer was considerably lenient given that enlisted service members could be sentenced to military prison for committing the same offense. Though Boswell was the first and last service member to be charged with this offense from 1950 to 1975, his lax punishment compared to those of Sergeant Mardis and Private Butler warned that participating in disorderly establishments maintained by others (absent any other criminal actions such as adultery, assault, or homicide) was a forgivable moral misdemeanor that the courts were willing to excuse for a minor fee.

Conclusion

Protecting the public morals of the military and civilian communities in which service members lived and worked after World

War II meant that the military justice system policed all crimes of moral turpitude that served as alternative outlets to marriage for the fulfillment of sexual needs and desires. Interpreting crimes of moral turpitude in terms of marriage and the nuclear family, the courts prosecuted behaviors that undermined both the attitudes about loyalty and morality that gentlemen were expected to exhibit in their relationships with women and children in public and the justice system's endorsement of natural sexual relations between a man and a woman for procreation rather than pleasure. These overtly public moral misdemeanors that challenged communal standards of decency were as threatening to the nuclear family ideal as crimes of marital infidelity and sodomy were because they drew public attention and criticism to the efficacy of the military justice system.

Not taking punitive action when servicemen engaged in public masturbation, communal viewings of pornographic matter, window peeping, and participation in the illicit sex trade compromised the U.S. military's international reputation as a morally righteous force in the global fight to contain communism and in the effort to expand the appeal of democratic institutions. But in the case of prostitution, the courts' intervention actually undermined command efforts to control servicemen's associations with notorious prostitutes by requiring the prosecution to prove that the prostitutes were, in fact, notorious. The effect, though unintentional, resulted in the wholesale decriminalization of servicemen's engagements with prostitutes, and it left overseas commanders ill equipped to prevent such associations.

The military justice system's regulation of crimes of moral turpitude was by no means unique in the postwar era. Mirroring dozens of state and federal laws that criminalized obscene and indecent language, gestures, and acts, the prosecution of service members' immoral behaviors at courts-martial kept pace with trends in civil law and signaled to the people and the world at large that the U.S. military was as moral as it was mighty. Prosecutorial trends also largely reflected predominating social mores and sexual values in civilian society. In the McCarthy era of the 1950s when sexual radicalism was associated with communism, prosecutions and convictions for service members who pushed the boundaries of sexual decency via pornographic consumption, exhibitionism and voyeurism, public masturbation, and prostitution-related activities reached their peak. Indecent exposure convictions, for instance, reached an astonishing rate of 95 percent in the immediate postwar era even though sustaining a guilty conviction for indecent exposure was difficult because, as with courts-martial for sodomy, typically little concrete evidence (other than the verbal testimony of the alleged victims) was available to prove the crime.[75]

As societal norms about sex and nudity relaxed in the midst of second-wave feminism and the LGBTQ civil rights movement in the 1960s and '70s, prosecution and conviction rates for crimes of moral turpitude generally declined (or stopped altogether in cases of pornographic consumption). This reduction was a result of both the liberalizing effects of the CMA's decisions to uphold service members' rights to due process and the shifting conceptions of gender roles that forced the courts to expand their definitions of masculinity and femininity to incorporate men and women who did not fit neatly into the established provider/protector and homemaker/helpmate roles. In the struggle to balance the dual demands of punishing criminal behaviors and protecting the due process rights of service members, the courts typically reached turning points after which more liberal conceptions of nudity and sex resulted in the decreasing prosecutions of sex crimes.

For indecent exposure, this turning point came comparatively early with the CMA's decision to decriminalize negligent exposure in 1958 upon realizing that a continued commitment to punishing incidents of indecent exposure would be a costly and absurd undertaking. In contrast, the turning point for pornography-related crimes did not occur until the 1990s when the CMA was forced to acknowledge that private consumption of adult pornography paled in comparison to the criminal indecency associated with the consumption or distribution of child pornography. Prosecution and conviction rates for pandering and maintaining brothels remained steady, however, because the courts expanded the traditional definition of the word "prostitute" to include men, thus addressing previously overlooked criminal behavior rooted in male promiscuity.

6

Policing Sex and
Marriage, 1976–2000

In 1988 a U.S. Air Force Court of Criminal Appeals convicted Sergeant Johnson, who had tested positive for the human immunodeficiency virus (HIV), of sodomy by fellatio, attempted sodomy, and aggravated assault for having unprotected sex with another airman. Though Johnson's commander had briefed him on how to prevent the transmission of HIV to his sexual partners, Johnson proceeded to have unprotected sex without informing his partner of his infection. In a unanimous and precedent-setting decision, the court ruled that Johnson's conduct was tantamount to aggravated assault for knowingly using his semen as a weapon to commit grievous and deadly bodily harm to another person.[1] Realizing that mere briefings on safe sexual practices were not enough to ensure that infected service members would follow them, commanders across the service branches in the aftermath of *Johnson* instituted official orders requiring HIV-infected service members to wear condoms and forewarn prospective sexual partners of their condition.[2] The army tested the legality of these command orders in the 1989 court-martial of Specialist Negron, whom a U.S. Army Court of Military Review (ACMR) convicted of willfully disobeying a superior's lawful order and of adultery in violation of Articles 90 and 134, respectively.

In August 1987 while Negron was living separately from his wife, he admitted to having intercourse on two occasions with

Private O. Though he wore a condom during both intimate encounters, out of embarrassment and fear of rejection he disclosed neither his infection nor his marital status to Private O.[3] Despite admitting his guilt, Negron challenged the legality of the command order on the grounds that it violated his constitutional right to privacy by unreasonably interfering with his intimate relationships. The convening authority upheld the regulation, however, arguing that it was a reasonably necessary measure to safeguard and protect the morale, discipline, and usefulness of a command. Though command regulations were admittedly not unlimited in their authority to regulate the private activities of service personnel, the *Negron* ruling ensured that HIV-infected service personnel would be held legally accountable for allowing their fear of sexual rejection to override their social obligation to protect innocent people from such a deadly virus.

The Court of Military Appeals (renamed the Court of Appeals of the Armed Forces [CAAF] in 1994) quelled any doubt about the legality of the HIV regulations in the 1994 case *United States v. Schoolfield*. In an almost identical scenario to that of *Negron*, Spc. K. Schoolfield of the army challenged his conviction for violating the HIV regulation on the grounds that it usurped his constitutional right to privacy by dictating the terms of his sexual encounters with women. He also challenged his aggravated assault conviction on the grounds that simply placing his penis in his partners' vaginas was not assault because he did not ejaculate. In a unanimous decision condemning Schoolfield's crime as one of detestable cowardice, the presiding CAAF judges affirmed both the aggravated assault charge and the legality of the HIV regulations. Likening Schoolfield's penis to a loaded gun, the judges rationalized that "because he is HIV positive, [Schoolfield's] gun is loaded and he assaults his victims by merely placing his penis in their vagina, whether or not he ejaculates in them."[4]

In the aftermath of these precedent-setting HIV cases, the courts consistently punished HIV-positive service members for unprotected sex as a felony crime. Similar to problems commanders faced when trying to control the spread of venereal disease, HIV-positive service members posed fatal health risks to their sexual partners. In response to increasing knowledge about the deadly effects of the virus and the steadily rising number of troops infected with it in the 1980s and 1990s, the courts created an entirely new category of sex crime that did not exist in the adultery and sodomy case law from 1950 to 1975. Consequently, the services generated a new (and evolving) set of regulations with which to police this unprecedented crime, justifying the expansion of the military's medical surveillance apparatus to routinely screen all service members for HIV. Despite service members' challenges to the constitutionality of the courts' surveillance and regulation of their "loaded guns," the military justice system of the twenty-first century stands poised to prosecute all servicewomen and servicemen whose irresponsible use of their "loaded guns" threatens to expose unknowing victims to this fatal infection.[5]

Though the last quarter of the twentieth century witnessed a general retreat of the government's legal surveillance over the marital and sexual affairs of citizens in the name of privacy, the opposite is true of the U.S. military justice system. The more expansive the armed forces became the more the military justice system's reach over the private sexual lives of active duty personnel grew. Astonishingly, the sheer number of courts-martial for crimes of marital infidelity and sodomy more than doubled in the last quarter of the twentieth century in comparison to the rates from 1950 to 1975. Out of an estimated total 2,298 sodomy courts-martial reviewed by military courts from 1950 to 2000, an astonishing 2,007 took place *after* 1975. Similarly, out of a total 600 adultery courts-martial from 1950 to 2000, 508 occurred after 1975.[6]

This drastic increase in prosecutions for crimes of sexual deviance occurred as military social issues worked their way into the mainstream media's discourse. Media coverage of the rise and fall of the controversial don't ask, don't tell policy, of top-ranking officers' extramarital affairs, and of rising rates of sexual assault catapulted the U.S. military's intimate strategies of social control to the forefront of the national news. Though neither legal scholars nor historians of gender, sexuality, and the military have offered a comprehensive review of the U.S. military justice system's regulation of sexual deviance in the last quarter of twentieth century, this task is essential for informing contemporary public policy debates about how to define and control sexual deviance and criminality.

The same punitive articles that authorized legal officials to prosecute sexual deviants in the military during the Cold War remain unchanged in the current edition of the Uniform Code of Military Justice; thus, the contemporary military justice system has astounding authority to police the private lives of the military community in the twenty-first century.[7] Moreover, critics of the military's seemingly antiquated legal code have questioned the constitutionality of military regulations that prohibit marriages between service members and citizens of host countries without express command approval and that criminalize consensual sodomy after the U.S. Supreme Court's landmark ruling in *Lawrence v. Texas*, which overruled all states' anti-sodomy laws.[8]

The following sections offer broad trends and patterns that emerged from the military courts' prosecution of crimes of sexual deviance from 1975 to 2000. Though summative in nature, this chapter offers evidence of the increasing importance of sex and marriage to the military's ongoing construction of gender and sexual deviance into the new millennium. Central to this process have been the courts' continued normalization and codification of heterosexual, monogamous marriage into military law. Using the courts' rulings, legal officials have defined and measured "deviance" and have justified the continued criminalization of service members whose marital and sexual behavior supposedly undermine the moral mission and reputation of the U.S. military community around the world.

Regulating Overseas Marriages into the Twenty-First Century

In 1978 the services updated the single joint directive on overseas marriages to clarify and justify the reasons for continued command interference in the marital choices of service members. At the same time that alien spouses became synonymous with potential national security threats, logistical command burdens, and embarrassments to the services, regulations endorsed the creation of "guidance classes" intended for those alien spouses whom commanders deemed worthy of marriage to American servicemen. The purpose of these command-sponsored guidance classes was to prevent the spouses from being overwhelmed by "adjustment problems upon arrival in the United States due to cultural change and [the] language barrier." By encouraging service members to enroll their fiancées in English classes and other appropriate courses aimed at teaching Western cultural values and customs, the regulations also led overseas commanders to initiate the assimilation and acculturation of their personnel's prospective alien spouses into U.S. society. By assisting these future U.S. citizens in learning English and Western values, guidance classes helped non-English-speaking spouses develop the "functional ability to live in the United States before [their] arrival in the country."[9]

Though a lack of available statistics renders an analysis of the effectiveness of these classes impossible, statistics for marriage approval processing from 1978 to 1980 in the Republic of Korea suggest that the procedural requirements for applicants persuaded many of them to reconsider their decisions to marry Korean nationals.[10] They also illustrate how rare command denials of marriage applications were at this time. Over a five-year period, service members submitted 16,608 applications to marry Korean nationals. In 1978 commanders approved 2,961 of a total of 4,137 applications received. Of the remaining 1,176 applications, applicants voluntarily withdrew them after deciding against marriage; none of these applications were denied. The same was true in 1979. Of a total 3,717 submitted applications, commanders denied none. Meanwhile, they approved 2,545, and 1,172 applicants withdrew their applications entirely. By 1980 the percentage of applicants who withdrew their applications increased to 38 percent, while the total number of applicants decreased by almost 12 percent. In that year, commanders denied only three applications and approved 2,048.

Table 1. U.S. Forces Korea marriage approval processing statistics, 1976–80

Year	Initiated	Completed	Disapproved	Withdrawn
1976	2,311	—	—	—
1977	3,154	—	—	—
1978	4,137	2,961	0	1,176 (28%)
1979	3,717	2,545	0	1,172 (32%)
1980	3,289	2,048	3	1,241 (38%)

Source: Eighth Army Provost Marshal, Special Investigations, letter, January 4, 1982, subject: Premarital Investigations; and Eighth Personnel Command letter, March 16, 1982, as cited in Branstetter, "Military Constraints," 5–22n38.

Although no records have been identified for the number of withdrawn applications for the years 1976 and 1977, the numbers provided indicate that the disapproval rate for that command was less than 1 percent between 1978 and 1980. The 30–40 percent withdrawal rate between 1978 and 1980 also suggests that a significant number of service members reconsidered their decisions after receiving counseling, additional time to reflect, and new information discovered during the investigation procedures. Proponents of the regulations contend that the withdrawal rate represented fewer logistical burdens for the U.S. Forces Korea (USFK) and increased mission readiness. What the statistics do not show are the number of Korean-American marriages that benefitted from the cross-cultural counseling and education these people received as part of the mandatory application process.[11] Though the USFK marriage statistics do not necessarily reflect those of other overseas commands, they do illustrate the effects of implementing the regulations in the command that boasts the highest number of international marriages annually (both historically and throughout the last quarter of the twentieth century).

Following the 1978 revision of the army regulations and the court-martial of Seaman Parker (as discussed in chapter 2), the issue of command regulation of international marriages received little attention until 1993 when the commandant of the U.S. Marine Corps Gen. Carl E. Mundy Jr. signed a directive prohibiting married recruits from joining the marines. Citing the high costs associated with supporting a marine's family as well as the low retention rate for married marines after completing their initial period of enlistment, the directive was set to go into effect on September 30, 1995.[12] The directive's few supporters praised it as a necessary step toward maximizing the corps's efficiency and effectiveness. Former assistant secretary of defense and secretary of the navy Jim Webb applauded the directive's intentions to minimize manpower losses while channeling money and resources into service members rather than their dependents.[13]

But the "constitutional questions [the directive] raised involving discrimination and privacy" rallied a host of critics, whose public outcry eventually secured its reversal. An outspoken critic,

Representative Pat Schroeder (D-CO) said, "If they are not allowed to be homosexuals and they're not allowed to be married, what are they supposed to do, take cold showers?" When President Bill Clinton's secretary of defense Les Aspin heard of the policy, he immediately reversed it on the grounds that the services' implementation of personnel policies that raised fundamental questions about "family values" was "sufficiently important [to] require his review."[14] Though General Mundy admitted that he "blind-sided" President Clinton and that it was "not one of [his] prouder moments in history," the quick demise of this directive was significant because, according to U.S. Army defense attorney and captain Dana Hollywood, it revealed that "although a Service may have legitimate ends in enacting personnel policy, it may prove to be so socially unpalatable and politically untenable that it becomes impossible to implement."[15]

Debates about the Mundy directive sparked public interest in the services' overseas marriage policy and ultimately led to its reversal in 1996.[16] For the first time since circular number 179's implementation in 1942, service members in every branch of the U.S. armed forces stationed overseas could marry foreign nationals (so long as these partners were of the opposite sex) without command interference. But this uncharacteristic freedom was short lived for service members stationed in the Republic of Korea. In 2007 the military issued a revision of AR 600-240 for U.S. Forces Korea (USFK 600-240) to address deteriorating U.S.-ROK relations over the problematic marriages of Korean women and American servicemen that resulted in large numbers of abandoned and waiting wives. Whereas *abandoned wives* referred to Korean women whose service husbands failed to assist them in obtaining visas and left them in Korea indefinitely when the servicemen returned to the United States, *waiting wives* were those who remained in Korea only because their visas had not been approved by the time their husbands' tours of duty ended.

The number of abandoned and waiting wives rose drastically after the overseas marriage regulation was rescinded in 1996. This increase was partly the result of the Defense Finance Accounting System's implementation of a new regulation in 2005 that alleviated the economic burdens of overseas marriage.[17] Granting an overseas housing allowance to all married service members whose dependents accompanied them on a non-command-sponsored tour, the regulation enabled single service members to upgrade their living quarters from the crowded confines of a barracks room to a spacious, fully furnished apartment or house off base. By marrying a foreign national in Korea, American service members also received more money each month.[18]

Without command regulations in place to enforce mandatory medical screening and counseling to service members on the potential immigration problems their intended spouses might encounter—a process that usually gave service members extra time both to learn more about their intended spouses and to change their minds about marriage—the rates of marriage, divorce, and abandonment of Korean spouses by American service members reached an all-time high. According to Captain Hollywood, from 1996 to the implementation of AR 600-240 for U.S. Forces Korea in 2007, the rising rate at which service husbands abandoned their Korean wives temporarily or permanently strained U.S.-ROK relations by draining the Korean economy and increasing anti-American sentiment among ROK citizens. Because access to U.S. military medical, housing, and shopping facilities stopped when their dependent ID cards expired ninety days after the sponsoring service member left the country, the abandoned and waiting wives and their children sought benefits through ROK social welfare programs.[19] To complicate the problem, many of the abandoned spouses were third-country citizens living in Korea on expired visas. Afraid of deportation and possible separation from their children (who gained U.S. citizenship through their fathers) if they sought help, countless abandoned spouses chose to "suffer in silence" and work low-paying, dangerous jobs as undocumented laborers.[20]

The high volume of abandoned and waiting wives and families was only one of a series of circumstances in the last quarter of the twentieth century that increased anti-American sentiment in Korea. The pro-democracy Kwangju Uprising was the turning point from which the U.S.-ROK relationship has never recovered. Later known as "South Korea's Tiananmen Square," this incident solidified anti-American sentiment when Koreans protesting the military rule of U.S.-backed dictator general Chun Doo-Hwan were massacred in the town of Kwangju in 1980. Charges of the Americans' complicity in the massacre planted the seed for more violent protests against the U.S. military's presence.[21]

U.S. Army private K. Markle's egregious murder of Korean prostitute K. E. Yoon in 1993 further strained the U.S.-ROK partnership. After raping Yoon and bludgeoning her to death with a soda bottle, Markle inserted a bottle into her vagina and an umbrella eleven inches into her rectum, and he covered her body and the crime scene with laundry detergent, believing it would act as lye and conceal the evidence. Yoon's death brought to the forefront of public discourse the disturbing issue of American servicemen's crimes against Korean citizens since the U.S. military occupation began in 1950. According to the National Campaign for Eradication of Crime by U.S. Troops in Korea (a non-profit organization of nearly fifty private ROK advocacy groups that formed in response to Yoon's murder), from 1967 to 1998 American troops committed almost forty thousand acts of criminal violence against Korean citizens.[22]

The growing presence of abandoned spouses and children generated so much "negative publicity" among Korean citizens about the immorality and irresponsibility of USFK troops that their commanding officers implemented USFK 600-240 to counter the force's deteriorating reputation.[23] Reinstituting the overseas marriage regulation was one of a few viable options to counter the negative publicity. According to Captain Hollywood, a more effective way to reduce the financial burden that abandoned families posed to Korea would have been a revision of the U.S.-ROK status of forces agreement. A revision promising a parental accountability standard for USFK troops would likely have strengthened the command's reputation by showing Korean citizens that Americans were willing to take financial and moral responsibility for the problems (and the people!) that the U.S. military's presence helped to create.[24]

In many ways USFK 600-240 is similar to its predecessors, not least in its similar paternalistic purpose to "ensure service members are protected against fraudulent marriage."[25] Its process also mirrors that of preceding regulations. In addition to requiring mandatory background checks, medical evaluations, parental consent forms for intended spouses younger than age eighteen, and the revocation of security clearances from those service members whose potential spouses pose intelligence threats to the United States, USFK 600-240 harkens back to the original 1953 regulation by requiring premarital counseling by the military chaplain on the particular challenges of interracial and cross-cultural marriages.[26] Additionally, whereas the 1978 regulation required one counseling session with the unit commander, USFK 600-240 requires two.

At the initial session, the commander is required to counsel the prospective couple about the importance of "understanding and accepting cultural differences." The second session is held without the fiancée and after a waiting period of at least forty-eight hours (which cannot be waived as the time is intended to allow troops to "reflect on the subjects discussed"). At this session, the service member may again meet with the commander to sign affidavits indicating that he received counseling on visa fraud and the possible involuntary extension of his assignment in Korea until all marriage and immigration requirements have been met.[27] By requiring two meetings with the commander and a forty-eight-hour reflection period, USFK 600-240 enforces a much more reasonable cooling-off period than the six-month period that led to Seaman Apprentice Nation's court-martial in 1958.

The main difference between USFK 600-240 and its predecessors is the inclusion of evidence of visa fraud among the preexisting reasons that warrant a commander's denial of a service member's marriage request. In response to cases such as that of U.S. Air Force staff sergeant G. Deguzman, whose sham marriage with a Korean national not only secured U.S. citizenship for the confidante of a drug lord and "master Korean criminal" but also opened the borders of the United States to the Korean mafia's black market activities, commanders also included evidence that the marriage is "solely for securing a visa for the intended spouse with no intention of living together as husband and wife" as grounds for command denial in the updated regulation.[28]

Just as legal officials questioned the logic of liability that commanders used to justify excluding suspected homosexuals from the services during the Cold War, military legal officials since 1975 have questioned the constitutionality of the overseas marriage regulations. In Captain Hollywood's opinion, USFK commanders are unqualified to counsel troops on immigration issues because they lack professional training in both immigration law and marital counseling. He also argues that command denial of marriage applications due to perceived financial instability, visa fraud, or the potential spouse's inability to obtain a visa is both subjective and unconstitutional given the U.S. Supreme Court's ruling in the 1978 case *Zablocki v. Redhail*. In determining that a Wisconsin statute requiring residents who were behind on child support payments to undergo financial and parental counseling before obtaining the court's permission to marry was unconstitutional, the majority of the court affirmed that the right to marry is so fundamental that courts should subject any law attempting to prevent it to a test of strict scrutiny.

At the same time, the court tempered this strict scrutiny rule with the confusing claim that not "every state regulation which relates in any way to the incidents of marriage must be subject to rigorous scrutiny."[29] At best *Zablocki* represented civil court's historic struggle to preserve both the private nature of marriage and the state's compelling interest to control it as a public institution. But it generated more questions than answers for military officials, who were uncertain whether civil courts would subject the overseas marriage regulations to the strict scrutiny standard if the opportunity arose. These questions reached their apex in 1996 when the services abandoned the regulations altogether. The ensuing nine years wherein servicemen married foreign nationals without any command oversight taught the services a tough lesson: when left unregulated, the problems generated by international marriages both undermined the U.S. military's reputation abroad and destabilized U.S. relationships with key democratic allies. Command leadership reinstated the overseas marriage regulations in the 2007 version of USFK 600-240 to salvage an already-strained partnership with the Republic of Korea.

That the U.S. Supreme Court will overturn the overseas marriage regulations is unlikely given the civil courts' deference to military decisions in the name of national security. The Supreme Court previously codified this deference into constitutional law in the 1953 case *Orloff v. Willoughby*, when it ruled that "the military constitutes a specialized community governed by a separate discipline from that of the civilian. Orderly government requires that the judiciary be as scrupulous not to interfere with legitimate Army matters as the Army must be scrupulous not to intervene in judicial matters."[30] The high court expanded its "specialized community" theory in 1974 by ruling that the need for obedience and effective discipline "may render permissible within the military that which would be constitutionally impermissible outside it."[31] This pattern of judicial deference gained momentum in later trials.[32] As a result, military laws and regulations flourish with little external interference despite the threats they pose to the fundamental constitutional rights of service members.

To date, USFK 600-240 still stands. Many USFK officials believe it has effectively prevented the problems leading to wives being abandoned or left waiting because the regulation has enabled commanders to suspend applicants' dates of expected return from overseas indefinitely until the U.S. Citizenship and Immigration Services approve visas for their wives.[33] The regulation is not, however, free from problems. In addition to raising constitutional concerns regarding the extent to which the military, as a "specialized community," can reasonably regulate the fundamental right of marriage among service members, USFK 600-240 offers no solution for cases where U.S. immigration services deny the visa applications of dependent wives. In these unfortunate instances, service members and their brides are faced with the same gut-wrenching decisions that confronted their predecessors. Do they terminate their marriages in defeat or commit to long-distance relationships for an indefinite time until the service members fulfill their terms of enlistment and return to the Republic of Korea permanently? Though this problem has no simple solutions, the mandatory counseling requirements at least ensure that prospective spouses are aware of this possibility when they decide to pursue their marriages.

The brief but fascinating history of overseas marriage regulations illustrates how the military's emergence as the world's premiere fighting force was highly gendered. As the foundational unit of social organization in the military in particular and the United States in general, marriage was a private relationship with profoundly public (and international) consequences. For this reason, military officials regulated the marital institution to ensure that marriages between service members and foreign nationals reinforced the military's reputation as a morally righteous and responsible global presence. As the USFK case reveals, prior to the implementation of USFK 600-240 in 2007, the unbridled marital aspirations of American service members in Korea threatened an already-fragile partnership when they abandoned their spouses and were not held accountable for financial support. In consideration of the Supreme Court's historic recognition of the armed forces as a specialized community that is largely immune to the dictates of civil law, that USFK 600-240 (and its twin variations in other overseas commands) will persist well into the twenty-first century is very likely.

Enforcing Monogamy and Natural Sex, 1976–2000

The courts enforced monogamy and so-called natural sex with a vengeance in the last quarter of the twentieth century by more than doubling the number of adultery and sodomy cases heard between 1950 and 1975. Male and female service members from all branches and ranks faced dismissals, dishonorable discharges, and confinement at hard labor for committing adultery both in isolation of other crimes and alongside more serious crimes such as rape, sodomy, indecent acts with minor children, and so on. The courts also continued to prosecute service-related crimes of bigamy, though without any significant changes or new obstacles from the pre-1975 cases.[34] But although the charges remained the same, the rules of the game changed. Military law regarding marital infidelity expanded to accommodate the increasing democratization of the armed forces. As more females enlisted in the services, more female enlistees were court-martialed on adultery charges. The introduction of new technologies such as video recorders and the internet, in combination with the increasing spread of deadly infections such as HIV, forced legal officials to redefine, expand, and sometimes create altogether new definitions of criminal activity that undermined the sanctity of monogamous marriage and natural sex.

A few noticeable trends emerged that differentiated many post-1975 courts-martial for adultery and sodomy from those of their predecessors. First, the courts increasingly combined charges of adultery with those of sodomy and indecent acts in the 1980s and 1990s. Recall from chapter 3 the courts stopped prosecuting "adultery by extension" of other crimes by 1970 because many convicted service members challenged the fairness of punishing them twice for a single offense. When the courts resumed prosecuting adultery via other crimes, the majority of the sodomy courts-martial from this time period included charges of adultery. The same is true of the increasing number of rape and sexual assault cases. Because a married serviceman's rape of a woman not his wife (or of a child) inherently constituted the commission of adultery, the courts increasingly prosecuted rapists for both the act of rape and the violation of monogamy that ensued. The result was an exponentially larger number of adultery prosecutions in the last quarter of the twentieth century.

Trends for sodomy courts-martial are equally intriguing. While the vast majority of consensual sodomy prosecutions during the 1950s and 1960s featured same-sex partners, effectively homosexualizing consensual sodomy (see chapter 4), service members convicted of consensual *heterosexual* sodomy increasingly appeared in courts-martial transcripts after 1975. As consensual sodomy became more heterosexualized in the 1980s and 1990s, the crime of consensual sodomy consequently underwent a period of de-homosexualization (but never carried the same negative stigma as same-sex sodomy). This trend does not necessarily suggest the emergence of a more tolerant legal attitude toward same-sex sodomy as the twentieth century progressed, but it does highlight the courts' increasing anxiety about (and commitment to) enforcing what they saw as natural sexual relations. This heightened effort to enforce natural sexual relations seemed to be partly a consequence of the rise of the New Right and the religious conservatives' call for a return to traditional family values since the military justice system's ongoing construction of gender and sexual deviance did not operate in complete isolation from the wider political climate of the country.[35]

As prosecutions for consensual heterosexual sodomy steadily increased in the last two decades of the twentieth century, so did the rate of *nonconsensual* sodomy courts-martial.[36] Where the courts of the immediate post–World War II era focused the majority of their attention on policing consensual same-sex sodomy (and hence ridding the services of "known homosexual liabilities"), after 1975 the courts shifted toward prosecuting coercive acts of both heterosexual and same-sex sodomy. As the number of female enlistees reached unprecedented heights in the 1980s and 1990s, documented incidents of sexual assault that resulted in courts-martial for nonconsensual sodomy and rape rose as well. This demographic shift resulted in another notable difference in pre- and post-1975 sodomy courts-martial: where the majority of nonconsensual sodomy victims in the 1950s and 1960s were civilian women (either dependent wives and daughters or women of occupied countries), active duty servicewomen increasingly became the primary victims of coercive sodomy in the 1980s and 1990s.[37] Consequently, the military justice system's role in policing crimes of sexual violence expanded exponentially in the last quarter of the twentieth century.

Protecting Public Morals into the Twenty-First Century

Policing public immorality in the military community in the last quarter of the twentieth century involved redefining crimes of moral turpitude within the broader context of the digital age. As emerging technologies such as the internet and webcams made the world of the obscene easier to access than ever before, the courts' attempts to expand their jurisdiction over the intimate lives of service members sometimes succeeded and at other times backfired. On the one hand, the court in pornography-related cases abandoned the practice of policing the private consumption of adult pornography in exchange for prosecuting child pornography cases. On the other hand, in voyeurism cases the courts expanded their jurisdiction by enlarging the traditional definition of window peeping to include spying with video recorders and webcams. Consequently, legal definitions of "sexual deviance" and "public immorality" have changed to meet the demands of military justice in the twenty-first century.

CHILD PORNOGRAPHY

Despite the hard line legal officials took against the consumption and exchange of pornography in the immediate postwar era, no pornography-related courts-martial occurred between 1967 and 1990. This absence of pornography-related prosecutions is puzzling when compared with the prosecution rate for other sex crimes over the same twenty-three-year period. During the 1970s and 1980s, convicted adulterers, sodomites, rapists, and those accused of other sexual indecencies colored the pages of military case law with a frequency that equaled or surpassed their prosecution rates during the 1950s and 1960s. How do we explain this phenomenon? Was it a result of changing attitudes about the indecency of adult pornography and its moral effects on service members or of changes in service members' consumption habits that made prosecutions difficult? Perhaps the volatile political climate of the Vietnam War demanded the courts' attention through 1975, or legal officials realized the futility of prosecuting a behavior that was deeply ingrained in military culture. Whatever the explanation, the twenty-three-year lull was—in retrospect—the calm before the storm.

When pornography-related courts-martial reemerged in the appellate record in 1991, military courts prosecuted service members for producing, possessing, and exhibiting child pornography. In doing so, legal officials upheld the constitutionality of the federal Protection of Children against Sexual Exploitation Act, which prohibited the possession and transport of child pornography among other things.[38] By continuing the zero-tolerance policy regarding service members' use of child pornography—even in the new medium of cyberspace, which made obscene material more widely accessible—the military justice system became a leader in the nationwide movement to extricate pedophiles from the broader community. In one judge's candid terms, military courts were in the business to "eradicate the evil of child pornography" in the military community.[39]

As a result, prosecutions for the private consumption of mainstream adult pornography quickly became obsolete. Only three courts-martial involved adult pornography between 1967 and 2000, with all occurring in 2000. In one case, the accused was charged with the robbery of his self-produced private sex video, which he had previously given to an X-rated video company, rather than with possession of pornography.[40] In another, the accused was dually charged with indecent acts with minors and for possession of pornography featuring adult women engaged in acts of bestiality.[41] In the final case, the court prohibited the use of government computers as a medium for the exchange, solicitation, distribution, and consumption of all obscene material involving both adults and children.[42]

Child pornography consumed the majority of the courts' attention in the last decade of the twentieth century. Air force major M. Talbert's court-martial in 1991 foreshadowed the insidious consequences that this mutated form of pornographic consumption had on the service community. Talbert was arraigned on three charges of conduct unbecoming an officer in violation of Article

133 after taking indecent liberties with three little girls at various times while he was stationed at Carswell Air Force Base in Texas. Upon admitting that he had photographed and videotaped the girls while they were sleeping, after removing their clothes and exposing their private parts with the intent of satisfying his sexual desires, the presiding judge permitted into evidence a briefcase that Office of Special Investigations agents had seized from Talbert's quarters. The briefcase contained more than two hundred pedophilic items including multiple photographs and videotapes of all three victims in the nude, countless pictures of toddlers and other children in swimsuits and various stages of undress, pages from catalogs displaying children modeling clothes, cut-outs from paperback books concerning sexual abuse of young children, newspaper articles about prosecutions of pedophiles, and an NBC video documentary of child molesters titled *Silent Shame*. In addition, the OSI agents found disturbing images of mutilated children in the briefcase.

Upon examining the contents of the briefcase, A. Clark, an expert witness and supervisor of sexual abuse investigations for the Texas Department of Human Services, concluded that Talbert was a "preferential child molester," or an individual sexually oriented toward children. She further testified that such individuals use photographs of "skimpily clad children" for sexual gratification and that such pictures are "just another step before they will be sexually abusing these children."[43] Seth L. Goldstein—another expert witness and director of the child abuse program in Napa Valley, California—testified that offenders such as Talbert, who fantasize while using child pornography, endanger the community because they "are constantly looking for more, which means more victims." Goldstein also argued that Talbert's possession of pictures of mutilated children indicated he posed a further danger to the community because "the potential for violence is there."[44] Despite Talbert's own acknowledgment that he was a pedophile, he appealed to the CMA on the grounds that the trial judge erred by allowing inadmissible expert opinion evidence concerning child molesters and that this error prevented him from receiving a fair and unbiased trial. The CMA, however, unanimously affirmed Talbert's sentence to dismissal and confinement at hard labor for five years.

The ruling and logic of *Talbert* laid the foundation for the military justice system's unflinching prosecution of service members caught with child pornography. The witness testimony against Talbert noting the causal link between consumers of child pornography and the sexual molestation of children dealt a damning blow to service members thereafter convicted of possessing child pornography regardless of their reasons for appeal. In 1993, for instance, the CAAF unanimously affirmed air force technical sergeant N. Tatum's guilty conviction for knowingly receiving child pornography through the mail and ruled the evidence did not substantiate his claim that government officials had entrapped him.[45]

One year later, the CAAF determined that solicitation of child pornography was equally as reprehensible as the crime of possession. In *United States v. Hartwig*, the CAAF unanimously ruled that soliciting children to participate in the production of pornographic matter constituted a violation of either Article 133 or 134, depending on the rank of the defendant. (In this case, the defendant solicited a school-aged girl to photograph herself in the nude and mail him a copy.)[46] Shortly thereafter, the CAAF issued another unanimous ruling condemning the solicitation of a mail-order catalog for the distribution of obscene videos and magazines depicting young children engaging in bondage, sadism, sodomy, bestiality, and male castration.[47]

Military courts expanded their jurisdiction over pornography-related crimes in 1995 when confronted with issues of extraterritoriality and the use of private computers and cyberspace for obtaining adult and child pornography. The issue of extraterritoriality emerged with the case of Staff Sergeant Pullen, who challenged his conviction for possession of child pornography on the grounds that the federal statute 18 U.S.C. 2252 (concerning the sexual exploitation of children) did not apply to him since he had committed the crime on a military installation in the Philippines. The U.S. Air Force Court of Criminal Appeals affirmed Pullen's conviction, ruling that the federal statute applied not only to the continental United States but also to all special maritime and territorial jurisdictions of the United States, as well as any land, building, or other natural or man-made structures owned by, leased to, or used by the U.S. government.[48] *Pullen* ensured that neither service members of the U.S. armed forces nor American civilian employees working on military installations around the world had immunity from prosecution under U.S. national standards of sexual decency.

The same year, in the landmark case *United States v. Maxwell*, the U.S. Air Force Court of Criminal Appeals expanded its jurisdictional authority to regulate pornographic material on service members' private computers. In this controversial case, Col. J. Maxwell, then acting commander of the Technical Training Center at Goodfellow Air Force Base in Texas, was convicted of conduct unbecoming an officer by possessing and distributing child pornography via his private email on his personal computer and was sentenced to dismissal from the air force. Maxwell appealed his case to the CAAF for consideration of whether the federal child pornography statute could constitutionally be applied to cyberspace. He also challenged the validity of the AFOSI agent's search warrant and seizure of his personal computer on probable cause grounds. Recognizing the importance of expanding jurisdictional authority to regulate sexual criminality in cyberspace, CAAF chief judge Cox summarized the challenges confronting military courts at the dawn of the new millennium: "New technologies create interesting challenges to long established legal concepts. . . . Now personal computers, hooked up to large networks, are so widely used that the scope of Fourth Amendment core concepts of 'privacy' as applied to them must be reexamined. Consequently, this opinion and the ones surely to follow will affect each one of us who has logged onto the 'information superhighway.'"[49] Concluding that Colonel Maxwell had been "traveling in the Gutter of the Information Highway," the CAAF affirmed his original sentence to dismissal from the air force.[50] By the end of Maxwell's appellate trial in 1996, the military justice system had effectively expanded its jurisdictional authority to include the regulation of the production, possession, and solicitation of all pornographic material on government and private computers both within the continental United States and on all U.S. military installations around the world.

Consequently, prosecutions for possessing child pornography reached an all-time high in the year 2000 when ten active duty personnel (six of whom were in the air force) were dismissed or dishonorably discharged from the services and imprisoned for their criminal conduct.[51] That the majority of those prosecuted at the dawn of the new millennium were convicted based on evidence on their personal computers or in private residences suggests the military justice system of the twenty-first century will freely exercise its jurisdictional authority to pursue active duty pedophiles in both public and private spaces.

INDECENT EXPOSURE

Similar to the statistics for pornography-related courts-martial, conviction rates for indecent exposure in the 1950s nearly equaled prosecution rates in the same decade because the Court of Military Appeals consistently denied service members' petitions for rehearings. After the CMA decriminalized negligent exposure in the 1958 *Manos* case, however, conviction rates paled in comparison to prosecution rates. Between 1959 and 1975, the majority of those service members who were initially court-martialed for the crime walked away free, especially when the 1972 *Caune* ruling distinguished public nudity as a crime only when the exposure occurred in the presence of the opposite sex. This liberal trend steadily continued from 1976 to 1985. Of the six service members prosecuted on charges of indecent exposure in this nine-year span, the CMA and the ACMR dismissed five cases on the grounds that the military judges committed prejudicial error in violation of the accused service members' due process rights.[52]

Convictions for indecent exposure became more common after 1985 as the courts struggled to clarify the blurry boundaries between crimes of indecent exposure, indecent acts, and taking indecent liberties with children. In the 1986 case of U.S. Air Force second lieutenant C. Ramirez Jr., for instance, the CMA ruled that public masturbation in the presence of minors was a more serious offense than indecent exposure and warranted the more severe punishment granted for convictions of indecent liberties/acts.[53] That same year, the CMA ruled that the offense of taking indecent liberties with children could be committed without any physical touching even though that same act also constituted indecent exposure.[54] The CMA expanded upon the new physical touching rule in 1987 when it established that the absence of physical touching did not automatically reduce the offense to indecent exposure.[55]

In the aftermath of this whirlwind of legal precedent setting in the mid-1980s that aimed to clarify the distinctions between indecent acts and indecent exposure, some service members fared better than others. A few enjoyed dismissals of their indecent exposure charges altogether, while a handful of others endured more serious punitive measures.[56] For the remaining majority, the courts affirmed the accused service members' guilt for committing the less serious offense of indecent exposure.[57] In the process, the courts also expanded the scope of the offense to include mooning (or the act of baring one's bum to unwilling members of the opposite sex), forms of exposure that had no adverse impact on the maintenance of good order and discipline (but that naturally disgraced the moral reputation of the armed forces), and willful (not negligent!) exposure that occurred in private locations such as bedrooms and personal residences (a new variation of the *Manos* precedent).[58]

By the 1990s the courts increasingly utilized incidents of indecent exposure to accuse servicemen of homosexuality. In the 1993 case *United States v. McGinty*, for example, the CAAF convicted a navy commander of indecent assault for running his fingers through a seaman's hair. Though the act was not violent, the judges argued that the sexual overture would have led to the criminal act of same-sex sodomy, though they had no way to prove this assertion. As a result, McGinty was forced to resign his position and retire.[59]

In its aftermath, the *McGinty* case set a precedent that the courts increasingly utilized after 1993 to convict suspected homosexuals of sexual deviance. By harnessing the logic that a questionably indecent gesture indicating homosexual attraction could potentially lead to same-sex sodomy, the CAAF opened the floodgates for hundreds of courts-martial against innocent servicemen. The implications of this were huge. Following the Clinton administration's implementation of the DADT policy, the CAAF set off a wave of legal homophobia that trickled down to the service review boards. At the same time, however, the courts overlooked thousands of indecent gestures that servicemen made toward women that, logically, could have led (and probably did) to the criminal act of rape or sexual assault.

Though the reasons for this remain unclear, the disturbing implication is hard to overlook: the military justice system in the last decade of the twentieth century was equally concerned with enforcing heterosexuality as it was with prosecuting sexual crimes that servicemen committed against women. This is not to say that the courts manipulated charges of indecent exposure to convict servicemen of homosexuality in *all* circumstances in which the opportunity presented itself. Indeed, convicted exhibitionists in numerous cases were avowedly heterosexual.[60] But in more cases than not, indecent exposure charges laid the groundwork for charges of homosexuality.[61] In an all-too-common scenario in which the circumstances mirrored earlier courts-martial for suspected homosexuals in the 1950s and 1960s, the CAAF convicted a dentist of homosexual acts, which constituted conduct unbecoming an officer and a gentleman. This charge originated in an indecent exposure charge. When OSI agents received a warrant to search Modesto's residence for evidence of the charge against him and found unrelated evidence that instead proved Modesto's "sexual perversity," the CAAF ruled that allowing it at trial did not constitute prejudicial error. The evidence in question consisted of multiple photographs showing Modesto dressed as a female impersonator, and in the court's opinion, they were proof beyond a reasonable doubt that his nonheterosexual tendencies were a threat to the heterosexual norm the courts were trying so hard to preserve. Given the courts' expansive additions to the list of actions and circumstances that constituted the offense of indecent exposure in the 1990s, the military justice system stands poised to police the exhibitionist ventures of service members well into the new millennium.

VOYEURISM, EXHIBITIONISM, AND VIDEOTAPING

Of all the moral misdemeanors under the purview of the courts in the second half of the twentieth century, officials prosecuted crimes of voyeurism the least. But the infrequency of their appearance in the case law bears no correlation to their significance. As the information age created new possibilities for human interaction on the internet, the crime of physical window peeping became more obsolete. To keep up with the changing times, the courts expanded the original definition of window peeping to incorporate similar conduct committed by using new technologies such as video cameras and webcams. In two of the three cases that occurred in the last quarter of the twentieth century, the courts argued that videotaping victims without their knowledge most closely resembled disorderly conduct in the absence of perverse or sexual overtones.[62] When sexual overtones or nudity were involved, window peeping via videotaping or using a webcam amounted to committing indecent acts. A U.S. Air Force Court of Military Review established this new precedent in its 1994 conviction of Tech. Sgt. R. McDaniel, whose charges of dereliction in the performance of duties, wrongfully videotaping certain female applicants for enlistment, and attempted wrongful videotaping of a certain female applicant for enlistment in violation of Articles 92, 134, and 80, respectively, led to his dishonorable discharge.

McDaniel's duties included processing enlistment applications and weighing recruits. His criminal conduct arose when, without the knowledge or consent of the victims of his covert gaze, he hid a camcorder in the storage room where the scales were located so he could watch female recruits in the nude. Under cross-examination by the AFOSI agent in charge of the undercover investigation, McDaniel admitted to having videotaped fourteen female recruits in this manner and to subsequently editing the videotapes to include only the portions where the women were disrobing, weighing themselves, and dressing again. Though McDaniel readily acknowledged at trial that his conduct was the product of a voyeur's curiosity, both the original court and the CMA treated his offenses as indecent acts—a more serious charge than that of voyeurism and a clear break from precedent in which the courts treated voyeurism as a crime of disorderly conduct.

The *McDaniel* precedent established a useful distinction between mere voyeurism and the more serious offense of indecent acts. Mere voyeurism, according to the court, was conduct in which the "actions occurred independent of any control or stimulus by the accused." The voyeur, in turn, acted "merely as a witness" to the circumstances unfolding before his eyes. But because Sergeant McDaniel videotaped the female recruits as they followed his directions, delivered remotely, to disrobe, to change positions, and to bounce up and down, McDaniel was clearly not simply a passive witness in an uncontrollable whirl of events. As the prosecution aptly summarized, "Had appellant merely videotaped these women without their knowledge and without doing anything to cause them to disrobe or pose . . . he would have engaged in a high-tech equivalent of voyeurism."[63] By redefining voyeurism to encompass the traditional act of window peeping with high-tech equipment such as video cameras and webcams, the courts saved the crime from becoming obsolete in the digital age.

PROSTITUTION AND PANDERING

Not surprising, the courts' leniency toward servicemen who associated with notorious prostitutes in the early Cold War carried over into the last quarter of the twentieth century. In the only court-martial of its kind from 1961 to 2000, the CAAF reversed the decision of an ACMR that convicted 1st Lt. D. Guaglione of publicly associating with prostitutes. The CAAF, in keeping with earlier court decisions, ruled that entering a red-light district or house of prostitution did not constitute the crime for which Guaglione was convicted. For the conviction to stand, the evidence had to establish beyond a reasonable doubt that Guaglione (and those service members who came after him) actually associated with a known prostitute inside the premises to the detriment of the armed forces' reputation. In effect, servicemen could freely enter red-light districts without fear of conviction so long as they did not associate with the sex workers therein.

To date, Guaglione was the last service member court-martialed for this crime.

Whether intentional or by accident, the *Guaglione* decision had the same effect of its predecessors. By making the crime of publicly associating with prostitutes nearly impossible to prove, the courts created an atmosphere of legal tolerance for service members to participate in the illicit sex trade. This leniency stood (and continues to stand) in direct contrast to legal officials' simultaneous efforts to enforce monogamy and public decency among U.S. military communities worldwide.[64]

At the same time the courts made the crime of publicly associating with prostitutes obsolete, they broadened the definition of prostitution and pandering to include "indiscriminate and promiscuous copulation with others" for pleasure in addition to sex for hire. The catalyst for this change was the court-martial of Lance Cpl. X. Gallegos, whom a U.S. Navy–Marine Corps Court of Criminal Appeals convicted of indecent acts and pandering. Though he admitted to arranging for three marines to have sex with his wife for his own viewing pleasure, Gallegos rejected the court's contention that his conduct was indecent and tantamount to pandering because he did not arrange the sexual acts for profit.[65]

In response, legal officials castigated Gallegos for allowing other men to so freely violate the sacred (and monogamous) marital bond that the courts preserved for husbands and wives alone. By affirming the charges, the CAAF vastly expanded the original meaning of pandering to encompass service members' promiscuous and indiscriminate copulation for pleasure. Though only six pandering cases came under the purview of the courts in the last quarter of the twentieth century, their 100 percent conviction rate signaled that the coming of the new millennium only strengthened the courts' historic commitment to eradicating promiscuous and indiscriminate sex for either hire or pleasure.[66]

Conclusion

What preliminary conclusions can we draw from an initial foray into the complex world of sex, marriage, and military justice in the last quarter of the twentieth century? On a fundamental level, this venture reveals that this subject involves much more than scholars outside the field of military justice ever suspected. Before beginning my research for this chapter, I incorrectly assumed that military courts followed a trajectory similar to that of civil courts in the 1980s and '90s, one that was characterized by a steady retreat from the private lives of citizens.[67] The CMA's increasing protection of suspected homosexuals at courts-martial during the Cold War and the steadily decreasing rate of prosecutions for crimes of adultery, bigamy, violation of command marriage regulations, pornographic consumption, voyeurism, exhibitionism, and prostitution and pandering indicated a general withdrawal from the intimate spaces of the service community. The Supreme Court's precedent-setting ruling in *O'Callahan*, which limited the military courts' jurisdiction to crimes that were specifically service connected, seemed to confirm this trend.

But I was mistaken. Prosecutions for adultery, bigamy, sodomy, indecent exposure, and pornographic consumption from 1976 to 2000 did not simply reach their Cold War rates; indeed, they dwarfed them. Such increased legal oversight was necessary, the courts asserted, to respond to the challenges that new forms of technology and the spread of new diseases posed to safety and morality. Nor did the end of either the Vietnam War or the Cold War stop the military's continued intervention in the marital decisions of service members stationed overseas who wished to wed non-Americans. Commanders argued that marriage regulation was critical to preserving the U.S.-ROK alliance, for example, because it prevented the creation of abandoned and waiting wives by ensuring that servicemen followed through on their marital commitments.

So how do we explain such a drastic reversal in prosecution rates from the third to the fourth quarter of the twentieth century? To some degree, it seems to have been a consequence of the convergence of two factors—technological advancement and the increasing commodification of sex in the last quarter of the twentieth century. The advent of new technologies such as the internet made "traveling in the Gutters of the Information Highway" (as one judge so aptly called it) so much easier and more accessible. With computers (and eventually laptops, cell phones, and tablets), service members who might never have explored pornographic material before had instant access to the world of the obscene. Video cameras and webcams had the same effect on crimes of indecent exposure and window peeping. By revolutionizing the medium through which these crimes could occur, voyeurs and exhibitionists no longer had to engage in criminal behavior in person.

This virtual world of criminal possibilities posed a host of new questions that forced the courts to revise old definitions of sexual deviance to keep up with the changing times. Does a relationship characterized solely by "virtual sex," for example, count as adulterous conduct if the partners do not have physical contact? Are service members' recordings of sexual encounters for private use criminally obscene, or do they fall within their constitutionally protected zone of privacy? Do these videos become obscene when made available to the public via social media sites such as Facebook? Should social media outlets such as Facebook, Twitter, Snapchat, and Instagram even be considered public terrain since members can dictate who has access to their personal posts, pictures, and videos? Is consensual, same-sex sodomy between gay service members still criminal conduct after the repeal of the don't ask, don't tell policy? To what extent are any of these behaviors service connected? Questions such as these will occupy the courts' attention for decades to come.

The political climate of the country also contributed to the rising rates for courts-martial for sexual deviance from 1976 to 2000. It is no coincidence that in the second half of the twentieth century, prosecutions for crimes of sexual deviance in the military dwindled as traditional family values faded during the civil rights and anti-war movements of the 1960s and early '70s and their calls for sexual and reproductive freedom. Conversely, prosecution rates peaked in the McCarthy era of the 1950s and again with the rise of the New Right in the 1980s. In both of these eras, many felt that sexual radicalism threatened the traditional family values that were embedded in the UCMJ and that made America the moral leader of the free world in the global war against communism. These general patterns suggest that the process of constructing and enforcing notions of sexual criminality and justice in the armed forces was, at least to some degree, influenced by the wider political culture.

So strong was the New Right's growing influence on military affairs, in fact, that no branch of government even attempted to challenge the military's anti-gay policy until 1993, when the military, the religious Right, and social conservatives mounted such fierce resistance to President Clinton's plan to abolish the policy that he was forced to compromise by endorsing the DADT directive. At best DADT was less a challenge to the military's historic exclusion policy than an extension of the vague and confusing policies of the postwar era in a less overtly discriminatory form.[68] Though intended to make sexual orientation a nonissue, DADT had the adverse effect of legalizing a basic inequity that the Constitution was supposed to guard against. By preventing gay service members from sharing their experiences, the policy of DADT shielded itself from scrutiny and interrogation and propagated an atmosphere of suspicion and fear for service members whose most innocent gestures often became the means for their court-martial.

The repeal of DADT in 2011 was, in part, the historic culmination of six decades of intense legal struggle among participants in the military justice system to equalize the court-martial process so that suspected homosexuals could benefit from the same rights to due process that their heterosexual counterparts enjoyed. According to the Servicemembers Legal Defense Network, though the policy's repeal represented "a significant step toward equality for all who want to serve their country in uniform," its implications for the future face of military justice remain uncertain.[69] Because Article 125 of the UCMJ has been neither revised to accommodate the repeal of DADT nor deleted in its entirety, the military courts still retain the authority to prosecute service members who engage in consensual same-sex or heterosexual sodomy. Nor have the general articles, Articles 133 and 134, been revised to specify what behaviors and mannerisms (effeminate gait, falsetto voice, associations with "notorious" prostitutes?) constitute conduct that is considered both unbecoming and prejudicial to good order and discipline. If the evidence is any indication, the U.S. military justice system's project of policing sex and marriage will continue well into the new millennium.

Conclusion

When discussing my research with a retired U.S. Air Force colonel one day in 2017, he asked what my argument was. I responded, "The U.S. military policed sex and marriage in the second half of the twentieth century in both subtle and overt ways to uphold standards of morality and democracy rooted in heterosexual monogamous marriage." The colonel disagreed. "The military justice system policed sex and marriage to maintain the good order and discipline of the armed forces," he replied, quoting verbatim the logic officials in the post–World War II era used to justify prosecuting and discharging suspected homosexuals. To a certain extent, this rationale makes sense. As a specialized community requiring its own rules of law to function as a unified force while defending the nation, criminalizing certain acts of sexual deviance such as adultery, coercive sodomy, pandering, and prostitution helped mitigate the violence sometimes associated with the commission of these crimes—violence that could compromise the military's mission by stirring up anti-U.S. sentiment among host populations in overseas locations.

But this logic leaves important questions unanswered. If the goal of policing sex and marriage was to maintain the good order and discipline of the forces, why were service personnel who provided invaluable contributions to the mission discharged or dismissed from the military for having consensual sexual relations where no evidence of disorder or violence was present? Why were service members prosecuted and discharged for committing no apparent crime besides that of possessing certain characteristics that officials perceived as signs of homosexual tendencies? Why did some commanders deny servicemen the right to marry women in host territories and legitimate their children where no evidence of ensuing disorder was apparent if the marital vows were taken? And why did the courts enforce the husband-wife privilege at the tragic expense of protecting the real victims of domestic violence and sexual abuse—that is, the wives and children of servicemen? (Indeed, it wasn't until the string of murder cases in postwar Germany and Japan featuring military wives who killed their husbands to escape their domestic prisons did the reality of domestic abuse in military families gain public attention.)

The answers to these puzzling questions seem to be in how the military defined "good order." The good order that the military justice system and countless regulations sought to maintain was a highly gendered one that idealized heterosexual monogamous marriage as the pillar of social stability in the military community. Marriage (in theory) provided a safe outlet for men's sexual needs by channeling them away from illicit sexual encounters and thus served the mission by keeping troops free of venereal disease (again, only theoretically). According to this ideal, acting as the provider and protector of a family of dependents fulfilled married servicemen's needs to feel masculine. But for this ideal to work in reality, military wives had to behave accordingly, acting as content homemakers and helpmates who serviced their husbands' sexual and emotional needs while remaining silent in the face of physical and emotional abuse. To maintain this good order, military wife guidebooks coached women in the language of feminine respectability so they could become acceptable members of the military community and encouraged women to police each other's behavior. Despite the military courts' loss of jurisdictional authority to try military dependents after 1957 as a result of the string of spousal murder cases, the courts helped to police military wives' behavior by penalizing those who refused to conform by revoking their rights to monthly allotment checks and by asserting the husband-wife privilege to punish wives (and, by extension, their children) who spoke out publicly about their husbands' wrongdoings.

For service husbands, maintaining the good order of the military community meant policing all sexual activities that threatened heterosexual monogamous marriage and standards of morality and decency. Despite the court's prophetic ruling in *United States v. Snyder* (see the vignette in the introduction), where judges asserted that the intention of the "good order and discipline" clause was not to invade the private bedrooms of service members, prosecuting the crimes of adultery, same-sex sodomy, voyeurism, exhibitionism, bigamy, pandering and prostitution, and viewing and sharing pornography enabled the military justice system to define "good order" in a gendered way that made sex and marriage extremely important areas of surveillance and control in the second half of the twentieth century. Good order was and continues to be inseparable from gendered notions of marriage, morality, sexuality, and decency in the United States military. Maintaining good order also meant defining and enforcing its opposite—that is, crimes of "disorder" and "deviance" that were equally influenced by gendered notions of order, stability, and normalcy. The justice system played a critical role in constructing notions of gender and sexual deviance, and the court-martial was a key site where those constructions were both validated and challenged.

Afterword

Upon entering Joint Base Elmendorf-Richardson in Anchorage, Alaska, I turn right onto Provider Drive and head toward the base exchange, the social meeting place for the military community that features a food court, a host of shops, and a commissary. On the way there, I encounter multiple vehicles with popular decals that say "Air Force Wife," "Wife—Toughest Job in the Army," and "Proud Navy Wife." At the exchange, I drop by the Military Clothing Sales Store, where military members can purchase uniforms and official military memorabilia as gifts for family and friends, to browse new service manuals in the small book section. In addition to the latest issue of *Military Spouse* magazine (which featured an attractive U.S. Marine husband and articles glamorizing being married to servicemen), I see titles such as *Married to the Military: A Survival Guide for Military Wives, Girlfriends, and Women in Uniform*; *Spouses Also Serve*; and *Portraits of the Toughest Job in the Army: Voices & Faces of Modern Army Wives.*[1]

When I opened one and read the first sentence that my eyes happened upon, I was struck by the similarities between this modern manual and the service wife guidebooks of the post–World War II era. Meredith Levya, military spouse and author, tells her audience, "By reading this book, you will be better able to support him [husband] in his mission and have a stronger relationship" and that the military wife's duty is "to control [her] family's destiny."[2] To do this, Levya argues, wives must educate themselves (with her manual) on the inner workings of military life, hierarchy, and language and on social and marital responsibility. Despite the appearance of male domination in the military and women's "second-class status," she assures her female readers that they are the true "commanders in chief" because they are "primarily responsible for raising the kids, managing the household finances, and establishing" themselves and their families "in the community."[3] Rather than encouraging wives to "sally forth in their best frocks" to social conventions for the benefit of their husbands' careers, Levya encouraged them to sally forth with their cell phones, tablets, and fashionable diaper bags.

Military customs that have prioritized the nuclear family as a key element to the success of the mission have enhanced the courts' efforts to enforce heterosexual, monogamous marriage as the foundational unit of American (and by extension U.S. military) society. Countless "family days" granted throughout the year (usually the day before or after national holidays) encourage service members to spend time with their spouses and children. The U.S. Army chaplains developed and implemented the "Strong Bonds" program (which the other service branches have adapted) in 2012 to "strengthen the bonds of marriage and family" by offering private marriage counseling services and effective communications classes for couples free of charge. Through special discounts and promotions for Alaska camping and fishing expeditions that are available only for married service members to enjoy with their families, military culture continues to idealize the nuclear family. (There are variations of family fun packages at every U.S. military base and post throughout the world.)

These and countless other examples reinforce the binary gender ideologies that the military justice system has idealized and enforced since the postwar era. As servicemen pass through the joint base's gates en route to and from work each day, they are reminded that to be true "arctic warriors," they must provide for and protect their families. Though the increasing number of servicewomen and single mothers who support themselves and their families has long challenged the notion that providing was a predominantly male task, military legal and social media discourse continues to cast representations of the provider as gendered male. Similar to Article 125, Articles 133 and 134 have not been amended to reflect the changing sex ratio of the U.S. armed forces.[4] They are still gendered masculine, meaning that, in the legal sense, only male officers can embody and deviate from the character traits traditionally associated with the male role of provider and protector. For female service members seeking justice in military courts, the implications are disturbing. In numerous case files of rape and sexual assault in the 1980s and '90s, active duty female victims were blamed for making themselves vulnerable to attack simply by pursuing careers in male-dominated fields.

The courts' construction and criminalization of sexual deviance forged a critical part of the military justice system's ongoing production of gender ideologies that buttressed heterosexual, monogamous marriage and the nuclear family during the second half of the twentieth century. From international (and interracial) marriages to sodomy to various acts of marital infidelity and indecency, policing the intimate realm of service members' lives played an important, though overlooked, role in America's transformation into a national security state (and the military's rapid expansion) during the Cold War. It also played an important role in the lives of millions of troops and their families. Though sex, marriage, deviance, and justice are typically not the first things that come to mind when considering how the military functions as a unique, specialized community, their regulation in the courts was essential to defining the values and gender ideologies that have made the world's most formidable fighting force as supposedly moral as it has been mighty.

NOTES

Author's Note

1. Though not impossible, tracking down the racial makeup of every defendant in this manuscript (let alone the entire body of case law) would be a difficult feat—even for the seasoned researcher. Aside from the U.S. census, other records that might contain information about a defendant's racial heritage are the military's enlistment and health files. For justifiable reasons, access to military personnel files is sometimes restricted to either the retiree or, in cases where the retiree is deceased, a family member. I am not claiming that the entire body of *Court-Martial Reports* offers scant evidence on the racial makeup of defendants, but they do for the cases involving adultery, bigamy, sodomy, prostitution and pandering, pornography, indecent exposure, and window peeping that inform my arguments in this book. Hillman's preliminary conclusions in *Defending America* suggest that a defendant's race negatively impacted sentencing for African American servicemen accused of rape and other nonsexual crimes from 1950 to 1975.

2. This legal protection stands in stark contrast to courts-martial proceedings during World War II that disproportionately accused black troops of raping French women and meted out the death sentence as a result. See Roberts, *What Soldiers Do*, 195–254. In the Cold War military, hostility often led to violence between black and white troops over the issue of sex with host women in occupied territories including South Korea, Germany, and Japan. Commanders attempted to mediate these hostilities by segregating houses of prostitution by rank and race. Segregated prostitution houses dated back to the Spanish-American War, however. See chapter 5 for a deeper discussion of the military's regulation of prostitution and the court-martial.

Introduction

1. *United States v. Snyder*, 4 C.M.R. 15 (1952).
2. *Snyder*, 4 C.M.R. at 17.
3. *Snyder*, 4 C.M.R. at 18.
4. Mary Louise Roberts's fascinating study *What Soldiers Do* is a notable exception to this trend, though she focuses specifically on American troops' sexual victimization of French women during World War II.
5. The creation of the Uniform Code of Military Justice after World War II and the Court of Military Appeals in 1950 made the postwar military justice system ripe for legal reform because the UCMJ streamlined the services' various policies by which the services prosecuted criminals and guaranteed all soldiers the right to due process regardless of their crimes. The CMA, in turn, was vested with supreme authority to interpret the provisions of the UCMJ in a manner that respected the due process rights of all service members. Accused service members often contested unfair trial proceedings and sentences by appealing to the CMA, which had the power to reverse, reduce, or dismiss court-martial sentences. For an extensive analysis of the history of the Court of Military Appeals, see Lurie, *Military Justice in America*.
6. Take, for example, a typical scenario of a married serviceman convicted of carnal knowledge for sleeping with a minor. The minor could not give legal consent due to her age, but she welcomed the advances of the service member. In the absence of physical violence, the service member was still convicted of carnal knowledge. Because he was married, the court also convicted him of adultery. In this way, an adultery court-martial could include the charge of rape or sodomy just as a pornography court-martial could include the charge of adultery or pandering. The boundaries separating sexually violent crimes from those of sexual deviance were blurry and fluid.
7. President Harry Truman signed the Uniform Code of Military Justice into law on May 5, 1950. It became effective May 31, 1951.
8. In attempting to answer these questions, I have chosen to omit a chapter dealing exclusively with rape. Rape and sexual assault

crimes certainly come into play in this volume when they inter-
sect with crimes of adultery, sodomy, and prostitution; however,
the courts did not prosecute rapists for the primary purpose of
enforcing monogamy, racial homogeneity, and heterosexuality. They prosecuted rapists to protect the public, deliver justice
to victims of a capital offense, and dispel public rumors about
unchecked sexual violence occurring on and around military
bases at home and abroad. Though the crimes of sexual deviance that I analyze in this book often involve harrowing stories of
violence, categorizing rape as a crime of sexual deviance grossly
undermines the tragedy, severity, and high stakes involved for the
victims, the accused, and their families. The high number of rape
courts-martial in the historical record, the extent of the current
rape crisis in the armed forces, and the unique struggles of military rape victims and rehabilitated rape offenders necessitate a
subfield of historical scholarship devoted solely to this issue.

9. Hillman, *Defending America*.
10. See Brandt, *No Magic Bullet*; and Belkin, *Bring Me Men*, 161–63.
11. See Canaday, *Straight State*, particularly 55–90; and Belkin, *Bring
Me Men*, 21–24, on the 1919 U.S. Navy's sodomy scandal in New-
port, Rhode Island.
12. Cott's *Public Vows* is the seminal work on state regulation of marriage and the institution's central role in structuring a patriarchal
society along gendered lines. See also Kerber, *No Constitutional
Right*, for an in-depth discussion of coverture laws. The first half
of Canaday's *Straight State*, 19–134, illustrates how federal immigration and welfare policy and the military's policies on homosexuality helped to normalize heterosexism and create the legal
and social category of "homosexual" in American society in the
first four decades of the twentieth century. Lehring, *Officially Gay*,
6, makes a similar argument about the U.S. military's construction of the modern homosexual subject through the creation and
implementation of homosexual exclusion policies. This new category of "homosexual" became the "new sight of regulation and a
new form of resistance." Holloway's *Sexuality, Politics, and Social
Control in Virginia* is an example of state regulation of sexuality
and citizenship in the first half of the twentieth century. Two out-

standing recent contributions to the literature on state regulation of sexuality and gender roles are Pliley, *Policing Sexuality*; and Ryan, *Red War on the Family*.

13. See Johnson, *Lavender Scare*, for the seminal work on the lavender scare. See Belkin, *Bring Me Men*, 21–24; and Canaday, *Straight State*, 55–90, for examples of military prosecutions of suspected homosexuals in the post–World War I era.

14. All other crimes of sexual deviance fell under the purview of the "general articles," Articles 133 and 134.

15. Enloe, *Maneuvers*. Enloe pioneered the field of military, gender, and sexuality studies with her landmark books *Does Khaki Become You?*; *Bananas, Beaches, and Bases*; and *Morning After*.

16. Hillman, *Defending America*, 1.

1. Engendering Military Marriages

1. I am inferring from the court transcript that W. Woolridge had a job in St. Louis. Based on her testimony, she had planned to visit the defendant to get her allotment checks during her "two-week vacation" before she realized he had already cashed them. *United States v. Woolridge*, 28 C.M.R. 78 (1959).

2. *United States v. Ryno*, 130 F Supp 685, 690 (SD Calif) (1955); and *United States v. Strand*, 20 C.M.R. 13 (1955). Both cited in *Woolridge*, 28 C.M.R. at 83.

3. See chapter 3 for an expansive analysis of the husband-wife privilege in military courts.

4. *Woolridge*, 28 C.M.R. at 76, 80.

5. In the dissenting opinion, Judge Latimer argued that depriving wives of their sole rights to monthly allotment checks would be far more than an injury according to the husband-wife privilege. Rather, it would be a "calamity" and would likely result in wives "applying for relief or going without the necessities of life." Latimer noted, "The far-reaching effect of the Court's decision [in this case] will make it impossible for the services to convict a serviceman for forging his dependent's allotment check." *Woolridge*, 28 C.M.R. at 82, 85.

6. May, *Homeward Bound*. Joanne Meyerowitz has complicated May's thesis by revealing the diversity of women's postwar expe-

riences as activists, wives, mothers, pacifists, and unionists, while Jessica Weiss illustrates how the postwar American family radically changed from its prewar counterpart. Fathers were encouraged to take a more hands-on role in raising their children and maintaining the home, while many wives and mothers chose to work outside the home. See Meyerowitz, *Not June Cleaver*; and Weiss, *To Have and to Hold*.

7. In *Consumer's Republic*, Cohen argues that mass consumption in postwar America became synonymous with patriotism, social equality, and the American dream. Participating in this mass consumer culture through the purchase of material goods such as vacuum cleaners, washing machines, and automobiles enabled consumer-citizens to purchase political power and effect social change. It also protected them from allegations of political and sexual radicalism at the height of the McCarthy era.

8. The manpower needs of the Cold War—of which the Korean and Vietnam Wars played an integral part—necessitated the expansion of all service branches in the post–World War II era. According to Hillman, *Defending America*, 8, the U.S. armed forces peaked around 3.5 million active duty service members from 1950 to 1953 and from 1968 to 1969 at the height of the Korean and Vietnam Wars, respectively. These statistics do not include the mounting number of civil service employees working for national security agencies in the 1950s and '60s. According to Höhn and Moon, *Over There*, 6–11, before the bombing of Pearl Harbor in 1941 the U.S. Navy and Marine Corps made up the majority of the U.S. military's meager 60,000 troops stationed in Cuba, Guam, Midway Atoll, Panama, the Philippines, Puerto Rico, the Virgin Islands, and Wake Island. By 1949, 582 overseas military installations had been established, mostly in Western Europe, northeastern Asia, and the Pacific. By 1960 the U.S. military occupied 815 bases overseas and had signed treaties with forty-three nations to have American troops stationed on their soil. The number of overseas U.S. military bases reached 1,014 at the height of the Vietnam War.

9. Alvah, *Unofficial Ambassadors*.

10. Despite their unique lens into the military's gendered expectations of military wives, these guidebooks do have limitations.

Most lack a distinction between guidance for officer's wives as compared to enlisted men's wives, thus eluding a class distinction with real meaning in military life. Making feminine respectability contingent upon homemaking also undoubtedly excluded those women who worked outside the home either by choice or out of economic necessity, and they represented roughly half the female population. Weiss, *To Have and to Hold*, 51–52, argues that by 1950, 52 percent of all women were working (recall W. Wooldridge, for example, in this chapter's opening anecdote). Nor do these guidebooks acknowledge the growing racial diversity of the post–World War II military by including examples or illustrations that would have been as culturally relevant to European, African American, or Asian service wives as they were to white service wives. Further, the authors also assumed that the prospective audience could read and comprehend English.

11. *Kinsella v. Krueger*, 351 U.S. 470 (1956); *Madsen v. Kinsella*, 348 U.S. 31 (1952); *Madsen v. Overholser*, 251 F. 2d 387 (DC Cir. 1958); *Reid v. Covert*, 351 U.S. 487 (1956); *Reid v. Covert*, 354 U.S. 3 (1957); *United States v. Covert*, 16 C.M.R. 465 (A.F.B.R. 1953); *United States v. Covert*, 19 C.M.R. 174 (1955); *United States v. Smith*, 10 C.M.R. 350 (A.B.R. 1952); *United States v. Smith*, 17 C.M.R. 314 (1954); and *United States v. St. Clair*, 21 C.M.R. 208 (1956).

12. Shea, *Army Wife* (1941), vii.

13. Shea, *Army Wife* (1941), vii–xvi.

14. Francine D'Amico and Laurie Weinstein note that etiquette books for military wives in the 1950s and '60s "were updated throughout the years to ensure that the behavior of the military wife complied with the role the military had set for her." See *Gender Camouflage*, 127.

15. Wier, *Army Social Customs*, 75.

16. May, *Homeward Bound*.

17. Murphy and Bowles Parker, *Fitting In*, 112.

18. Military and women's historians wrote little about military wives until the 1990s, following the lead of military sociologists interested in the unique lifestyle's effects on dependents. Betty Sowers Alt and Bonnie Domrose Stones's *Campfollowing* laid the foundation for the legitimate historical study of military wives on their own terms rather than as extensions of their husbands.

19. Enloe, *Morning After*, 195–96. Enloe argues that "without women to objectify, men's military service would be less confirming of their manhood, perhaps even of their citizenship." She coined the phrase "militarized masculinity," which depends largely upon men's self-perceptions of their own masculinity.

20. For a detailed analysis of the military as a gendered institution, see Herbert, *Camouflage Isn't Only for Combat*.

21. Collins, *Army Woman's Handbook*, 177.

22. Shea, *Army Wife* (1941), 90, 147.

23. Collins, *Army Woman's Handbook*, 184.

24. Pye and Shea, *Navy Wife*, 26, 57.

25. Shea, *Air Force Wife*, 4, xi.

26. Jerome and Shea, *Marine Corps Wife*, 38, 87.

27. Murphy and Parker, *Fitting In*, 47.

28. Bowles, *Hints from Heloise*, 1.

29. Redmond, *Handbook for Army Wives*, 3.

30. Redmond, *Handbook for Army Wives*, 3, 4.

31. Collins, *Army Woman's Handbook*, 177–78.

32. Bowles, *Hints from Heloise*, 1.

33. Shea, *Army Wife* (1941), 90–93, 100, 147.

34. Wier, *Army Social Customs*, 75.

35. Shea, *Air Force Wife*, 48–173; and Jerome and Shea, *Marine Corps Wife*, 174–94.

36. Bowles, *Hints from Heloise*, 7–8.

37. Shea, *Army Wife* (1941), 133–34.

38. Wier and Hickey, *Air Force Social Customs*, 136.

39. Pye and Shea, *Navy Wife*, 76. They believe officers' wives have more responsibility in maintaining a peaceful home environment than enlisted wives do because officers make command decisions that influence hundreds of people, while enlisted men's smaller responsibilities do not affect as many people.

40. Murphy and Parker, *Fitting In*, 20, 29.

41. Bowles, *Hints from Heloise*, 2–3.

42. Shea, *Army Wife* (1948), 135–36.

43. Collins, *Army Woman's Handbook*, 182.

44. Shea, *Army Wife* (1948), 240; Shea, *Air Force Wife*, 223; and Jerome and Shea, *Marine Corps Wife*, 220–21.

45. Wier, *Army Social Customs*, 78.

46. Murphy and Parker, *Fitting In*, 90.

47. Kinzer and Leach, *What Every Army Wife*, 41.

48. Gross, *Mrs. NCO*, 38–39.

49. For example, see Schlesinger, "Crisis of American Masculinity."

50. Wier, *Army Social Customs*, 79.

51. Shea, *Army Wife* (1948), 7.

52. Shea, *Army Wife* (1941), 6.

53. Pye and Shea, *Navy Wife*, 76.

54. Collins, *Army Woman's Handbook*, 181.

55. Wier, *Army Social Customs*, 79–80.

56. Greiner and Bedrick, *Something on Protocol*, 1–2.

57. Kinzer and Leach, *What Every Army Wife*, 30.

58. Shea, *Army Wife* (1948), 86, xvi.

59. Wier and Hickey, *Air Force Social Customs*, 78.

60. Shea, *Army Wife* (1948), 15.

61. Wier and Hickey, *Air Force Social Customs*, 75.

62. Greiner and Bedrick, *Something on Protocol*, 8, 10.

63. Redmond, *Handbook for Army Wives*, 98.

64. Collins, *Army Woman's Handbook*, 187.

65. Wier, *Army Social Customs*, 57.

66. Collins, *Army Woman's Handbook*, 187.

67. Wier, *Army Social Customs*, 79.

68. Gross, *Mrs. NCO*, 3.

69. For guidebook references to wives' informal networking, see, for example, Collins, *Army Woman's Handbook*, 204; Murphy and Parker, *Fitting In*, 108–51; and Wier, *What Every Air Force Wife*, 102–12.

70. Alvah, *Unofficial Ambassadors*, 14–81.

71. Shea, *Army Wife* (1948), 108, 294.

72. Shea, *Air Force Wife*, 245.

73. Wier and Hickey, *Air Force Social Customs*, 65–75.

74. Wier, *What Every Air Force Wife*, 131–32.

75. Kinzer and Leach, *What Every Army Wife*, 93–94.

76. Alvah, *Unofficial Ambassadors*, 1–13.

77. Goldstein, *War and Gender*, as cited in Belkin, *Bring Me Men*, 27.

78. Enloe, *Maneuvers*.

79. See, for example, Wicks, *Warriors and Wildmen*; Huebner, *Warrior Image*; and Higate, *Military Masculinities*, as cited in Belkin, *Bring Me Men*, 27–29. Scholar Aaron Belkin argues that uncertainty about what constitutes the masculine causes identity confusion in service members who simultaneously strive for warrior toughness while engaging in acts such as sodomy and hazing that require troops to take on feminine characteristics. Same-sex sodomy and rape, by penetrating and being penetrated, are just a few of the more striking examples of how troops display both masculine and feminine traits.

80. Article 99 of the code idealizes character traits such as courage, responsibility, and integrity in combat situations, for instance. It criminalizes cowardly and irresponsible actions, including but not limited to running away before the enemy; "shamefully abandoning, surrendering or delivering up"; endangering the safety of a command, unit, place, or military property through disobedience, neglect, or intentional misconduct; casting away arms or ammunitions; engaging in cowardly conduct; and willfully failing to do one's utmost to encounter, engage, capture, or destroy enemy troops, combatants, vessels, aircraft or any other thing. The MCM defines *cowardice* as "misbehavior through fear. Fear is a natural feeling of apprehension when going into battle and the mere display of such apprehension would not constitute the offense, but the refusal or abandonment of a performance of duty before or in the presence of the enemy as a result of fear does constitute the offense." *Manual for Courts-Martial*, section 151b (2).

81. Article 134 violations—most notably, miscellaneous crimes of moral turpitude—are the subject of chapter 5.

82. As chapter 4 suggests, the courts' struggles simultaneously to enforce heterosexism as the norm while ensuring due process to all accused service members resulted in the construction of competing notions of masculinity.

83. These subjects are the foci of chapters 3 and 5.

84. See, for example, *United States v. Perkins*, 8 C.M.R. 855 (A.F.B.R. 1952); *United States v. McFerrin*, 28 C.M.R. 255 (1959); and *United States v. Sheeks*, 37 C.M.R. 50 (1966). In addition to service husbands who received swift and harsh punishment for failing to ade-

quately provide for or protect their families, husband-wife teams were court-martialed for a variety of criminal acts including running brothels out of government quarters (see chapter 5); committing arson (see *United States v. Fuller*, 23 C.M.R. 584 [A.B.R. 1957]; and *United States v. Fuller*, 25 C.M.R. 405 [1958]) and larceny (see *United States v. Wade*, 27 C.M.R. 637 [A.B.R. 1958]; *United States v. Green*, 29 C.M.R. 868 [A.F.B.R. 1960]; and *United States v. Rogers*, 32 C.M.R. 623 [A.B.R. 1962]); participating in black market activity (see *United States v. Reed*, 33 C.M.R. 932 [A.B.R. 1963]); and staging death to receive the service member's death gratuity benefit (see *United States v. Nuckols*, 20 C.M.R. 471 [A.B.R. 1955]).

85. Command regulation of marriages between service members stationed in overseas locations and citizens of the host country is the subject of chapter 2.

86. In this book, I have included child abuse cases that illustrate broader trends in prosecutions of sexual deviance. For a few examples of parent-inflicted physical and/or sexual abuse of dependent children, see *United States v. Francis*, 12 C.M.R. 695 (A.F.B.R. 1953); *United States v. Clemens*, 34 C.M.R. 778 (A.F.B.R. 1964); and *United States v. Menchaca*, 47 C.M.R. 709 (A.F.B.R. 1973).

87. For cases of servicemen murdering their wives in relation to adulterous affairs, see chapter 3. For examples of non-adultery-related cases and those featuring evidence of domestic violence, see *United States v. McKay*, 18 C.M.R. 629 (A.F.B.R. 1955); *United States v. Madison*, 34 C.M.R. 435 (A.F.B.R. 1964); and *United States v. Smeal*, 49 C.M.R. 751 (A.F.B.R. 1975).

88. According to the Court of Military Appeals, Downard committed his offense prior to May 31, 1951, the effective date of the Uniform Code of Military Justice; and his trial was held after this date. Article of War 95, which Downard was accused of violating, was interpreted to mean that a service member found guilty of conduct unbecoming an officer and a gentleman should be dismissed from the service. Article 133 of the UCMJ, however, held that dismissal was not mandatory for officers found guilty of violating the article; rather, the punishment was at the court's discretion, with dismissal being the severest of numerous sentences available to the courts. For the original trial transcript, see *United States v.*

Downard, 1 C.M.R. 405 (A.B.R. 1951). For the appellate transcript, see *United States v. Downard*, 3 C.M.R. 80 (1952).

89. U.S. Department of the Army, AR 600-30, 1.

2. Policing International Military Marriages

1. *United States v. Reese*, 22 C.M.R. 614 (A.B.R. 1956). Though the trial records did not contain specific references to Reese's racial background or ethnicity, it is safe to assume he was Caucasian. From 1950 to 1975, military courts normalized whiteness by explicating only the races or ethnicities of accused service members who deviated from this norm, or who identified themselves as "nonwhite." Reese's case was one of thousands in which the defendant's whiteness was implicated through the transcript's silence on his racial makeup. Reese's first name was never mentioned in the court transcripts.

2. *Reese*, 22 C.M.R. at 614–15.

3. Very few scholars have uncovered statistics on the number of command approvals and denials between American service members and European nationals, though recent scholarship suggests that command denials between African American servicemen and German women were common in postwar Germany. Heide Fehrenbach, author of *Race after Hitler*, reveals how the U.S. military's policy at the time was to reject any claims of paternity made by German mothers and to forbid these men from marrying the mothers of their children. Fehrenbach estimates that some five thousand "brown babies" were born to German women and African American servicemen between 1945 and 1955, and many of these children were adopted by American military families in the continental United States without ever having the chance to meet their biological parents. For more on this topic, see Regina Griffin's documentary *Brown Babies: The Mischlingskinder Story* (Regina Griffin Films, 2014); and "'Brown Babies' Long Search for Family, Identity," CNN, November 20, 2011, http://inamerica.blogs.cnn.com/2011/11/20/germanys-brown-babies-still-searching-for-their-american-fathers/. For additional reading on relationships between American service members and European and Asian women

and the children born of these relationships during the Cold War, see Höhn, *GIS and Fräuleins*; and Kim, *Adopted Territory*.

4. *Maynard v. Hill*, 125 U.S. 190, 211 (1888).

5. See Cott, *Public Vows*.

6. U.S. Forces Korea/Eighth U.S. Army (USFK/EA) Pamphlet 600-091, paragraph 4 states: "Each month approximately 300 Korean-American couples make application to marry in the Republic of Korea. Some studies indicate that as high as 80 percent of these Korean-American (GI) marriages end in divorce within two years of their return to the United States. In lieu of or accompanying a divorce can be a high rate of domestic violence, suicide acts, psychological and sociological dysfunction, financial problems, social stigma, and problems of assimilation in society. . . . The service member and the commander can be faced with increased absenteeism, inefficiency, AWOL, behavioral problems, and poor retention." The "studies" regarding Korean-American divorces to which USFK/EA Pamphlet 600-091 refers appear to have been a single report from Fort Lewis, Washington. See D. Moon, reserve chaplain, "Study of Problems of Korean Wives" (1976), as cited in Branstetter, "Military Constraints," 5–22.

7. Höhn, "You Can't Pin Sergeant's Stripes," 124, 142–43fn49. These cumbersome procedures included requiring GIS who were younger than the age of twenty-one to get parental approval and instituting strict time restraints for filing applications and consummating marriages. Applications could be filed no earlier than six months and no later than three months before the wedding, the wedding had to occur one month before the soldier's return to the United States to prevent the German spouse from becoming a financial burden for the military by remaining in Germany and receiving military support and services, and the intended spouse had to undergo extensive screenings to ensure her physical and mental health, moral character, and political loyalties to U.S. democracy.

8. See, for example, Johns, "Right to Marry."

9. *United States v. Nation*, 26 C.M.R. 504, 507 (1958).

10. U.S. Department of the Army, AR 600-240 (1965).

11. Ngai, *Impossible Subjects*.

12. For a superb analysis of war brides in the twentieth century, see Zeiger, *Entangling Alliances*. See also Friedman, *Citizenship in Cold War America*, 48–79, for an analysis of a German war bride whose two-year imprisonment on Ellis Island reveals in painful clarity how competing notions of race and gender influenced the discourse and public policy on national security.

13. Goldman, "Trends in Family Patterns."

14. Little, *Military Family*.

15. Alt and Stone, *Campfollowing*, xi–63.

16. Wood, "Army Laundresses," 26–34.

17. Wilson-Buford, "'Troublesome Hellions,'" 13–29.

18. Brig. Gen. and U.S. Army judge advocate general W. M. Dunn (38 Records of the Bureau 47) as cited in *United States v. Jordan*, 30 C.M.R. 427 (A.B.R. 1960).

19. Command VA2a, *Digest of the Opinions of the Judge Advocate General of the Army* (1879), and 43 Records of the Bureau 109 as cited in Branstetter, "Military Constraints," 8.

20. *Digest of the Opinions of the Judge Advocate General of the Army* (1912), 266, as cited in *Jordan*, 30 C.M.R. at 427.

21. Budreau, *Answering the Call*, 26.

22. C.M. 121330 (1918), cited at sec. 454 (68), in U.S. Department of the Army, Office of the Judge Advocate General, *Digest of Opinions*.

23. U.S. Department of the Army, AR 615-360; and U.S. Department of the Army, AR 600-750.

24. D'Amico and Weinstein, *Gender Camouflage*, 121; and Hillman, *Defending America*, 79.

25. Military Affairs Division, Office of the Judge Advocate of the Army (SPJGA), 291.1 (June 1, 1942), as cited in *Jordan*, 30 C.M.R. at 427–28. Military courts consistently upheld the legality of reasonable overseas marriage regulations into the twenty-first century. See chapter 6 for an analysis of these regulations in the last quarter of the twentieth century and into the twenty-first century.

26. U.S. War Department, Cir. No. 179, sec 1.

27. War Brides Act of 1945, Pub. L. No. 79-271, Stat. 659.

28. S. Rep. No. 1515, 81st Cong., 1st sess.

29. Alien Fiancées and Fiancés Act of 1946, Pub. L. No. 79-471, 60 Stat. 339.
30. Harry S. Truman, Immigration Bill Veto, 1952, *U.S. Code Congressional and Administrative News*, 921, 926, as cited in Branstetter, "Military Constraints," 9. This anti-Asian immigration policy dated back to the Chinese Exclusion Act of 1882.
31. For examples of this ostracization, see Yuh, *Beyond the Shadow*; Barrett and Calvi, *GI Brides*; and Shukert and Scibetta, *War Brides*.
32. The single joint directive had different names for each branch. See U.S. Department of the Army, AR 600-240 (1953).
33. U.S. Department of the Army, AR 600-240 (1965). Diseases that were considered contagious or evidentiary of sexual promiscuity included actinomycosis, amebiasis, blastomycosis, favus, filariasis, gonorrhea, granuloma inguinale, keratoconjunctivitis, infections, leishmaniasis, leprosy, lymphogranuloma venereum, mycetoma, paragonimiasis, ringworm of the scalp, schistosomiasis, chancroid, syphilis in the infection stage, trachoma, trypanosomiasis, and yaws.
34. U.S. Department of the Army, AR 600-240 (1965), 6.
35. U.S. Department of the Army, AR 600-240 (1965), 1.
36. U.S. Department of the Army, AR 600-240 (1965), 7.
37. *United States v. Nation*, 26 C.M.R. 504, 506 (1958). For the history of marriage counseling, see Davis, *More Perfect Unions*. Davis illustrates how marriage counseling emerged in the 1930s and became a tool not just for personal happiness but also for the state and clergy in an effort to strengthen American families. On the history of the chaplaincy, see Whitt, *Bringing God to Men*; and Loveland, *Change and Conflict*.
38. U.S. Department of the Army, AR 600-240 (1965), 3.
39. U.S. Department of the Army, AR 600-240 (1965), 3.
40. U.S. Department of the Army, AR 600-240 (1965), 3.
41. *United States v. Nation*, 26 C.M.R. 504, 507 (1958).
42. *Nation*, 26 C.M.R. at 507.
43. *Nation*, 26 C.M.R. at 506.
44. *Nation*, 26 C.M.R. at 508. This rule of reasonable control and regulation was established in the cases *United States v. Martin*, 1

USCMA 674, 5 C.M.R. 102 (1952); and *United States v. Milldebrandt*, 8 USCMA 635, 25 C.M.R. 139 (1957).

45. Kristin Celello provides an illuminating picture of the anxiety that rising divorce rates invoked in *Making Marriage Work*. The irony is that in attempting to keep divorce rates down in the Cold War military, commanders sometimes prevented the marital unions on which the military's social structure depended.

46. *United States v. Guidry*, 22 C.M.R. 614, 617 (1957).

47. *Guidry*, 22 C.M.R. at 618.

48. As cited in *United States v. Avery*, 9 C.M.R. 648, 651 (A.F.B.R. 1953).

49. *Guidry*, 22 C.M.R. at 614.

50. Hillman, *Defending America*, 80, notes that "the regulations limiting marriage sometimes made it more difficult for well-intentioned servicemen to legitimize their relationships with foreign women."

51. Hillman, *Defending America*, 80–83.

52. *United States v. Jordan*, 30 C.M.R. 424, 430 (A.B.R. 1960).

53. *Jordan*, 30 C.M.R. at 429–30.

54. *United States v. Levinsky*, 30 C.M.R. 461, 462–65 (1960). The full text of COMNAVPHIL 5800.1E 60 (November 5, 1958) is located in the Levinsky transcript. The "reasonably necessary" rule was established in the case *United States v. Martin*, 1 USCMA 674, 5 C.M.R. 102 (1952).

55. *United States v. Wheeler*, 30 C.M.R. 387, 389 (1961). Wheeler's first name was not documented in court transcripts.

56. *Wheeler*, 30 C.M.R. at 391.

57. U.S. Department of the Army, AR 600-240 (1965), with a revision effective April 24, 1966. New revisions also included rules for civilian U.S. citizens working within overseas commands. Though working on overseas bases did not require civilian Americans to obtain command permission to marry non-U.S. citizens, the regulations instructed command personnel to encourage their civilian brothers to undergo counseling with the military chaplain about the "legal, moral and procedural problems involved in oversea marriages." The regulation was revised again in 1975 and 1978 to accommodate the administrative changes required by the Privacy Act of 1974.

58. *Loving v. Virginia*, 388 U.S. 1 (1967).
59. U.S. Department of the Army, AR 600-240 (1977), paras. 1A and 1B.
60. U.S. Department of the Army, AR 600-240 (1977), paras. 1A and 1B.
61. U.S. Department of the Army, AR 600-240 (1978), 5.
62. U.S. Department of the Army, AR 600-240 (1978), para. 4a.
63. U.S. Department of the Army, AR 600-240 (1978), paras. 4c–4f.
64. *United States v. Parker*, 5 M.J. 922 (N.C.M.R. 1978).
65. U.S. Department of the Army, AR 600-3, 2.
66. See chapter 6 for an analysis of the armed forces' use of overseas marriage regulations from 1975 to the present.
67. Statistics on command denial of marriages between South Korean women and American servicemen during the Cold War were collected by Capt. Ross Branstetter, an active duty judge advocate general who was stationed in Korea and had access to this data. As chapter 6 illustrates, marriages between American servicemen and South Korean women were so common that these relationships began to corrode U.S.-ROK relations. Though collecting marriage data on all overseas commands would enable us to draw more definitive conclusions about the scope and consequences of the marriage regulations, we must postpone the formation of such conclusions until more data becomes available.

3. Enforcing Monogamy

1. *United States v. O'Brien*, 9 C.M.R. 201 (A.B.R. 1952). The first O'Brien child was born in 1947 and the second in 1948.
2. *O'Brien*, 9 C.M.R. at 204.
3. *O'Brien*, 9 C.M.R. at 205, 206.
4. *O'Brien*, 9 C.M.R. at 206, 207.
5. *United States v. O'Brien*, 11 C.M.R. 108 (1953).
6. *O' Brien*, 9 C.M.R. 207 (1952).
7. *O'Brien*, 11 C.M.R. 107 (1953).
8. *O'Brien*, 11 C.M.R. 108 (1953).
9. European Command, "Kan. Pen to Hang Ex-wo Who Slew Wife in Munich," *Stars and Stripes*, July 31, 1954, 7.
10. Cott, *Public Vows*.

11. Wholly deserving of its own chapter, the history of legal officials' use of Article 125 to enforce heterosexism and "natural" sexual relations is the subject of chapter 4.

12. *Manual for Courts-Martial*, section 151b (2).

13. *United States v. McDonald*, 32 C.M.R. 692 (N.B.R. 1963).

14. *McDonald*, 32 C.M.R. at 693.

15. *United States v. Leach*, 22 C.M.R. 183 (1956). See Linda K. Kerber's keen analysis of the *feme covert* and the evolution of coverture laws in *No Constitutional Right*.

16. *Funk v. United States*, 290 U.S. 371, 54 S. Ct. 212 (1933).

17. *Hawkins v. United States*, 358 U.S. 74, 79 S. Ct. 136 (1958).

18. *United States v. McDonald*, 32 C.M.R. 692 (1963).

19. *United States v. Moore*, 34 C.M.R. 416–17 (1964).

20. *Moore*, 34 C.M.R. at 421.

21. See *State v. Wilcox*, 185 Iowa 90, 169 NW 646, 4 ALR 1066 (1918); and *Wilkinson v. People*, 86 Colo. 406, 282 P 257 (1929).

22. *United States v. Leach*, 22 C.M.R. 190 (1956).

23. *Leach*, 22 C.M.R. at 190.

24. *United States v. Benn*, 28 C.M.R. 424 (A.B.R. 1958).

25. *United States v. Massey*, 34 C.M.R. 930 (A.F.B.R. 1963).

26. Quinn as cited in *United States v. Massey*, 35 C.M.R. 255 (1965).

27. *United States v. Nees*, 39 C.M.R. 31 (1968).

28. *United States v. Moore*, 34 C.M.R. 422 (1963).

29. *Moore*, 34 C.M.R. 422 (1963).

30. See *United States v. Parker*, 32 C.M.R. 482 (A.B.R. 1962); and *United States v. Parker*, 33 C.M.R. 111 (1963).

31. *United States v. Hanna*, 7 C.M.R. 571 (A.F.B.R. 1952).

32. See Rowland, *Boundaries of Her Body*, 486–92, for a provocative analysis of the historical trajectory of seduction crimes in America.

33. *Hanna*, 7 C.M.R. at 578.

34. *United States v. Lyon*, 35 C.M.R. 280 (1965).

35. *Lyon*, 35 C.M.R. at 286.

36. See *C.M. v. J.M.*, 726 A.2D 998, 1001 (N.J. Super. Ct. 1999), citing *Magierowski v. Buckley*, 39 N.J. Super. Ct. 534, 555 (App. Div. 1956), in Rowland, *Boundaries of Her Body*, 488. Seduction actions for minors are still the cause for civil action suits in many states today.

37. See *Hodges v. Howell*, 4 P.3D 803, 805 (Utah App. 2000), citing *Bowers v. Carter*, 59 Utah 249, 252 (1921), in Rowland, *Boundaries of Her Body*, 489–90.

38. *United States v. Hanna*, 7 C.M.R. 579 (A.F.B.R. 1952).

39. Hillman, *Defending America*, 81, contends that bigamists in the ranks "made commanding officers anxious about both the military's public image and fraud against the government."

40. Hillman, *Defending America*, 195n116, also notes that there were thirty-nine bigamy convictions between 1950 and 1975, and half of them were prosecuted during first five years of the UCMJ's existence.

41. *United States v. Hadsell*, 42 C.M.R. 766 (A.B.R. 1970).

42. *United States v. Burkhart*, 40 C.M.R. 1009 (A.F.B.R. 1969).

43. *United States v. Guidry*, 22 C.M.R. 614, 617 (1957).

44. Hillman, *Defending America*, 81–82, summarizes military bigamy cases as follows: "The usual bigamy court-martial involved an airman who failed to extricate himself from a hastily arranged first marriage before entering into a second marriage, usually in a different geographic location."

45. *United States v. Grogen*, 34 C.M.R. 680 (N.B.R. 1963).

46. *Grogen*, 34 C.M.R. at 680.

47. For the most common type of bigamy trials (which legal officials labeled "mistake of fact" cases), see *United States v. Williams*, 7 C.M.R. 548 (A.F.B.R. 1952); *United States v. Avery*, 9 C.M.R. 648 (A.F.B.R. 1953); *United States v. Duff*, 12 C.M.R. 802 (A.F.B.R. 1953); *United States v. Noe*, 22 C.M.R. 198 (1956); *United States v. Williamson*, 14 C.M.R. 676 (A.F.B.R. 1953); *United States v. Bateman*, 23 C.M.R. 312 (1957); *United States v. Grogen*, 34 C.M.R. 677 (N.B.R. 1963); *United States v. Bradshaw*, 35 C.M.R. 118 (1964); and *United States v. Pruitt*, 38 C.M.R. 236 (1968). Though rare, military courts also prosecuted service members for committing multiple bigamy offenses in *United States v. Green*, 26 C.M.R. 508 (1958); and *United States v. McDonald*, 32 C.M.R. 689 (N.B.R. 1962). Absent in the case law are courts-martial for the offense of polygamy.

48. See *United States v. Jones*, 11 C.M.R. 855 (A.F.B.R. 1953); *United States v. Matthews*, 23 C.M.R. 790 (A.F.B.R. 1957); and *United States v. Howell*, 29 C.M.R. 528 (1960).

49. *United States v. Whitaker*, 31 C.M.R. 334 (A.B.R. 1960).

50. *United States v. Burkhart*, 40 C.M.R. 1009 (A.F.B.R. 1969).
51. *United States v. Hadsell*, 42 C.M.R. 768 (1970).
52. See *United States v. Ortega*, 45 C.M.R. 576 (A.B.R. 1972).
53. Judge George Latimer's dissenting opinion in *United States v. Melville*, 25 C.M.R. 106 (1958).
54. *United States v. Leach*, 22 C.M.R. 191 (1956).
55. *United States v. Bailey*, 12 C.M.R. 564 (A.B.R. 1953).
56. *United States v. Smith*, 35 C.M.R. 662 (A.B.R. 1965). The U.S. Army Review Board's decision in this case to classify wrongful cohabitation as a general disorder mirrored the trajectory of the civil courts' historic prosecutions of nonmarital living arrangements as misdemeanors rather than felonies.
57. *United States v. Melville*, 25 C.M.R. 101 (1958).
58. *Melville*, 25 C.M.R. 105 (1958).
59. *Melville*, 25 C.M.R. 106 (1958).
60. *Melville*, 25 C.M.R. 106 (1958).
61. *United States v. Parker*, 12 C.M.R. 213, 214–15 (A.B.R. 1953).
62. *United States v. Knight*, 13 C.M.R. 447 (A.B.R. 1953).
63. Hillman, *Defending America*, 84.
64. Alvah, *Unofficial Ambassadors*.
65. *United States v. Hudson*, 7 C.M.R. 163 (A.B.R. 1952).
66. Hillman, *Defending America*, 88, 201n160, argues that only four officers were convicted of spousal abuse from 1950 to 1975, but she overlooks the most extreme cases in which service husbands murdered their wives. In combination with spousal homicide, conviction rates for domestic violence (excluding child abuse) are more than double Hillman's original estimation and include both enlisted men and officers. In addition, the *Court Martial Reports* are full of cases in which evidence of the husbands' violent abuse of their wives emerged in the trial record in relation to the commission of unrelated crimes such as extortion, larceny, and numerous others. Though the majority of service husbands who abused their wives escaped legal prosecution and punishment, the cacophony of witnesses testifying about the common occurrence provides irrefutable evidence that domestic violence was a rampant problem in military marriages from 1950 to 1975, but legal officials chose to let them slip under the regulatory radar. This

is ironic given the herculean efforts of military courts to prevent sexual deviance between spouses.

67. *United States v. Smith*, 34 C.M.R. 185 (1964).

68. To illustrate the discipline problems that marital infidelity incited among the service community, as well as the extent of the domestic violence servicemen (and occasionally service wives) perpetrated against their spouses, I focus specifically on cases in which adultery provoked service husbands to acts of assault and homicide. See *United States v. O'Brien*, 9 C.M.R. (1952); *United States v. Marymont*, 28 C.M.R. 904 (A.F.B.R. 1959); *United States v. Marymont*, 29 C.M.R. 561 (1960); *United States v. Erb*, 30 C.M.R. 938 (A.F.B.R. 1961); *United States v. Erb*, 31 C.M.R. 110 (1961); *United States v. Weaver*, 31 C.M.R. 662 (A.F.B.R. 1962); and *United States v. Fields*, 41 C.M.R. 119 (1969).

69. O'Brien was the only soldier to receive the death sentence for the charge of premeditated murder of a spouse between 1952 and 1975. Military courts rarely used the death sentence for spousal homicide cases.

70. *Marymont*, 28 C.M.R. at 904; and *Marymont*, 29 C.M.R. at 561.

71. *United States v. Thomas*, 37 C.M.R. 520 (A.F.B.R. 1965). For the appellate transcript, see *United States v. Thomas*, 37 C.M.R. 367 (1967).

72. *United States v. Riska*, 33 C.M.R. 941 (A.F.B.R. 1963).

73. *United States v. Tobin*, 38 C.M.R. 423 (1968). For the original trial transcript, see *United States v. Tobin*, 38 C.M.R. 885 (A.B.R. 1967). See also *United States v. Gagnon*, 43 C.M.R. 933 (A.F.B.R. 1970); *United States v. Gagnon*, 44 C.M.R. 214 (1972); *United States v. Hurt*, 40 C.M.R. 207 (1970); and *United States v. Alphin*, 34 C.M.R. 461 (1964). The *Alphin* case is notable because the CMA, despite the clear evidence that Alphin was guilty of the voluntary manslaughter of Mrs. Alphin's illicit lover, dismissed the case on grounds of prejudicial error.

74. *Mercer v. Dillon*, Misc. Docket No. 69-57, 41 C.M.R. 264 (A.F.B.R. 1969–70).

75. *O'Callahan v. Parker*, 395 U.S. 258 (1969).

76. *United States v. Francis*, 12 C.M.R. 695 (A.F.B.R. 1953).

77. *United States v. Farrell*, 18 C.M.R. 684 (A.F.B.R. 1954). For unknown reasons, Farrell petitioned the CMA to review his case

although he was found not guilty of either charge. The CMA denied the petition.

78. *United States v. Norris*, 28 C.M.R. 903 (A.B.R. 1959).

79. See *Manual for Courts-Martial*, para. 76(a)(8). Because the law officer presiding over Norris's trial failed to instruct the court to regard the two offenses as a single offense for the purpose of punishment, the convening authority reduced Norris's sentence from eighteen months to twelve months of hard labor confinement.

80. As cited in *Norris*, 28 C.M.R. at 903.

81. *United States v. Pruitt*, 38 C.M.R. 238 (1968).

82. In the 1980s and '90s, courts-martial for marital infidelity more than doubled compared to courts-martial for those charges from 1950 to 1975. See chapter 6.

4. Normalizing Heterosexism

1. It is curious that Sandoval brought a charge of sodomy against Adkins since he consented to Adkins's sexual advance and Sandoval's compliance made him an accomplice to the crime.

2. *United States v. Adkins*, 18 C.M.R. 116, 120 (1955).

3. *Adkins*, 18 C.M.R. at 121. The *Manual for Courts-Martial*, para. 138(e), defines an *expert witness* as one who is "skilled in some art, trade, profession, or science or who has knowledge and experience in relation to matters which are not generally within the knowledge of men of common education and experience."

4. Johnson, *Lavender Scare*. Where this chapter focuses almost exclusively on courts-martial for suspected homosexuality of male service members from 1950 to 1975, Margot Canaday's masterful chapter "Finding a Home in the Army," in *Straight State*, 175–213, draws on records, reports, and administrative discharge files to evaluate the impact of military exclusion policies on women suspected of lesbianism.

5. Hillman, *Defending America*. See chapter 2, 29–43.

6. Johnson, *Lavender Scare*, deftly illustrates how the lavender scare laid the groundwork for the gay rights movement by forging a collective identity for sexual minorities who were victims of the federal government's wholesale persecution in the 1950s.

7. Sinclair, "Homosexuality and the Military," 704.

8. For a detailed account of Matlovich's story, see Hippler, *Matlovich*.
9. This phenomenon was part of a larger evolution in U.S. criminal procedure termed "constitutionalization," which increased protections for all accused persons, not only those convicted of same-sex sodomy. Only two soldiers in active war zones were court-martialed for same-sex sodomy during the Korean and Vietnam Wars. Second Lt. G. Jackson was discharged for making lewd comments and improper advances to an enlisted soldier under his command in Korea in 1953. The CMA denied Jackson's petition for appellate review. In 1971 E-4 T. Conway was convicted of sodomy and assault with intent to commit sodomy on a fellow troop at Camp Evans, Republic of Vietnam. The convening authority reversed the charges and dismissed the case altogether. See *United States v. Jackson*, 12 C.M.R. 403 (A.B.R. 1953); and *United States v. Conway*, 43 C.M.R. 779 (A.B.R. 1971).
10. Lehring, *Officially Gay*.
11. For an exhaustive history of anti-sodomy law in U.S. history, see Eskridge, *Dishonorable Passions*.
12. Shilts, *Conduct Unbecoming*, 16–17.
13. Berube, *Coming Out under Fire*.
14. D'Amico, "Race-ing and Gendering," 6.
15. *Manual for Courts-Martial*, para. 204, 367.
16. Hillman, *Defending America*, 33. Hillman's analysis of some homosexual sodomy courts-martial suggests that the extremely homophobic culture of the Cold War military made it nearly impossible for alleged homosexual service members to receive impartial trials. This chapter expands and challenges her preliminary conclusions. For her analysis of homosexual sodomy cases, see *Defending America*, 32–43, 59–64, 111, 114–127.
17. Citing 1 Peter 4:8 in *United States v. Radford*, 17 C.M.R. 604 (A.F.B.R. 1954).
18. USCMA judge Kilday describing sodomy in the majority opinion of *United States v. Goodman*, 33 C.M.R. 195, 199 (1963).
19. The two cases of heterosexual sodomy between 1950 and 1975 that did not involve child victims were *United States v. Doherty*, 17 C.M.R. 287 (1954); and *United States v. Parker*, 32 C.M.R. 482 (A.B.R. 1962). See *United States v. Parker*, 33 C.M.R. 111 (1963) for the appellate trial record.

20. Winthrop, *Military Law and Precedents*, 711–12, as cited in *United States v. Yeast*, 36 C.M.R. 890, 904 (A.F.B.R. 1965), explains that a violation of Article 134, according to the *Manual for Courts-Martial*, "must offend so seriously against law, justice, morality or decorum as to expose disgrace, socially or as a man, the offender, and at the same time must be of such a nature or committed under such circumstances as to bring honor or disrepute upon the military profession which he represents."

21. Secretary of the Navy, Directive No. 1620.1, as cited in *United States v. Betts*, 30 C.M.R. 214 (1961). These regulations were similar in form and content for all services. Navy regulations applied to both U.S. Navy and Coast Guard members.

22. U.S. Department of the Army, AR 635-443; and U.S. Department of the Air Force, AFR 35-66. AR 635-443 was implemented on January 12, 1950, and was superseded by AR 600-443 on April 10, 1953. On January 12, 1955, AR 600-443 was superseded by AR 635-89, which was later superseded by AR 635-212 and AR 635-100. Meanwhile, the revised version of AFR 35-66 became effective May 31, 1954.

23. Canaday, *Straight State*, 197. See 190–98 especially for a detailed description of the trauma and humiliation women endured during investigations. Canaday bases her comparative conclusions about the relatively "clear-cut" nature of male homosexuality investigations on thirty-two discharge files for male homosexuality between 1948 and 1951. Though her hypothesis here is compelling, it risks misrepresenting historical reality by overlooking thousands of other discharge files that were processed in this time frame (this omission is understandable given that many of these files were still classified as she conducted her research) and by projecting this trend onto the years 1952–59. See 190n60.

24. According to Lehring, *Officially Gay*, 6, the U.S. military's exclusionary policies were central to the creation of the modern homosexual subject. This new homosexual "identity" became the "new sight of regulation and a new form of resistance." Religion, medicine, and psychiatry consolidated an official lexicon that made modern homosexuality synonymous with unnatural sexual deviance, disease, and mental sickness. The Cold War military used these discur-

sive "truth creations" and wrote them into military policies. These truth creations all attempted to define what and who homosexuals were and, in so defining them, created the need for surveillance and punishment apparatuses to control these deviant subjects.

25. AR 635-89 as cited in *United States v. Goins*, 23 C.M.R. 542, 543–44 (A.B.R. 1956).

26. *Goins*, 23 C.M.R. at 543.

27. Canaday makes a compelling argument that this increasing surveillance of servicewomen took the form of witch hunts similar to those the federal government waged against suspected communist-leaning government officials during McCarthy's Red Scare. Canaday, *Straight State*, 189.

28. *Goins*, 23 C.M.R. at 544.

29. Canaday, *Straight State*, 200n101. See 199–200 for an analysis of the famous *Clackum* case in which a servicewoman suspected of lesbianism became the victim of entrapment and demanded a trial by court-martial in lieu of an undesirable discharge so she could challenge the investigation's evidence (or lack thereof). Authorities discharged her anyway. Clackum was the first service member to sue the military for denial of due process rights in federal courts. Because I use primarily courts-martial transcripts, I cannot offer a statistical analysis of the rate at which male service members refused dishonorable discharges and opted for trial by court-martial.

30. Prosecution via court-martial was rare and represented the most extreme among a wide variety of administrative tools available to punish suspected sexual deviants.

31. AFR 35-66 as cited in *United States v. Adams*, 21 C.M.R. 733, 739–40 (A.F.B.R. 1956).

32. AR 635-89 as cited in *Goins*, 23 C.M.R. at 544.

33. AR 635-89 as cited in *Goins*, 23 C.M.R. at 544.

34. *Goins*, 23 C.M.R. at 543.

35. *United States v. Smith*, 28 C.M.R. 782, 783 (A.F.B.R. 1959).

36. *Smith*, 28 C.M.R. at 784.

37. *Goins*, 23 C.M.R. at 542.

38. *Goins*, 28 C.M.R. at 543.

39. AR 635-89 as cited in *Goins*, 28 C.M.R. at 544.

40. *Goins*, 28 C.M.R. at 543.

41. *United States v. Sheehan*, 29 C.M.R. 887, 889 (A.F.B.R. 1960).

42. *United States v. Green*, 29 C.M.R. 370 (A.B.R. 1957).

43. *Green*, 29 C.M.R. at 371.

44. AR 635-89 as cited in *Green*, 29 C.M.R. at 371.

45. *Green*, 29 C.M.R. at 371.

46. See, for instance, *Betts*, 30 C.M.R. 215 (1961); and *United States v. Rivera*, 31 C.M.R. 93 (1961).

47. *United States v. Yeast*, 36 C.M.R. 890, 893 (A.F.B.R. 1965).

48. *Yeast*, 36 C.M.R. at 897.

49. *Yeast*, 36 C.M.R. at 891.

50. *Yeast*, 36 C.M.R. at 901.

51. *Yeast*, 36 C.M.R. at 908–9.

52. *Yeast*, 36 C.M.R. at 902.

53. *Yeast*, 36 C.M.R. at 903.

54. *Yeast*, 36 C.M.R. at 909.

55. Crittendon, *Crittenden Report*.

56. *United States v. Davisson*, 6 C.M.R. 174, 176 (A.B.R. 1952).

57. *Davisson*, 6 C.M.R. at 175.

58. Secretary of the Navy, Directive No. 1620.1, as cited in *Betts*, 30 C.M.R. 215 (1961).

59. For the most comprehensive overview of the history of the Court of Military Appeals (later renamed the U.S. Court of Appeals for the Armed Forces), see Lurie, *Military Justice in America*.

60. *United States v. Knudson*, 7 C.M.R. 438, 442 (N.B.R 1952).

61. *Knudson*, 7 C.M.R. at 440.

62. *Knudson*, 7 C.M.R. at 443–44.

63. *United States v. Knudson*, 16 C.M.R. 164 (1954).

64. *United States v. Warren*, 20 C.M.R. 135, 137 (1955).

65. *Warren*, 20 C.M.R. at 138.

66. *Warren*, 20 C.M.R. at 145.

67. *Warren*, 20 C.M.R. at 144.

68. *Warren*, 20 C.M.R. at 144.

69. *United States v. Bird*, 24 C.M.R. 447, 448–49 (A.B.R. 1957).

70. *Bird*, 24 C.M.R. at 450.

71. Voir dire examination was a procedural safeguard of the UCMJ that required the defendant's attorney to question all court mem-

bers about their biases toward issues related to homosexuality before the trial began to enforce the defendant's right to an impartial hearing. Court members who were found to harbor prejudice about homosexuality that would bias their judgment were replaced.

72. *United States v. Lackey*, 22 C.M.R. 384, 387 (A.B.R. 1954).

73. *Lackey*, 22 C.M.R. at 388.

74. *Lackey*, 22 C.M.R. at 388.

75. *United States v. Kennedy*, 24 C.M.R. 61, 62 (1957).

76. *Kennedy*, 24 C.M.R. at 62.

77. *United States v. Haynes*, 24 C.M.R. 881, 887 (A.B.R. 1957).

78. *Sherman v. United States*, as cited in *United States v. Haynes*, 27 C.M.R. 60, 63 (1958).

79. *Haynes*, 24 C.M.R. at 886.

80. *United States v. Hillan*, 26 C.M.R. 771, 795 (N.B.R. 1957).

81. *Hillan*, 26 C.M.R. at 805.

82. *United States v. Battista*, 33 C.M.R. 282, 283 (1963).

83. *Battista*, 33 C.M.R. at 285.

84. *United States v. Woodard*, 39 C.M.R. 6 (1968).

85. *United States v. Ortega*, 45 C.M.R. 576 (1972).

86. Dissenting opinion, *Ortega*, 45 C.M.R. at 581. In an exceptional case, the CMA also upheld the procedural rights of an alleged homosexual soldier whom a review board convicted of the first-degree murder of his male sexual partner in *United States v. Weems*, 13 C.M.R. 25 (1953).

87. Approximately 130 homosexual sodomy cases were reported in the *Court-Martial Reports* between 1950 and 1975, only one of which featured a female defendant.

88. Concurring opinion of *United States v. Hillan*, 26 C.M.R. 805 (1957).

89. It is interesting to note Vinet's reference to the young "men" whom homosexuals seduced in the services given that this case was about a woman who supposedly sexually assaulted, rather than seduced, another woman. Perhaps male judges were just as shocked at the idea of female homosexuality as were the military police Canaday discusses. They were apparently so stunned upon discovering two female service members having oral sex in a car that they left the scene.

90. The Stonewall riots broke out after police violently raided a popular gay bar in California, dragging dozens of bar patrons out into the street and publicly beating and shaming them. Many historians of gender and sexuality mark the Stonewall riots as the catalyst for the national gay liberation movement.

5. Protecting the Public Morals

1. *United States v. Stewart*, 7 C.M.R. 226 (A.B.R. 1951).
2. *Stewart*, 7 C.M.R. at 223.
3. For the original trial transcripts, see *United States v. Jewson*, 7 C.M.R. 216 (A.B.R. 1951); and *Stewart*, 7 C.M.R. at 222. For the appellate transcripts reviewed by the Court of Military Appeals, see *United States v. Jewson*, 5 C.M.R. 80 (1952); and *United States v. Stewart*, 5 C.M.R. 76 (1952).
4. *Stewart*, 7 C.M.R. at 224–25.
5. *Jewson*, 7 C.M.R. at 216.
6. *Stewart*, 7 C.M.R. at 222.
7. *Stewart*, 7 C.M.R. at 226.
8. *Stewart*, 7 C.M.R. at 226.
9. *Jewson*, 7 C.M.R. at 219.
10. *United States v. Manos*, 24 C.M.R. 627 (A.F.B.R. 1956).
11. *Manual for Courts-Martial*, para. 212 at 380.
12. Winthrop, *Military Law and Precedents*, 711–12, as cited in *United States v. Yeast*, 36 C.M.R. 904 (A.F.B.R. 1965).
13. Article 134, in *Manual for Courts-Martial*, para 213(a) at 381, "refers only to acts directly prejudicial to good order and discipline and not to acts which are prejudicial only in a remote or indirect sense. An irregular or improper act on the part of a member of the military service can scarcely be conceived which may not be regarded as in some indirect or remote sense prejudicing discipline, but this article does not contemplate such distant effects and is confined to cases in which the prejudice is reasonably direct and palpable."
14. Military masculinity has been the subject of numerous scholarly investigations. A notable and more recent example is Belkin's *Bring Me Men*. Belkin argues that the U.S. military's unique culture of masculinity is rooted in bizarre aspects of human nature

such as filth, masochism, penetration, sexual conquest, and weakness, and these conceptions of masculinity became the templates for how the U.S. military conducted its operations from the Spanish-American War through the end of the twentieth century.

15. *United States v. Caune*, 46 C.M.R. 201 (1973).

16. See Strub, *Perversion for Profit*, for an overview of anti-obscenity campaigns in American civil law.

17. *Duncan v. United States*, 48 F2d 128, 132fn 3 (9th Cir. 1931), as cited in *United States v. Stewart*, 7 C.M.R. 226 (A.B.R. 1951).

18. See *United States v. Cowan*, 12 C.M.R. 374 (A.B.R. 1953).

19. *Cowan*, 12 C.M.R. at 377.

20. See *United States v. White*, 37 C.M.R. 791 (A.F.B.R. 1966).

21. *United States v. Schneider*, 27 C.M.R. 566, 567 (A.B.R. 1958).

22. See *United States v. Ford*, 31 C.M.R. 353 (A.B.R. 1961).

23. *United States v. Manos*, 25 C.M.R. 238, 241 (1958).

24. *United States v. Royston*, 4 C.M.R. 263 (A.B.R. 1951).

25. *Royston*, 4 C.M.R. at 266.

26. After graduating from Tuskegee College in 1934 and Howard University Law School in 1940, Royston enlisted in the army in 1941 and was promoted to the rank of master sergeant in eighteen months. He graduated from Officers' Candidate School in 1942 and served as a law member, trial judge advocate, and defense counsel of general courts-martial and as a legal officer of a quartermaster depot before arriving at Camp Edwards in December 1950.

27. *Royston*, 4 C.M.R. at 265.

28. See *United States v. White*, 6 C.M.R. 424 (A.B.R. 1952); and *United States v. Franklin*, 8 C.M.R. 513 (A.B.R. 1952), for cases following the *Royston* precedent. The army review boards indicted Franklin and White on similar charges and under similar circumstances to those in Royston's case with one critical difference. Where Royston's skin color was explicated in the trial record, the absence of any notations pertaining to the racial heritage of Franklin and White indicated that both were Caucasian. That all three were convicted on similar charges suggests that the precedent established in *Royston*—public masturbation was sufficient evidence of willful intent to indecently expose one's private parts to public view—was enforced among service members of different racial

makeups. Significantly, however, Franklin and White were not subjected to lineups. The CMA denied Franklin's petitions for review two times, whereas White did not attempt an appeal. Cases involving child victims of indecent exposure have largely been omitted from this book. I will examine these and other child abuse cases in future publications.

29. *United States v. Anderson*, 8 C.M.R. 212 (A.B.R. 1952).

30. *Anderson*, 8 C.M.R. at 214.

31. *United States v. Fletcher*, 23 C.M.R. 911 (A.F.B.R. 1956). Fletcher did not petition the Court of Military of Appeals for a review of his case.

32. *Fletcher*, 23 C.M.R. at 914.

33. *United States v. Manos*, 25 C.M.R. 238 (1958).

34. For the original trial transcript, see *United States v. Manos*, 24 C.M.R. 626, 629 (A.F.B.R. 1956). Manos's charge of window peeping arose out of a neighbor's complaint that she had seen Manos peering into the window of another neighbor's home at night. As a result, the military police put Manos's residence under surveillance, and the complainant's home became the "headquarters" of spying operations to confirm the truth of the accusation. When the complainant witnessed Manos in the nude while she was spying on him from the bushes, she then complained to his commander that she was the victim of indecent exposure. See this chapter's subsequent section on voyeurism for a complete overview. By affirming the original review board's window-peeping conviction against Manos in 1958, the CMA acknowledged the military justice system's responsibility to "protect . . . the public from being involuntary subjects of the voyeur's curiosity" in the second half of the twentieth century.

35. According to Judge Latimer in *Manos*, 25 C.M.R. at 240, English common law criminalized negligent indecent exposure as early as 1809 in the case *Rex v. Crunden*. The court ruled that the accused's intention to bathe naked in the sea was irrelevant since his conduct near a group of houses tended to "outrage decency and to corrupt the public morals."

36. *Manos*, 25 C.M.R. at 239, 243. The "reasonable person" rule was established in the case of *State v. Martin*, 125 Iowa 715, 101 NW 637 (1904).

37. Only three indecent exposure courts-martial featuring adult victims between 1959 and 1975 resulted in guilty convictions. These cases included *United States v. Loppi*, 37 C.M.R. 625 (A.B.R. 1966); *United States v. McCord*, 39 C.M.R. 929 (A.F.B.R. 1968); and *United States v. Austin*, 44 C.M.R. 550 (A.F.B.R. 1971).
38. *United States v. Conrad*, 34 C.M.R. 124 (A.F.B.R. 1963).
39. *United States v. Conrad*, 35 C.M.R. 411 (1965); and *United States v. Stackhouse*, 37 C.M.R. 99 (1967).
40. *United States v. Caune*, 46 C.M.R. 200, 201 (1973).
41. *Caune*, 46 C.M.R. at 201. This case also illustrates the heterosexual normative standard against which the criminal conduct of service members was consistently judged during the Cold War (and into the twenty-first century, as discussed in chapter 6).
42. *United States v. Clark*, 22 C.M.R. 888 (A.F.B.R. 1956).
43. In C.M. 263231, Baker, 41 B.R. 209, the presiding judges ruled that evidence that the accused peered into the window of a female's bedroom constituted disorderly and service-discrediting conduct in violation of Article of War 96 (the predecessor of Articles 133 and 134). Prior to the publication of the *Court Martial Reports*, pre-UCMJ courts-martial decisions were published in the *Boards of Review of the Army*, which commence with C.M. 187168, Greene, 1 B.R. 1 (July 10, 1929).
44. *Clark*, 22 C.M.R. at 888–91.
45. *United States v. Merrill*, 34 C.M.R. 901, 903 (A.F.B.R. 1963).
46. *United States v. Schoenberg*, 37 C.M.R. 45 (1966).
47. Moon, *Sex among Allies*. Policing prostitution and venereal disease (VD) was unique neither to the U.S. military nor to the twentieth century. See, for example, Levine, *Prostitution, Race and Politics*; Edwards, *Comfort Women*; Henson, *Comfort Woman*; Remick, *Regulating Prostitution in China*; and Hershatter, *Dangerous Pleasures*.
48. For U.S. military regulation of prostitution in Asia, see Sturdevant and Stoltzfus, *Let the Good Times Roll*. For regulation in South Korea, see Moon, *Sex among Allies*; and Moon, "Regulating Desire." For regulation in Japan, see Takeuchi, "'Pan-Pan Girls.'" For prostitution and VD regulation in Puerto Rico, see

Briggs, *Reproducing Empire*. For regulation during World War II in Hawaii, see Bailey and Farber, *First Strange Place*; in France, see Roberts, *What Soldiers Do*, 195–254; and in Germany, see Höhn, "You Can't Pin Sergeant's Stripes." See Belkin, *Bring Me Men*, 161–63, for a discussion on military regulation of prostitution in the Philippines in 1898. Brandt's *No Magic Bullet* illustrates that attempts to regulate venereal disease were not unique to the post–World War II era in the United States. Clement's *Love for Sale* and Brandt's *No Magic Bullet* address the military's general regulation of venereal disease during World War II.

49. See preceding notes 47 and 48 of this chapter for examples of scholarship on the U.S. military's regulation of prostitution and venereal disease in around military installations in overseas locales outside of the continental United States.

50. *United States v. Mallory*, 17 C.M.R. 409 (A.B.R. 1954).

51. *United States v. Moss*, 3 C.M.R. 773, 775 (A.F.B.R. 1951).

52. *Webster's New International Dictionary*, 2nd ed., unabridged, as cited in *Moss*, 3 C.M.R. at 775.

53. *United States v. Rice*, 14 C.M.R. 316, 318–19 (A.B.R. 1953). At trial Pvt. M. Shaffer, the enlisted man who accompanied Rice to the prostitution house, testified that while en route to Uijongbu village Rice stated that he "intended to get a little dicking." Shaffer does not appear to have been court-martialed for his participation in this escapade.

54. *Manual for Courts-Martial*, subpar. 127(c), p. 221.

55. *United States v. Plummer*, 30 C.M.R. 18 (1960).

56. *United States v. Barcomb*, 3 C.M.R. 623 (A.F.B.R. 1951).

57. *United States v. Barcomb*, 3 C.M.R. 149 (1951).

58. Service members were charged with the pandering of minors in two notable cases from 1950 to 1975. In *United States v. Bohannon*, 20 C.M.R. 870 (A.F.B.R. 1955), U.S. Air Force second lieutenant S. Bohannon was convicted on three separate charges of carnal knowledge and enticing a fourteen-year-old girl to commit acts of prostitution in violation of Articles 120 and 134. The evidence established that Bohannon assisted the girl in running away from home and supporting herself through prostitution on and around Ellington Air Force Base in Houston, Texas. He was sentenced to

dismissal, total forfeiture of all pay and allowances, and two years in hard labor confinement. The second case—*United States v. Hodges*, 33 C.M.R. 235 (1963)—involved an air force tech sergeant who was charged with incest, carnal knowledge, and pandering of his fifteen-year-old daughter. The Court of Military Appeals dismissed the pandering charge on the grounds of insufficient evidence, but it affirmed the other charges and sentenced Hodges to a dishonorable discharge, total forfeiture of all pay and allowances, and three years in hard labor confinement.

59. *United States v. Brown*, 24 C.M.R. 65 (1957).

60. *Brown*, 24 C.M.R. at 66. The CMA judges commonly referred to each other as "brothers" not only as a sign of affection and respect but also as a way to reaffirm the heterosexual nature of their close relationships. This linguistic custom functioned largely to express unity amid constant criticism from military commanders and judge advocates who resented the new appellate court for undermining the authority the court-martial had enjoyed before the UCMJ was created. This exclusive fraternity of presidentially appointed civilian judges depended upon the strength of its "brotherhood" to sustain the Court of Military Appeals in its fledgling years. The paternalistic overtones of the judges' brotherhood references conferred on their decisions an air of benevolence and authority. The brotherhood also signified the larger cult of masculinity that governed the manner in which the judges related to each other. Relating to and referencing each other as brothers displayed the heterosexual and familial nature of the judges' close relationships to each other and quelled any suspicions, especially during the lavender scare of the McCarthy era, that these government employees might be national security threats with homosexual tendencies.

61. *Black's Law Dictionary*, 4th ed., 626, as cited in *Brown*, 24 C.M.R. at 68. In *United States v. Gentry*, 23 C.M.R. 238 (1957), the CMA ruled that the act of merely transporting service members to a house of prostitution for profit did not amount to pandering since the accused's conduct "only made it easier for four soldiers to reach a place where they could engage in sexual activities." The evidence established that Gentry accepted ten dollars from several

soldiers whom he transported to and from a house of prostitution. For the act to equate to pandering, it "must be more than [transporting to a house of prostitution] or the driver of a car can be charged with a sexual offense merely because he solicited passengers to pay for transportation to a house of illfame [*sic*]." In comparing Gentry's case to that of Brown, Judge Ferguson explained that "although [Brown] did not transport the trainees to a house of illfame, he did what we consider even worse—he brought a house of illfame to the trainees." See *Brown*, 24 C.M.R. at 69.

62. *Brown*, 24 C.M.R. at 68.
63. *United States v. Adams*, 40 C.M.R. 22 (1969).
64. *Adams*, 40 C.M.R. at 23.
65. *Adams*, 40 C.M.R. at 25.
66. *Adams*, 40 C.M.R. at 24.
67. *United States v. Wright*, 48 C.M.R. 295 (A.F.C.M.R. 1974). Wright was charged with four offenses of pandering in violation of Article 134. On May 31, 1972, Wright transported three young women onto K. I. Sawyer Air Force Base, Michigan, for the purpose of putting on a strip show at the alert facility later that night. Although prosecution witnesses testified that Wright was collecting money from his brothers-in-arms for entry into the show (which was cut short when the headquarters squadron's first sergeant crashed the party), Wright denied earning any sort of proceeds.
68. *United States v. Butler*, 11 C.M.R. 445, 447 (A.B.R. 1953).
69. Private Butler was also charged with breaking restriction on multiple occasions and assault and battery upon a female German national.
70. Table of maximum punishments in *Manual for Courts-Martial*, subpar. 127(c), 275.
71. *United States v. Mardis*, 20 C.M.R. 340 (1956).
72. *Mardis*, 20 C.M.R. at 346.
73. *Mardis*, 20 C.M.R. at 345. Again this issue is a male dominated one.
74. *United States v. Boswell*, 35 C.M.R. 491 (A.B.R. 1963).
75. The rate of 95 percent is based on my own calculations from my own research.

6. Policing Sex and Marriage

1. *United States v. Johnson*, 27 M.J. 798 (A.F.C.M.R. 1988).

2. See, for example, U.S. Department of the Army, AR 600-110.
3. *United States v. Negron*, 28 M.J. 775 (A.C.M.R. 1989).
4. *United States v. Schoolfield*, 40 M.J. 132, 133 (1994). Chief Judge Sullivan cited the expert testimony of Doctor Redfield, who presented evidence that "a male can transmit the human immunodeficiency virus even though there may not be an ejaculation in the vagina." This case is distinguishable from *United States v. Perez*, 33 M.J. 1050 (1991), in which the CAAF ruled that the accused, although HIV positive, was not guilty of aggravated assault because his surgical vasectomy prevented him from transmitting the virus through ejaculation.
5. I did not encounter courts-martial featuring HIV-positive female defendants.
6. These statistics are based on the author's own preliminary calculations of cases published by the Judge Advocate General of the Armed Forces in *Military Justice Reporter*, vols. 1–54.
7. The UCMJ has undergone multiple revisions, but the contents of the punitive articles have remained unchanged.
8. *Lawrence v. Texas*, 539 U.S. 558 (2003). This landmark Supreme Court decision overturned all state anti-sodomy laws on the grounds that such laws violate the citizens' rights to privacy.
9. U.S. Department of the Army, AR 600-240 (1977), paras. 1A and 1B.
10. I focus on the U.S.-ROK relationship because it has generated the most data.
11. Branstetter, "Military Constraints," 16.
12. Montalvo, "Constitutional Right to Marry," 239–40.
13. James Webb, "The Military Is Not a Social Program," *New York Times*, August 18, 1993, A19.
14. Clifford Krauss, "The Marines Want Singles Only, but They Are Quickly Overruled," *New York Times*, August 12, 1993, A1.
15. Hollywood, "End to 'Til Deros Do Us Part,'" 151.
16. Rescinded on January 1, 1996, by Department of the Army, Pamphlet 25-33, "User's Guide," ch. 1. See Legal Assistance Branch of the Administrative and Civil Law Department of the Judge Advocate General's School, JA 263, *Family Law Guide*.
17. Prior to this regulation, service members who married foreign nationals while on overseas tours did not receive a housing allowance after acquiring a dependent. This usually meant that

newly married couples had to live separately because the service member could not afford to pay rent off the base or post, and the Korean spouse was not allowed to live in the barracks.

18. According to Branstetter, "Military Constraints," 14n37, "The absence of direct appeal procedures in cases where authority to marry in an overseas command has been withheld does not mean the soldier is thereby absolutely denied the ability to marry. A disappointed soldier has a number of alternatives. The service member may attempt, through military channels, to have the denial changed by complaint to the service Inspector General or a request for redress from a commander higher that the approved authority. The applicant may also request a 'fiancée visa' which permits the service member to bring the proposed spouse to the U.S. to marry without the necessity for command approval. In any event, if the service member married notwithstanding denial of permission, the marriage is valid if recognized in the country where it took place. If the soldier does marry without permission, there is a possibility of some punishment even though there are no reported Army cases of trial by court-martial in such instances and the Army regulations on the subject are not punitive as were the directives in *Nation*, *Wheeler*, and *Parker*."

19. Kim, "Productive Welfare."

20. Hollywood, "End to 'Til Deros Do Us Part,'" 163.

21. For information on the Kwangju Uprising, see Becky Branford, "Lingering Legacy of Korean Massacre," BBC News, May 18, 2005, http://news.bbc.co.uk/2/hi/asia-pacific/4557315.stm.

22. Button, "Social-Cultural Changes," 199, 203; and Moon, *Sex among Allies*, 59, 12–14, 40–41.

23. USFK, Regulation 600-240, "Summary" (March 2, 2007), as cited in Hollywood, "End to 'Til Deros Do Us Part,'" 163: "Insufficient regulation of international marriages involving U.S. Forces, Korea (USFK) personnel has resulted in numerous void marriages and others in which the 'spouse' is ineligible for marriage and/or immigration to the United States, creating a logistical burden and negative publicity for USFK." Hollywood also notes that this regulation applied to roughly twenty-eight thousand troops when it was implemented in 2007.

24. Hollywood, "End to 'Til Deros Do Us Part,'" 163–64.
25. PFC Antuan Rofe, "New USFK Marriage Regulation Protects Service Members," U.S. Army, March 20, 2007, https://www.army.mil/article/2326/new_usfk_marriage_regulation_protects_servicemembers/.
26. Regarding intelligence threats, one Russian woman confided to Captain Hollywood that "she and other 'juicy girls' could earn extra money by acquiring operational information from Soldiers and selling it to Russian mafia handlers who would offer it to the Russian government." See Hollywood, "End to 'Til Deros Do Us Part,'" 185n206.
27. Hollywood, "End to 'Til Deros Do Us Part,'" 184–85.
28. *United States v. Deguzman*, 1988 C.M.R. Lexis 543 (A.F.C.M.R.).
29. Hollywood, "End to 'Til Deros Do Us Part,'" 189–90; and *Zablocki v. Redhail*, 434 U.S. 374 (1978).
30. *Orloff v. Willoughby*, 345 U.S. 83, 94 (1953).
31. *Parker v. Levy*, 417 U.S. 733, 758 (1974).
32. See, for example, *Goldman v. Weinberger*, 475 U.S. 503 (1986); and *Rostker v. Goldberg*, 453 U.S. 57 (1981).
33. Hollywood, in "End to 'Til Deros Do Us Part,'" 193, contends, "While precise data on abandoned or waiting spouses was always indeterminate, there is no denying that the regulation has significantly curbed further swelling of this lamentable population. Command involvement now ensures that Soldiers act responsibly in assisting their dependents in seeking immigration to the United States."
34. See, for example, *United States v. Prater*, 32 M.J. 433 (1991); *United States v. Murphy*, 36 M.J. 1137 (1993); *United States v. Good*, 39 M.J. 615 (1994); *United States v. Wheeler*, 40 M.J. 242 (1994); *United States v. Bulger*, 41 M.J. 194 (1994); *United States v. Hatfield*, 44 M.J. 22 (1996); *United States v. Eversole*, 53 M.J. 132 (2000); *United States v. Swift*, 53 M.J. 439 (2000); and *United States v. Munar*, 2000 A.F.C.C.A. Lexis 234. For the first and only court-martial for bigamy featuring a female service member, see *United States v. Vidal*, 1994 C.M.R. Lexis 100.
35. For a few examples (out of thousands) of courts-martial featuring prosecutions for both consensual heterosexual sodomy and

adultery, see *United States v. Wilson*, 23 M.J. 899 (A.C.M.R. 1987); *United States v. Rivera*, 26 M.J. 638 (A.C.M.R. 1988); *United States v. Harrison*, 1989 C.M.R. Lexis 793; *United States v. Breland*, 32 M.J. 801 (A.C.M.R. 1991); *United States v. Sumbry*, 33 M.J. 564 (A.C.M.R. 1991); *United States v. Heath*, 1991 C.M.R. Lexis 907 (A.F.C.M.R.); *United States v. Giroux*, 37 M.J. 553 (A.C.M.R. 1993); *United States v. Bevacqua*, 37 M.J. 996 (C.G.C.M.R. 1993); *United States v. Miller*, 1993 C.M.R. Lexis 70 (A.C.M.R.); and *United States v. Sullivan*, 38 M.J. 746 (A.C.M.R. 1993). For a few notable examples of consensual same-sex sodomy and adultery courts-martial, see *United States v. Timmerman*, 28 M.J. 531 (A.F.C.M.R. 1989); and *United States v. Fell*, 33 M.J. 628 (A.C.R. 1991).

36. For a few examples of courts-martial featuring prosecutions for either nonconsensual sodomy or rape and adultery, see *United States v. Turner*, 17 M.J. 997 (A.C.M.R. 1984); *United States v. Horalan*, 1994 C.C.A. Lexis 69 (A.F.C.C.A.); *United States v. Gittens*, 36 M.J. 594 (A.F.C.M.R. 1992); *United States v. Doyle*, 1991 C.M.R. Lexis 862 (N.M.C.C.M.R.); and *United States v. Moore*, 22 M.J. 523 (N.M.C.C.M.R. 1986).

37. For an all-too-common scenario in which a serviceman's commission of forcible sodomy against a servicewoman resulted in the victim's death, see *United States v. Whitehead*, 26 M.J. 613 (A.C.M.R. 1988). Unfortunately, many of the perpetrators whose guilt legal officials established beyond a reasonable doubt walked free as a result of procedural errors at trial.

38. Protection of Children against Sexual Exploitation Act, 18 U.S.C. 2252.

39. *United States v. Maxwell*, 45 M.J. 406, 424 (1996).

40. See *United States v. Bolkan*, unpublished decision (A.F. Ct. Crim. App. 2000).

41. See *United States v. Whitson*, unpublished decision (N.M. Ct. Crim. App. 2000).

42. See *United States v. Monroe*, 52 M.J. 326 (2000).

43. *United States v. Talbert*, 33 M.J. 244, 245 (1991).

44. *Talbert*, 33 M.J. at 246.

45. *United States v. Tatum*, 36 M.J. 302 (1993).

46. *United States v. Hartwig*, 39 M.J. 125 (1994).

47. *United States v. Bilby*, 39 M.J. 467 (1994).
48. *United States v. Pullen*, 41 M.J. 886 (A.F. Ct. Crim. App. 1995).
49. *United States v. Maxwell*, 45 M.J. 406, 410 (1996). Maxwell was also convicted of indecent language, but the court reversed this conviction on the grounds that Maxwell's Fourth Amendment right to reasonable privacy was violated.
50. *Maxwell*, 45 M.J. at 428.
51. For U.S. Air Force courts-martial for possession of child pornography in 2000, see *United States v. Monroe*, 52 M.J. 326 (2000); *United States v. Murray*, 52 M.J. 423 (2000); *United States v. Sapp*, 53 M.J. 90 (2000); *United States v. Augustine*, 53 M.J. 95 (2000); *United States v. Allen*, 53 M.J. 402 (2000); and *United States v. Gallo*, 53 M.J. 556 (A.F. Ct. Crim. App. 2000). For the U.S. Navy, see *United States v. James*, 53 M.J. 612 (N.M. Ct. Crim. App. 2000); and *United States v. Madigan*, 54 M.J. 515 (N.M. Ct. Crim. App. 2000). For the U.S. Marine Corps, see *United States v. Mader*, unpublished opinion (N.M. Ct. Crim. App. 2000). For the U.S. Coast Guard, see *United States v. Brantner*, 54 M.J. 595 (C.G. Ct. Crim. App. 2000).
52. *United States v. Douglas*, 1 M.J. 354 (1976); *United States v. Fail*, 13 M.J. 91 (1982); *United States v. Edwards*, 15 M.J. 159 (1983); *United States v. Haston*, 21 M.J. 559 (A.C.M.R. 1985); and *United States v. Flores*, 21 M.J. 160 (1985). In the only case in which a service member was convicted of indecent exposure between 1976 and 1985, *United States v. Miller*, 2 M.J. 301 (A.F.C.M.R. 1976), the AFCMR affirmed Miller's conviction of larceny, assault, and indecent exposure, as well as his sentence to eighteen months' confinement at hard labor. Miller appealed to the court, seeking relief from what he believed was an excessive sentence. It affirmed his sentence on the grounds that it was hardly excessive considering that the maximum punishment for the three combined offenses amounted to a punitive discharge, total forfeiture of all pay and allowances, reduction to the grade of airman basic, and confinement at hard labor for eighteen months.
53. *United States v. Ramirez*, 21 M.J. 353 (1986).
54. *United States v. Scott*, 21 M.J. 345 (1986). Scott was charged with three separate offenses of indecent exposure to minor females at Camp Lejeune, North Carolina.

55. *United States v. Thomas*, 25 M.J. 75 (1987). In this strange case, the CAAF affirmed the appellant's original conviction of indecent acts rather than indecent exposure for dancing with minors in the nude.

56. For dismissals, see *United States v. Timmerman*, 28 M.J. 531 (A.F.C.M.R. 1989); and *United States v. Lange*, 2000 C.A.A.F. Lexis 399. For cases with more punitive measures, see *United States v. Murray-Cotto*, 25 M.J. 784 (A.C.M.R. 1988); and *United States v. Eberle*, 44 M.J. 374 (1996).

57. *United States v. Jackson*, 30 M.J. 1203 (A.F.C.M.R. 1990); and *McGray v. Grande*, 38 M.J. 657 (A.C.M.R. 1993). Though *McGray v. Grande* did not expand the scope of the offense of indecent exposure, it established a precedent that enabled appellate courts to grant extraordinary relief to service members accused of indecent exposure who were illegally confined at hard labor while awaiting trial.

58. In the comical case *United States v. Choate*, 32 M.J. 423 (1991), the accused mooned another serviceman's wife through his window in base housing. For the original trial transcript concerning exposure not having adverse impact on good order and discipline, see *United States v. Hanson*, 30 M.J. 657 (A.C.M.R. 1990); and for its appellate transcript, see *United States v. Hanson*, 32 M.J. 309 (1991). Finally, for the willful exposure case, see *United States v. Graham*, 54 M.J. 605 (N.M. Ct. Crim. App. 2000).

59. *United States v. McGinty*, 38 M.J. 131 (1993).

60. See, for example, *United States v. Langston*, 53 M.J. 335 (2000); and *United States v. Huberty*, 53 M.J. 369 (2000). These cases saw the first indecent exposure prosecutions of the twenty-first century. Both featured servicemen whose indecent exposure to female victims led to charges of adultery.

61. See *United States v. Modesto*, 39 M.J. 1055 (A.C.M.R. 1994); and *United States v. Modesto*, 43 M.J. 315 (1995).

62. See *United States v. Johnson*, 4 M.J. 770 (A.C.M.R. 1978); and *United States v. Foster* 13 M.J. 789 (A.C.M.R. 1981), pet. denied, 14 M.J. 206 (1982).

63. *United States v. McDaniel*, 39 M.J. 173 (1994).

64. *United States v. Guaglione*, 27 M.J. 268 (1988).

65. *United States v. Gallegos*, 41 M.J. 446 (1995).

66. Aside from the courts-martial of Guaglione and Gallegos, the remaining pandering cases included *United States v. Moore*, 22 M.J. 523 (N.M.C.C.M.R 1986); *United States v. Allen*, 53 M.J. 402 (2000); and *United States v. Miller*, 53 M.J. 504 (2000), in which the U.S. Air Force Court of Criminal Appeals sustained a pandering conviction against Master Sgt. P. Miller for soliciting minor females to engage in sexual acts with him for money at Offutt Air Force Base. Miller apparently initiated his solicitations and activities while his wife and daughter were out of town. The CAAF affirmed Allen's pandering charge based on evidence that he solicited his ex-wife to have sex with other men both to earn extra money with which to pay bills and to enhance their own sexual relationship. For the original trial transcript, see *United States v. Allen*, 44 M.J. 549 (A.F. Ct. Crim. Appeals 1996).

67. See my conclusion in Wilson-Buford, "From Exclusion to Acceptance."

68. D'Amico, "Race-ing and Gendering," 7.

69. Cid Standifer, "DADT Repeal Has Less Impact than Expected, Survey Shows," *Air Force Times*, March 29, 2012, 12.

Afterword

1. Levya, *Married to the Military*; Booher, *Spouses Also Serve*; and Mock, *Portraits of the Toughest Job*.

2. Levya, *Married to the Military*, 4–5.

3. Levya, *Married to the Military*, 1.

4. The end of military conscription and the transition to an all-volunteer force in 1973 enabled women to serve in the armed forces in record high numbers. According to Segal and Segal in a report titled "America's Military Population," 27, women comprised less than 2 percent of the active duty population from World War II to 1972. In 1980 the percentage of women in the services increased to almost 8.4 percent. It peaked at 15 percent in 2002 and has remained steady since.

BIBLIOGRAPHY

Court Cases, Laws, and Military Regulations

Alien Fiancées and Fiancés Act of 1946, Pub. L. No. 79-471, 60 Stat. 339 (1946).

Bowers v. Carter, 59 Utah 249, 252 (1921).

C.M. 187168, Greene, 1 B.R. 1 (July 10, 1929).

C.M. 263231, Baker, 41 B.R. 209.

C.M. v. J.M., 726 A.2D 998, 1001 (N.J. Super. Ct. 1999).

Department of the Army. Pamphlet 25-33, "User's Guide for Army Publications and Forms." Washington DC: Department of the Army Headquarters, 1996.

Duncan v. United States, 48 F2d 128, 132fn 3 (9th Cir. 1931).

Funk v. United States, 290 U.S. 371, 54 S. Ct. 212 (1933).

Goldman v. Weinberger, 475 U.S. 503 (1986).

Hawkins v. United States, 358 U.S. 74, 79 S. Ct. 136 (1958).

Hodges v. Howell, 4 P.3D 803, 805 (Utah App. 2000).

Judge Advocate General of the Armed Forces. *Court-Martial Reports*, volumes 1–50. Rochester: Lawyers Co-operative Publishing, 1950–75.

———. *Military Justice Reporter*, volumes 1–54. St. Paul MN: The West Group, 1976–2000.

Judge Advocate General's School, U.S. Army. *Civil Affairs, Military Government: Selected Cases and Materials*. Charlottesville VA: U.S. Army, 1958.

Kinsella v. Krueger, 351 U.S. 470 (1956).

Lawrence v. Texas, 539 U.S. 558 (2003).

Legal Assistance Branch of the Administrative and Civil Law Department of the Judge Advocate General's School. JA 263, *Family Law Guide*. Charlottesville VA: U.S. Army, 1998.

Loving v. Virginia, 388 U.S. 1 (1967).

Madsen v. Kinsella, 348 U.S. 31 (1952).

Madsen v. Overholser, 251 F. 2d 387 (DC Cir. 1958).

Magierowski v. Buckley, 39 N.J. Super. Ct. 534, 555 (App. Div. 1956).

Manual for Courts-Martial, United States. Washington DC: U.S. Government Printing Office, 1951.

Maynard v. Hill, 125 U.S. 190 (1888).

McGray v. Grande, 38 M.J. 657 (A.C.M.R. 1993).

Mercer v. Dillon, 41 C.M.R. 264 (A.F.B.R. 1969–70).

O'Callahan v. Parker, 395 U.S. 258 (1969).

Orloff v. Willoughby, 345 U.S. 83 (1953).

Parker v. Levy, 417 U.S. 733 (1974).

Protection of Children against Sexual Exploitation Act, 18 U.S.C. 2252 (1994).

Reid v. Covert, 351 U.S. 487 (1956).

Reid v. Covert, 354 U.S. 3 (1957).

Rostker v. Goldberg, 453 U.S. 57 (1981).

Secretary of the Navy. Directive No. 1620.1. Effective December 1, 1949.

S. Rep. No. 1515, 81st Cong., 1st sess. 1948.

State v. Martin, 125 Iowa 715, 101 NW 637 (1904).

State v. Wilcox, 185 Iowa 90, 169 NW 646, 4 ALR 1066 (1918).

United States v. Adams, 21 C.M.R. 733 (A.F.B.R. 1956).

United States v. Adams, 40 C.M.R. 22 (1969).

United States v. Adkins, 18 C.M.R. 116 (1955).

United States v. Allen, 44 M.J. 549 (A.F. Ct. Crim. Appeals 1996).

United States v. Allen, 53 M.J. 402 (2000).

United States v. Alphin, 34 C.M.R. 461 (1964).

United States v. Anderson, 8 C.M.R. 212 (A.B.R. 1952).

United States v. Augustine, 53 M.J. 95 (2000).

United States v. Austin, 44 C.M.R. 550 (A.F.B.R. 1971).

United States v. Avery, 9 C.M.R. 648 (A.F.B.R. 1953).

United States v. Bailey, 12 C.M.R. 564 (A.B.R. 1953).

United States v. Barcomb, 3 C.M.R. 149 (1951).

United States v. Barcomb, 3 C.M.R. 623 (A.F.B.R. 1951).

United States v. Bateman, 23 C.M.R. 312 (1957).

United States v. Battista, 33 C.M.R. 282 (1963).

United States v. Benn, 28 C.M.R. 424 (A.B.R. 1958).

United States v. Betts, 30 C.M.R. 214 (1961).

United States v. Bevacqua, 37 M.J. 996 (C.G.C.M.R. 1993).

United States v. Bilby, 39 M.J. 467 (1994).

United States v. Bird, 24 C.M.R. 447 (A.B.R. 1957).

United States v. Bohannon, 20 C.M.R. 870 (A.F.B.R. 1955).

United States v. Bolkan, unpublished decision (A.F. Ct. Crim. App. 2000).

United States v. Boswell, 35 C.M.R. 491 (A.B.R. 1963).

United States v. Bradshaw, 35 C.M.R. 118 (1964).

United States v. Brantner, 54 M.J. 595 (C.G. Ct. Crim. App. 2000).

United States v. Breland, 32 M.J. 801 (A.C.M.R. 1991).

United States v. Brown, 24 C.M.R. 65 (1957).

United States v. Bulger, 41 M.J. 194 (1994).

United States v. Burkhart, 40 C.M.R. 1009 (A.F.B.R. 1969).

United States v. Butler, 11 C.M.R. 445 (A.B.R. 1953).

United States v. Caune, 46 C.M.R. 201 (1973).

United States v. Choate, 32 M.J. 423 (1991).

United States v. Clark, 22 C.M.R. 888 (A.F.B.R. 1956).

United States v. Clemens, 34 C.M.R. 778 (A.F.B.R. 1964).

United States v. Conrad, 34 C.M.R. 124 (A.F.B.R. 1963).

United States v. Conrad, 35 C.M.R. 411 (1965).

United States v. Conway, 43 C.M.R. 779 (A.B.R. 1971).

United States v. Covert, 16 C.M.R. 465 (A.F.B.R. 1953).

United States v. Covert, 19 C.M.R. 174 (1955).

United States v. Cowan, 12 C.M.R. 374 (A.B.R. 1953).

United States v. Davisson, 6 C.M.R. 174 (A.B.R. 1952).

United States v. Deguzman, 1988 C.M.R. Lexis 543 (A.F.C.M.R.).

United States v. Doherty, 17 C.M.R. 287 (1954).

United States v. Douglas, 1 M.J. 354 (1976).

United States v. Downard, 1 C.M.R. 405 (A.B.R. 1951).

United States v. Downard, 3 C.M.R. 80 (1952).

United States v. Doyle, 1991 C.M.R. Lexis 862 (N.M.C.C.M.R.).

United States v. Duff, 12 C.M.R. 802 (A.F.B.R. 1953).

United States v. Eberle, 44 M.J. 374 (1996).

United States v. Edwards, 15 M.J. 159 (1983).

United States v. Erb, 30 C.M.R. 938 (A.F.B.R. 1961).

United States v. Erb, 31 C.M.R. 110 (1961).

United States v. Eversole, 53 M.J. 132 (2000).

United States v. Fail, 13 M.J. 91 (1982).

United States v. Farrell, 18 C.M.R. 684 (A.F.B.R. 1954).

United States v. Fell, 33 M.J. 628 (A.C.R. 1991).

United States v. Fields, 41 C.M.R. 119 (1969).

United States v. Fletcher, 23 C.M.R. 911 (A.F.B.R. 1956).

United States v. Flores, 21 M.J. 160 (1985).

United States v. Ford, 31 C.M.R. 353 (A.B.R. 1961).

United States v. Foster, 13 M.J. 789 (A.C.M.R. 1981).

United States v. Francis, 12 C.M.R. 695 (A.F.B.R. 1953).

United States v. Franklin, 8 C.M.R. 513 (A.B.R. 1952).

United States v. Fuller, 23 C.M.R. 584 (A.B.R. 1957).

United States v. Fuller, 25 C.M.R. 405 (1958).

United States v. Gagnon, 43 C.M.R. 933 (A.F.B.R. 1970).

United States v. Gagnon, 44 C.M.R. 214 (1972).

United States v. Gallegos, 41 M.J. 446 (1995).

United States v. Gallo, 53 M.J. 556 (A.F. Ct. Crim. App. 2000).

United States v. Gentry, 23 C.M.R. 238 (1957).

United States v. Giroux, 37 M.J. 553 (A.C.M.R. 1993).

United States v. Gittens, 36 M.J. 594 (A.F.C.M.R. 1992).

United States v. Goins, 23 C.M.R. 542 (A.B.R. 1956).

United States v. Good, 39 M.J. 615 (1994).

United States v. Goodman, 33 C.M.R. 195 (1963).

United States v. Graham, 54 M.J. 605 (N.M. Ct. Crim. App. 2000).

United States v. Green, 29 C.M.R. 370 (A.B.R. 1957).

United States v. Green, 26 C.M.R. 508 (1958).

United States v. Green, 29 C.M.R. 868 (A.F.B.R. 1960).

United States v. Grogen, 34 C.M.R. 680 (N.B.R. 1963).

United States v. Guaglione, 27 M.J. 268 (1988).

United States v. Guidry, 22 C.M.R. 614 (1957).

United States v. Hadsell, 42 C.M.R. 766 (A.B.R. 1970).

United States v. Hanna, 7 C.M.R. 571 (A.F.B.R. 1952).

United States v. Hanson, 30 M.J. 657 (A.C.M.R. 1990).

United States v. Hanson, 32 M.J. 309 (1991).

United States v. Harrison, 1989 C.M.R. Lexis 793.

United States v. Hartwig, 39 M.J. 125 (1994).

United States v. Haston, 21 M.J. 559 (A.C.M.R. 1985).

United States v. Hatfield, 44 M.J. 22 (1996).

United States v. Haynes, 24 C.M.R. 881 (A.B.R. 1957).

United States v. Haynes, 27 C.M.R. 60 (1958).

United States v. Heath, 1991 C.M.R. Lexis 907 (A.F.C.M.R.).

United States v. Hillan, 26 C.M.R. 771 (N.B.R. 1957).

United States v. Hodges, 33 C.M.R. 235 (1963).

United States v. Horalan, 1994 C.C.A. Lexis 69 (A.F.C.C.A.).

United States v. Howell, 29 C.M.R. 528 (1960).

United States v. Huberty, 53 M.J. 369 (2000).

United States v. Hudson, 7 C.M.R. 163 (A.B.R. 1952).

United States v. Hurt, 40 C.M.R. 207 (1970).

United States v. Jackson, 12 C.M.R. 403 (A.B.R. 1953).

United States v. Jackson, 30 M.J. 1203 (A.F.C.M.R. 1990).

United States v. James, 53 M.J. 612 (N.M. Ct. Crim. App. 2000).

United States v. Jewson, 7 C.M.R. 216 (A.B.R. 1951).

United States v. Jewson, 5 C.M.R. 80 (1952).

United States v. Johnson, 4 M.J. 770 (A.C.M.R. 1978).

United States v. Johnson, 27 M.J. 798 (A.F.C.M.R. 1988).

United States v. Jones, 11 C.M.R. 855 (A.F.B.R. 1953).

United States v. Jordan, 30 C.M.R. 427 (A.B.R. 1960).

United States v. Kennedy, 24 C.M.R. 61 (1957).

United States v. Knight, 13 C.M.R. 447 (A.B.R. 1953).

United States v. Knudson, 7 C.M.R. 438 (N.B.R. 1952).

United States v. Knudson, 16 C.M.R. 164 (1954).

United States v. Lackey, 22 C.M.R. 384 (A.B.R. 1954).

United States v. Lange, 2000 C.A.A.F. Lexis 399.

United States v. Langston, 53 M.J. 335 (2000).

United States v. Leach, 22 C.M.R. 183 (1956).

United States v. Levinsky, 30 C.M.R. 461 (1960).

United States v. Loppi, 37 C.M.R. 625 (A.B.R. 1966).

United States v. Lyon, 35 C.M.R. 280 (1965).

United States v. Mader, unpublished opinion (N.M. Ct. Crim. App. 2000).

United States v. Madigan, 54 M.J. 515 (N.M. Ct. Crim. App. 2000).

United States v. Madison, 34 C.M.R. 435 (A.F.B.R. 1964).

United States v. Mallory, 17 C.M.R. 409 (A.B.R. 1954).

United States v. Manos, 24 C.M.R. 627 (A.F.B.R. 1956).

United States v. Manos, 25 C.M.R. 238 (1958).

United States v. Mardis, 20 C.M.R. 340 (1956).

United States v. Martin, 1 USCMA 674, 5 C.M.R. 102 (1952).

United States v. Marymont, 28 C.M.R. 904 (A.F.B.R. 1959).

United States v. Marymont, 29 C.M.R. 561 (1960).

United States v. Massey, 34 C.M.R. 930 (A.F.B.R. 1963).

United States v. Massey, 35 C.M.R. 255 (A.F.B.R. 1965).

United States v. Matthews, 23 C.M.R. 790 (A.F.B.R. 1957).

United States v. Maxwell, 45 M.J. 406 (1996).

United States v. McCord, 39 C.M.R. 929 (A.F.B.R. 1968).

United States v. McDaniel, 39 M.J. 173 (1994).

United States v. McDonald, 32 C.M.R. 689 (N.B.R. 1962).

United States v. McDonald, 32 C.M.R. 692 (N.B.R. 1963).

United States v. McFerrin, 28 C.M.R. 255 (1959).

United States v. McGinty, 38 M.J. 131 (1993).

United States v. McKay, 18 C.M.R. 629 (A.F.B.R. 1955).

United States v. Melville, 25 C.M.R. 106 (1958).

United States v. Menchaca, 47 C.M.R. 709 (A.F.B.R. 1973).

United States v. Merrill, 34 C.M.R. 901 (A.F.B.R. 1963).

United States v. Milldebrandt, 8 USCMA 635, 25 C.M.R. 139 (1957).

United States v. Miller, 2 M.J. 301 (A.F.C.M.R. 1976).

United States v. Miller, 1993 C.M.R. Lexis 70 (A.C.M.R.).

United States v. Miller, 53 M.J. 504 (2000).

United States v. Modesto, 39 M.J. 1055 (A.C.M.R. 1994).

United States v. Modesto, 43 M.J. 315 (1995).

United States v. Monroe, 52 M.J. 326 (2000).

United States v. Moore, 34 C.M.R. 422 (1963).

United States v. Moore, 34 C.M.R. 416 (1964).

United States v. Moore, 22 M.J. 523 (N.M.C.C.M.R. 1986).

United States v. Moss, 3 C.M.R. 773 (A.F.B.R. 1951).

United States v. Munar, 2000 A.F.C.C.A. Lexis 234.

United States v. Murphy, 36 M.J. 1137 (1993).

United States v. Murray, 52 M.J. 423 (2000).

United States v. Murray-Cotto, 25 M.J. 784 (A.C.M.R. 1988).

United States v. Nation, 26 C.M.R. 504 (1958).

United States v. Nees, 39 C.M.R. 31 (1968).

United States v. Negron, 28 M.J. 775 (A.C.M.R. 1989).

United States v. Noe, 22 C.M.R. 198 (1956).

United States v. Norris, 28 C.M.R. 903 (A.B.R. 1959).

United States v. Nuckols, 20 C.M.R. 471 (A.B.R. 1955).

United States v. O'Brien, 9 C.M.R. 201 (A.B.R. 1952).

United States v. O'Brien, 11 C.M.R. 108 (1953).

United States v. Ortega, 45 C.M.R. 576 (A.B.R. 1972).

United States v. Parker, 12 C.M.R. 213 (A.B.R. 1953).

United States v. Parker, 32 C.M.R. 482 (A.B.R. 1962).

United States v. Parker, 33 C.M.R. 111 (1963).

United States v. Parker, 5 M.J. 922 (N.C.M.R. 1978).

United States v. Perez, 33 M.J. 1050 (1991).

United States v. Perkins, 8 C.M.R. 855 (A.F.B.R. 1952).

United States v. Plummer, 30 C.M.R. 18 (1960).

United States v. Prater, 32 M.J. 433 (1991).

United States v. Pruitt, 38 C.M.R. 236 (1968).

United States v. Pullen, 41 M.J. 886 (A.F. Ct. Crim. App. 1995).

United States v. Radford, 17 C.M.R. 604 (A.F.B.R. 1954).

United States v. Ramirez, 21 M.J. 353 (1986).

United States v. Reed, 33 C.M.R. 932 (A.B.R. 1963).

United States v. Reese, 22 C.M.R. 614 (A.B.R. 1956).

United States v. Rice, 14 C.M.R. 316 (A.B.R. 1953).

United States v. Riska, 33 C.M.R. 941 (A.F.B.R. 1963).

United States v. Rivera, 31 C.M.R. 93 (1961).

United States v. Rivera, 26 M.J. 638 (A.C.M.R. 1988).

United States v. Rogers, 32 C.M.R. 623 (A.B.R. 1962).

United States v. Royston, 4 C.M.R. 263 (A.B.R. 1951).

United States v. Sapp, 53 M.J. 90 (2000).

United States v. Schneider, 27 C.M.R. 566 (A.B.R. 1958).

United States v. Schoenberg, 37 C.M.R. 45 (1966).

United States v. Schoolfield, 40 M.J. 132 (1994).

United States v. Scott, 21 M.J. 345 (1986).

United States v. Sheehan, 29 C.M.R. 887 (A.F.B.R. 1960).

United States v. Sheeks, 37 C.M.R. 50 (1966).

United States v. Smeal, 49 C.M.R. 751 (A.F.B.R. 1975).

United States v. Smith, 10 C.M.R. 350 (A.B.R. 1952).

United States v. Smith, 17 C.M.R. 314 (1954).

United States v. Smith, 28 C.M.R. 782 (A.F.B.R. 1959).

United States v. Smith, 34 C.M.R. 185 (1964).

United States v. Smith, 35 C.M.R. 662 (A.B.R. 1965).

United States v. Snyder, 4 C.M.R. 15 (1952).

United States v. Stackhouse, 37 C.M.R. 99 (1967).

United States v. St. Clair, 21 C.M.R. 208 (1956).

United States v. Stewart, 7 C.M.R. 226 (A.B.R. 1951).

United States v. Stewart, 5 C.M.R. 76 (1952).

United States v. Sullivan, 38 M.J. 746 (A.C.M.R. 1993).

United States v. Sumbry, 33 M.J. 564 (A.C.M.R. 1991).

United States v. Swift, 53 M.J. 439 (2000).

United States v. Talbert, 33 M.J. 244 (1991).

United States v. Tatum, 36 M.J. 302 (1993).

United States v. Thomas, 37 C.M.R. 520 (A.F.B.R. 1965).

United States v. Thomas, 37 C.M.R. 367 (1967).

United States v. Thomas, 25 M.J. 75 (1987).

United States v. Timmerman, 28 M.J. 531 (A.F.C.M.R. 1989).

United States v. Tobin, 38 C.M.R. 885 (A.B.R. 1967).

United States v. Tobin, 38 C.M.R. 423 (1968).

United States v. Turner, 17 M.J. 997 (A.C.M.R. 1984).

United States v. Vidal, 1994 C.M.R. Lexis 100.

United States v. Wade, 27 C.M.R. 637 (A.B.R. 1958).

United States v. Warren, 20 C.M.R. 135, 137 (1955).

United States v. Weaver, 31 C.M.R. 662 (A.F.B.R. 1962).

United States v. Weems, 13 C.M.R. 25 (1953).

United States v. Wheeler, 30 C.M.R. 387 (1961).

United States v. Wheeler, 40 M.J. 242 (1994).

United States v. Whitaker, 31 C.M.R. 334 (A.B.R. 1960).

United States v. White, 6 C.M.R. 424 (A.B.R. 1952).

United States v. White, 37 C.M.R. 791 (A.F.B.R. 1966).

United States v. Whitehead, 26 M.J. 613 (A.C.M.R. 1988).

United States v. Whitson, unpublished decision (N.M. Ct. Crim. App. 2000).

United States v. Williams, 7 C.M.R. 548 (A.F.B.R. 1952).

United States v. Williamson, 14 C.M.R. 676 (A.F.B.R. 1953).

United States v. Wilson, 23 M.J. 899 (A.C.M.R. 1987).

United States v. Woodard, 39 C.M.R. 6 (1968).

United States v. Woolridge, 28 C.M.R. 78 (1959).

United States v. Wright, 48 C.M.R. 295 (A.F.C.M.R. 1974).

United States v. Yeast, 36 C.M.R. 890 (A.F.B.R. 1965).

U.S. Department of the Air Force. AFR 35-66, "Discharge of Homosexuals," January 12, 1951.

U.S. Department of the Army. AR 600-3, "Chaplain Support Activities." Washington DC: U.S. Department of Defense, October 19, 1971.

———. AR 600-30, "Character Guidance Program," March 1, 1965.

———. AR 600-110, "Personnel-General: Identification, Surveillance, and Administration of Personnel Infected with Human Immunodeficiency Virus (HIV)," March 11, 1988.

———. AR 600-240, Naval Personnel (NAVPERS) 15858, Air Force (AFR) 34-12, and Marine Corps (MCO) 1752.1, "Marriage in Oversea Commands," 1953.

———. AR 600-240/NAVPERS 15858A/AFR 211-18A/MCO 1752.1A, "Marriage in Oversea Commands," December 17, 1965.

———. AR 600-240/Bureau of Naval Personnel Instruction (BUPERSINST) 1756.1-Ch.1/AFR 211-18/MCO 1752.1C, "Marriage in Oversea Commands," March 15, 1977.

———. AR 600-240, "Marriage in Oversea Commands," June 1, 1978.

———. AR 600-240, "Marriage in Oversea Commands," March 2, 2007.

———. AR 600-750, "Marriage in Oversea Commands," 1939.

———. AR 615-360, "Marriage in Oversea Commands," 1935.

———. AR 635-443, "Personnel Separations," January 12, 1950.

U.S. Department of the Army, Office of the Judge Advocate General. *Digest of Opinions of the Judge Advocate General of the Army, 1912–1940.* Washington DC: U.S. Government Printing Office, 1943.

U.S. Forces Korea. Regulation 600-240, "International Marriages of USFK Personnel." Washington DC: U.S. Department of Defense, March 2007.

U.S. Forces Korea/Eighth U.S. Army. Pamphlet 600-091, "Commander's Guide to Marriage Counseling." Washington DC: U.S. Government Printing Office, January 14, 1981.

U.S. War Department. Cir. No. 179, Sec. 1, June 8, 1942.

War Brides Act of 1945, Pub. L. No. 79-271, Stat. 659 (1945).

Wilkinson v. People, 86 Colo. 406, 282 P 257 (1929).

Zablocki v. Redhail, 434 U.S. 374 (1978).

Published Sources

Alexander, M. Jacqui, and Chandra Mohanty, eds. *Feminist Geneologies, Colonial Legacies, Democratic Futures.* New York: Routledge, 1997.

Alt, Betty Sowers, and Bonnie Domrose Stone. *Campfollowing: A History of the Military Wife.* New York: Praeger, 1991.

Alvah, Donna. *Unofficial Ambassadors: American Military Families Overseas and the Cold War, 1946–1965.* New York: New York University Press, 2007.

Anderson, Warwick. *Colonial Pathologies: American Tropical Medicine, Race, and Hygiene in the Philippines.* Durham NC: Duke University Press, 2006.

Bacevich, Andrew. *Breach of Trust: How Americans Failed Their Soldiers and Their Country.* New York: Metropolitan Books, 2013.

———. *The Limits of Power: The End of American Exceptionalism.* New York: Holt, 2008.

———. *The New American Militarism: How Americans Are Seduced by War.* New York: Oxford University Press, 2013.

———. *Washington Rules: America's Path to Permanent War.* New York: Metropolitan Books, 2011.

Bailey, Beth L., and David Farber. *The First Strange Place: Race and Sex in World War II Hawaii.* Baltimore: Johns Hopkins University Press, 1994.

Baker, Anni. *American Soldiers Overseas: The Global Military Presence.* New York: Praeger, 2004.

Barrett, Duncan, and Nuala Calvi. *GI Brides: The Girls Who Crossed the Atlantic for Love.* William Morrow, 2014.

Belkin, Aaron. *Bring Me Men: Military Masculinity and the Benign Façade of American Empire, 1989–2001.* Oxford: Oxford University Press, 2012.

Bernardin, Susan, Melody Graulich, Lisa MacFarlane, and Nicole Tonkovich. *Trading Gazes: Euro-American Women Photographers and Native North Americans, 1880–1940.* New Brunswick NJ: Rutgers University Press, 2003.

Berube, Allan. *Coming Out under Fire: The History of Gay Men and Women in World War II.* Chapel Hill: University of North Carolina Press, 1990.

Booher, Tiffany A. *Spouses Also Serve.* Mustang OK: Tate Publishing, 2007.

Bowles, Heloise. *Hints from Heloise: From the Air Force to Air Force Wives.* Washington DC: U.S. Government Printing Office, 1973.

Brandt, Allan. *No Magic Bullet: A Social History of Venereal Disease since 1880.* Oxford: Oxford University Press, 1987.

Branstetter, Capt. Ross W. "Military Constraints upon Marriages of Service Members Overseas, or if the Army Wanted You to Have a Wife." *Military Law Review* 102 (Fall 1983): 5–22.

Braudy, Leo. *From Chivalry to Terrorism: War and the Changing Nature of Masculinity*. New York: Vintage, 2005.

Briggs, Laura. *Reproducing Empire: Race, Sex, Science, and U.S. Imperialism in Puerto Rico*. Berkeley: University of California Press, 2002.

Brown, Melissa. *Enlisting Masculinity: The Construction of Gender in US Military Recruiting Advertising during the All-Volunteer Force*. Oxford: Oxford University Press, 2012.

Budreau, Lisa M. *Answering the Call: The U.S. Army Nurse Corps, 1917–1919: A Commemorative Tribute to Military Nursing in World War I*. Washington DC: Defense Department, Office of Medical History & Office of the Surgeon General, 2008.

Button, Edward J. "Social-Cultural Changes in South Korea since 1991: An American View." *International Journal of Korean Studies*, no. 1 (Fall/Winter 2004).

Canaday, Margot. *The Straight State: Sexuality and Citizenship in Twentieth-Century America*. Princeton: Princeton University Press, 2009.

Celello, Kristin. *Making Marriage Work: A History of Marriage and Divorce in the Twentieth-Century United States*. Chapel Hill: University of North Carolina Press, 2012.

Chomsky, Noam. *Failed States: The Abuse of Power and the Assault on Democracy*. New York: Holt, 2007.

——. *Hegemony or Survival: America's Quest for Global Dominance*. New York: Metropolitan Books, 2003.

Clement, Elizabeth Alice. *Love for Sale: Courting, Treating, and Prostitution in New York City, 1900–1945*. Chapel Hill: University of North Carolina Press, 2006.

Cockburn, Cynthia, and Dubravka Zarkov. *The Postwar Moment: Militaries, Masculinities, and International Peacekeeping*. London: Lawrence and Wishart, 2002.

Cohen, Lizabeth. *A Consumer's Republic: The Politics of Mass Consumption in Postwar America*. New York: Vintage Books, 2003.

Collins, Clella R. *Army Woman's Handbook*. 4th ed. New York: Whittlesey House, 1942.

Cott, Nancy. *Public Vows: A History of Marriage and the Nation.* Cambridge MA: Harvard University Press, 2000.

Crittendon, Secretary of the Navy Capt. S. H. *The Crittenden Report: Report of the Board Appointed to Prepare and Submit Recommendations to the Secretary of the Navy for the Revision of Policies, Procedures and Directives Dealing with Homosexuals, 21 December 1956–15 March 1957.* Washington DC: U.S. Government Printing Office, 1957.

D'Amico, Francine. "Race-ing and Gendering the Military Closet." In *Gay Rights, Military Wrongs: Political Perspectives on Lesbians and Gays in the Military,* edited by Craig A. Rimmerman, 3–46. New York: Garland Publishing, 1996.

D'Amico, Francine, and Lauri Weinstein. *Gender Camouflage: Women and the U.S. Military.* New York: New York University Press, 1999.

Davis, Rebecca. *More Perfect Unions: The American Search for Marital Bliss.* Cambridge MA: Harvard University Press, 2010.

Domosh, Mona. *American Commodities in an Age of Empire.* New York: Routledge, 2006.

Edwards, Wallace. *Comfort Women: A History of Japanese Forced Prostitution during the Second World War.* Absolute Crime. Amazon Digital Services, 2013.

Ellinghaus, Katherine. *Taking Assimilation to Heart: Marriages of White Women and Indigenous Men in the United States and Australia, 1887–1937.* Lincoln: University of Nebraska Press, 2009.

Elshtain, Jean Bethke. *Women and War.* New York: Basic Books, 1987.

Elshtain, Jean Bethke, and Sheila Tobias, eds. *Women, Militarism, and War.* Lanham MD: Rowman and Littlefield, 1990.

Enloe, Cynthia. *Bananas, Beaches, and Bases: Making Feminist Sense of International Politics.* Berkeley: University of California Press, 1990.

———. *Does Khaki Become You? The Militarization of Women's Lives.* London: Pandora Press, 1988.

———. *Maneuvers: The International Politics of Militarizing Women's Lives.* Berkeley: University of California Press, 2000.

———. *The Morning After: Sexual Politics at the End of the Cold War.* Berkeley: University of California Press, 1993.

Eskridge, William J., Jr. *Dishonorable Passions: Sodomy Laws in America, 1861–2003.* New York: Viking, 2008.

Fehrenbach, Heide. *Race after Hitler: Black Occupation Children in Postwar Germany and America*. Princeton: Princeton University Press, 2007.

Friedman, Andrea. *Citizenship in Cold War America: The National Security State and the Possibilities of Dissent*. Amherst: University of Massachusetts Press, 2014.

Gaddis, John Lewis. *The Cold War: A New History*. New York: Penguin Books, 2006.

——— . *Strategies of Containment: A Critical Appraisal of the American National Security Policy during the Cold War*. Oxford: Oxford University Press, 2005.

Gibson, E. Lawrence. *Get Off My Ship: Ensign Berg v. The U.S. Navy*. New York: Avon, 1978.

Goldman, Nancy Loring. "Trends in Family Patterns of the U.S. Military Personnel during the 20th Century." In *The Social Psychology of Military Service*, edited by Nancy Loring Goldman and David Segal, vol. 6. Beverly Hills: Sage, 1976.

Goldstein, Joshua. *War and Gender: How Gender Shapes the War System and Vice Versa*. Cambridge: Cambridge University Press, 2001.

Grayzel, Susan R. *Women's Identities at War*. Chapel Hill: University of North Carolina Press, 1999.

Greiner, Virginia, and Charlott Bedrick. *Something on Protocol*. 10th ed. Panama City FL: Boyd Brothers, 1963.

Gross, Mary Preston. *Mrs. NCO*. 3rd ed. Chuluota FL: Beau Lac Publishers, 1969.

Henson, Maria Rosa. *Comfort Woman: A Filipina's Story of Prostitution and Slavery under the Japanese Military*. Lanham MD: Rowman and Littlefield, 1999.

Herbert, Melissa S. *Camouflage Isn't Only for Combat: Gender, Sexuality, and Women in the Military*. New York: New York University Press, 1998.

Hershatter, Gail. *Dangerous Pleasures: Prostitution and Modernity in Twentieth-Century Shanghai*. Berkeley: University of California Press, 1999.

Higate, Paul R. *Military Masculinities: Identity and the State*. Santa Barbara: Praeger, 2003.

Hillman, Elizabeth Lutes. *Defending America: Military Culture and the Cold War Court-Martial.* Princeton: Princeton University Press, 2005.

Hippler, M. *Matlovich: The Good Soldier.* Boston: Alyson, 1989.

Hoganson, Kristin. *Consumers' Imperium: The Global Production of American Domesticity, 1865–1920.* Chapel Hill: University of North Carolina Press, 2007.

Höhn, Maria. *GIs and Fräuleins: The German-American Encounter in 1950s West Germany.* Chapel Hill: University of North Carolina Press, 2001.

———. "You Can't Pin Sergeant's Stripes on an Archangel: Soldiering, Sexuality, and U.S. Army Policies in Germany." In Höhn and Moon, *Over There,* 109–45.

Höhn, Maria, and Martin Klimke. *A Breath of Freedom: The Civil Rights Struggle, African American GIs, and Germany.* New York: Palgrave Macmillan, 2010.

Höhn, Maria, and Seungsook Moon, eds. *Over There: Living with the U.S. Military Empire from World War Two to the Present.* Durham: Duke University Press, 2010.

Holloway, Pippa. *Sexuality, Politics, and Social Control in Virginia, 1920–1945.* Chapel Hill: University of North Carolina Press, 2006.

Hollywood, Capt. Dana Michael. "An End to 'Til Deros Do Us Part': The Army's Regulation of International Marriages in Korea." *Military Law Review* 200 (Summer 2009): 154–94.

Huebner, Andrew J. *The Warrior Image: Soldiers in American Culture from the Second World War to the Vietnam Era.* Chapel Hill: University of North Carolina Press, 2008.

Hughes, Michael J. *Forging Napoleon's Grande Armée: Motivation, Military Culture, and Masculinity in the French Army, 1800–1808.* New York University Press, 2012.

Jacobs, Margaret D. *White Mother to a Dark Race: Settler Colonialism, Maternalism, and the Removal of Indigenous Children from the American West and Australia, 1880–1940.* Lincoln: University of Nebraska Press, 2009.

Janiewski, Dolores. "Engendering the Invisible Empire: Imperialism, Feminism, and U.S. Women's History." *Australian Feminist Studies* 16, no. 36 (2001).

Jerome, Sally, and Nancy Brinton Shea. *The Marine Corps Wife: What She Ought to Know about the Customs of the Service and the Management of a Navy Household*. New York: Harper & Row, 1955.

Johns, Richard B. "The Right to Marry: Infringement by the Armed Forces." *Family Law Quarterly* 10, no. 4 (1977): 357–87.

Johnson, Chalmers. *Blowback: The Costs and Consequences of American Empire*. New York: Metropolitan Books, 2000.

——— . *Dismantling the Empire: America's Last Best Hope*. New York: Metropolitan Books, 2010.

——— . *Nemesis: The Last Days of the American Republic*. New York: Metropolitan Books, 2007.

——— . *The Sorrows of Empire: Militarism, Secrecy, and the End of the Republic*. New York: Metropolitan Books, 2004.

Johnson, David K. *The Lavender Scare: The Cold War Persecution of Gays and Lesbians in the Federal Government*. Chicago: University of Chicago Press, 2006.

Kaplan, Amy. *The Anarchy of Empire in the Making of U.S. Culture*. Cambridge MA: Harvard University Press, 2005.

Kerber, K. Linda. *No Constitutional Right to Be Ladies: Women and the Obligations of Citizenship*. New York: Hill and Wang, 1998.

Kim, Eleana J. *Adopted Territory: Transnational Korean Adoptees and the Politics of Belonging*. Durham: Duke University Press, 2010.

Kim, Young-hwa. "Productive Welfare: Korea's Third Way?" *International Journal of Social Welfare* 12, no. 1 (January 2003): 61–67.

Kinzer, Betty, and Marion Leach. *What Every Army Wife Should Know*. 2nd ed. Harrisburg PA: Stackpole Books, 1968.

Kontour, Kyle. "War, Masculinity and Gaming in the Military Entertainment Complex: A Case Study of *Call of Duty 4: Modern Warfare*." PhD diss., University of Colorado–Boulder, 2011.

Lee, Jin-kyung. *Service Economies: Militarism, Sex Work, and Migrant Labor in South Korea*. Minneapolis: University of Minnesota Press, 2010.

Leffler, Melvyn P. *For the Soul of Mankind: The United States, the Soviet Union and the Cold War*. New York: Hill and Wang, 2008.

——— . *The Specter of Communism: The United States and the Origins of the Cold War*. New York: Hill and Wang, 1994.

Lehr, Doreen Drewry. "Military Wives: Breaking the Silence." In *Gender Camouflage: Women and the U.S. Military*, edited by Francine D'Amico and Laurie Weinstein, 117–42. New York: New York University Press, 1999.

Lehring, Gary L. *Officially Gay: The Political Construction of Sexuality by the U.S. Military*. Philadelphia: Temple University Press, 2003.

Levine, Philippa. *Prostitution, Race, and Politics: Policing Venereal Disease in the British Empire*. London: Routledge, 2003.

Levya, Meredith. *Married to the Military: A Survival Guide for Military Wives, Girlfriends, and Women in Uniform*. New York: Simon & Schuster, 2003.

Litoff, Judy Barrett, and David C. Smith, eds. *American Women in a World at War: Contemporary Accounts from World War II*. Wilmington DE: Scholarly Resources, 1997.

Little, Roger W. *The Military Family: Handbook of Military Institutions*. Beverly Hills: Sage, 1971.

Loveland, Anne. *Change and Conflict in the U.S. Army Chaplain Corps since 1945*. Knoxville: University of Tennessee Press, 2014.

Lurie, Jonathan. *Military Justice in America: The U.S. Court of Appeals for the Armed Forces, 1775–1980*. Abridged ed. Lawrence: University Press of Kansas, 2001.

Lutz, Catherine, ed. *The Bases of Empire: The Global Struggle against U.S. Military Posts*. New York: New York University Press, 2009.

May, Elaine Tyler. *Homeward Bound: American Families in the Cold War Era*. New York: Basic Books, 2008.

McCormick, Thomas J. *America's Half-Century: United States Foreign Policy in the Cold War and After*. 2nd ed. Baltimore: Johns Hopkins University Press, 1995.

McEnaney, Laura. *Civil Defense Begins at Home: Militarization Meets Everyday Life in the Fifties*. Princeton: Princeton University Press, 2000.

Meyerowitz, Joanne. *Not June Cleaver: Women and Gender in Postwar America, 1945–1960*. Philadelphia: Temple University Press, 1994.

Mitchell, Pablo. *Coyote Nation: Sexuality, Race, and Conquest in Modernizing New Mexico, 1880–1920*. Chicago: University of Chicago Press, 2005.

Mock, Janelle H. *Portraits of the Toughest Job in the Army: Voices & Faces of Modern Army Wives*. Lincoln NE: iUniverse, 2007.

Molina, Natalie. *Fit to Be Citizens? Public Health and Race in Los Angeles, 1879–1939*. Berkeley: University of California Press, 2006.

Montalvo, Eric S. "The Constitutional Right to Marry . . . Fundamental Right or Façade? A Review of the Constitutionality of Military Restrictions on the Right to Marry . . . and Even if They Could . . . Whether They Should." *Naval Law Review* 52 (2005).

Moon, Katharine H. S. *Sex among Allies: Military Prostitution in U.S.-Korean Relations*. New York: Columbia University Press, 1997.

Moon, Seungsook. "Regulating Desire, Managing the Empire: U.S. Military Prostitution in South Korea, 1945–1970." In Höhn and Moon, *Over There*, 39–77.

Murphy, Mary Kay, and Carol Bowles Parker. *Fitting In as a New Service Wife*. Harrisburg PA: Stackpole Books, 1966.

Ngai, Mae. *Impossible Subjects: Illegal Aliens and the Making of Modern America*. Princeton: Princeton University Press, 2004.

O'Neill, Colleen. *Working the Navajo Way: Labor and Culture in the Twentieth Century*. Lawrence: University Press of Kansas, 2005.

Painter, David S. *The Cold War: An International History*. New York: Routledge, 1999.

Pascoe, Peggy. *What Comes Naturally: Miscegenation Law and the Making of Race in America*. Oxford: Oxford University Press, 2009.

Paterson, Thomas G. *On Every Front: The Making and Unmaking of the Cold War*. 3rd ed., rev. New York: W. W. Norton, 1993.

Pliley, Jessica R. *Policing Sexuality: The Mann Act and the Making of the FBI*. Cambridge MA: Harvard University Press, 2015.

Pye, Anne Briscoe, and Nancy Shea. *The Navy Wife: What She Ought to Know about the Customs of the Service and the Management of a Navy Household*. 7th ed. New York: Harper & Brothers, 1942.

Redmond, Catherine. *Handbook for Army Wives and Mothers and All Other Dependents*. Washington DC: Infantry Journal, Penguin Books, 1944.

Remick, Elizabeth. *Regulating Prostitution in China: Gender and Local Statebuilding, 1900–1937*. Palo Alto CA: Stanford University Press, 2014.

Roberts, Mary Louise. *What Soldiers Do: Sex and the American GI in World War II France*. Chicago: University of Chicago Press, 2013.

Rotskoff, Lori. *Love on the Rocks: Men, Women, and Alcohol in Post–World War II America*. Chapel Hill: University of North Carolina Press, 2002.

Rowland, Debran. *Boundaries of Her Body: A Troubling History of Women's Rights in America*. Naperville IL: Sphinx Publishing, 2004.

Ryan, Erica J. *Red War on the Family: Sex, Gender, and Americanism in the First Red Scare*. Philadelphia: Temple University Press, 2015.

Schlesinger, Arthur, Jr. "The Crisis of American Masculinity." *Esquire*, November 1958, 63–65.

Segal, David R., and Mady Wechsler Segal. "America's Military Population." *Population Bulletin: A Publication of the Population Reference Bureau* 59, no. 4 (December 2004): 1–40.

Shah, Nayan. *Contagious Divides: Epidemics and Race in San Francisco's Chinatown*. Berkeley: University of California Press, 2001.

Shea, Nancy. *The Air Force Wife: What She Ought to Know about the Customs of the Service and the Management of an Air Force Household*. New York: Harper & Row, 1951.

——— . *The Army Wife: What She Ought to Know about the Customs of the Service and the Management of an Army Household*. 3rd ed. New York: Harper & Brothers, 1948. First edition, 1941.

Shilts, Randy. *Conduct Unbecoming: Gays and Lesbians in the U.S. Military*. New York: St. Martin's Press, 1993.

Shukert, Elfrieda Berthiaume, and Barbara Smith Scibetta. *War Brides of World War II*. New York: Presidio Press, 1988.

Sinclair, G. D. "Homosexuality and the Military: A Review of the Literature." *Journal of Homosexuality* 56 (2009): 701–18.

Stoler, Ann Laura. *Carnal Knowledge and Imperial Power: Race and the Intimate in Colonial Rule*. Berkeley: University of California Press, 2002.

Streets, Heather. *Martial Races: The Military, Race and Masculinity in British Imperial Culture, 1985–1914*. Manchester: Manchester University Press, 2011.

Strub, Whitney. *Perversion for Profit: The Politics of Pornography and the Rise of the New Right*. New York: Columbia University Press, 2013.

Sturdevant, Saundra Pollack, and Brenda Stoltzfus. *Let the Good Times Roll: Prostitution and the U.S. Military in Asia*. New York: New Press, 1993.

Takeuchi, Michiko. "'Pan-Pan Girls' Performing and Resisting Neocolonialism(s) in the Pacific Theater: U.S. Military Prostitution in Occupied Japan, 1945–1952." In Höhn and Moon, *Over There*, 78–108.

Warner, Maj. Mark M., USAF. "The Air Force Wife—Her Perspective." *Air University Review*, May–June 1984.

Weiss, Jessica. *To Have and to Hold: Marriage, the Baby Boom, and Social Change*. Chicago: University of Chicago Press, 2000.

Westad, Odd Arne. *The Global Cold War: Third World Interventions and the Making of Our Times*. Cambridge: Cambridge University Press, 2007.

Wexler, Laura. *Tender Violence: Domestic Visions in an Age of U.S. Imperialism*. Chapel Hill: University of North Carolina Press, 2000.

Whitfield, Steven J. *The Culture of the Cold War*. Baltimore: Johns Hopkins University Press, 1991.

Whitt, Jacqueline E. *Bringing God to Men: American Military Chaplains and the Vietnam War*. Chapel Hill: University of North Carolina Press, 2014.

Wicks, Stephen. *Warriors and Wildmen: Men, Masculinity, and Gender*. Westport CT: Bergin & Garvey, 1996.

Wier, Ester. *Army Social Customs*. Harrisburg PA: Military Service Publishing, 1958.

———. *What Every Air Force Wife Should Know*. 3rd ed. Harrisburg PA: Stackpole Books, 1966.

Wier, Ester, and Dorothy Coffin Hickey. *The Answer Book on Air Force Social Customs*. Harrisburg PA: Military Service Publishing, 1957.

Wilson-Buford, Kellie. "From Exclusion to Acceptance: A Case History of Homosexuality in the U.S. Court of Military Appeals." In *Evolution of Government Policy Towards Homosexuality in the US Military: The Rise and Fall of DADT*, edited by James E. Parco and David A. Levy. New York: Routledge, 2014.

———. "'Troublesome Hellions' and 'Belligerent Viragos': Enlisted Wives, Laundresses, and the Politics of Gender on Nineteenth-Century Army Posts." *Military History of the West* 41 (2011): 13–29.

Winthrop, Col. William. *Military Law and Precedents*. 2nd ed., rev. Washington DC: U.S. Government Printing Office, 1920.

Wood, Cynthia. "Army Laundresses and Civilization on the Western Frontier." *Journal of the West* 41 (Summer 2002): 26–34.

Yuh, Ji-Yeon. *Beyond the Shadow of Camptown: Korean Military Brides in America.* New York: New York University Press, 2002.

Zeiger, Susan. *Entangling Alliances: Foreign War Brides and American Soldiers in the Twentieth Century.* New York: New York University Press, 2010.

aliens: counseling for, 211; investigations into background of, 58–61, 211; legal and illegal, 52; as military spouses, 42, 50–52, 55–58, 62–65, 69, 72–76, 205, 208–10, 212–15

allotment checks, 17, 237, 246n1, 246n5

Alvah, Donna, 36–37

Anderson, W., 173–74

appellate reviews, 151, 153, 175, 184, 219, 281n57. *See also* ABR (Army Board of Review); Air Force Court of Criminal Appeals; CAAF (Court of Appeals of the Armed Forces); CMA (Court of Military Appeals)

Aquino, Domingo P., 65

Army, U.S., 52–56, 126, 131–35, 138

Army Board of Review. *See* ABR (Army Board of Review)

Army Court of Military Review (ACMR), 201, 224, 228

The Army Wife (Shea), 21–22, 37

Army Woman's Handbook (Collins), 24–25

Asians, 58–59, 256n30

Aspin, Les, 208

automobiles as crime scenes, 110–11, 175, 178, 190–91, 268n99, 274n61

Ayars, Judge Advocate, 67, 148

B., Sally, 195

Barcomb, J., 189

Barkin, Judge, 171

Battista, C., 152–53

Bedrick, Charlott, 33

Benn, W., 89

Berger, Herbert, 175

Berube, Allan, 124

bigamy, 66–67, 98–102, 260nn39–40, 260n44

Bird, R., 146

Bissell, William B., 79

Boards of Review of the Army, 272n43

Bohannon, S., 273n58

Booth, Lieutenant Colonel, 136–37

Boswell, C., 196–97

Bowles, Heloise, 25, 28–29

Brandenburg, Judge Advocate, 70

Branstetter, Ross, 258n67

"brothers" (CMA judges), 191, 274n60

Brown, C., 190–91, 274n61

"brown babies," 253n3

Bullard, Colonel, 159–60

Burkhart, J., 101

Butler, Mrs., 193–95

Butler, R., 193–95, 275n69

CAAF (Court of Appeals of the Armed Forces), 202, 221–23, 225–26, 228–29, 276n4, 281n55. *See also* CMA (Court of Military Appeals)

Canady, Margot, 126–27, 265n23, 266n27

Carey, M., 65–66

Caune, N., 178–79

chaplains, 61, 70–71, 73, 240, 256n37, 257n57

Character Guidance program, 42–43

children: abandoned, 69–70; adopted, 91, 253n3; illegitimate, 47–48, 51, 65, 67–68, 253n3; in seduction cases, 97, 259n36; sexually exploited, 89–91, 111–12, 128–29, 182, 219, 224, 273n58, 281n55, 282n66

Chun Doo-Hwan, 210

CID (Criminal Investigations Detachment), 170–72

civil law, 49, 83, 85–86, 95–96, 198–99, 213, 259n36, 261n56

Clark, A., 220

Clark, D., 180–81

CMA (Court of Military Appeals), 261n66; in abuse cases, 42, 112, 115, 252n88; in adultery cases, 82, 102, 104, 202; in alienation of affections cases, 95, 97; in bigamy cases, 101–2; in entice-ment cases, 2–3; in exposure cases, 171, 173–74, 176–79, 223–24; in homicide cases, 110, 262n77; on husband-wife privilege, 17–18, 87–92; in international marriage cases, 63–64, 69–71, 75–76; in interracial marriage cases, 75; judges on, 274n60; legal rights protected by, 141–45, 147, 148–53, 154–55, 199–200, 230; in pandering cases, 189, 191–92, 274n58, 274n61; in pornogra-phy cases, 165–66, 169, 221; in prostitution-related cases, 188,

195–96; role of, 6, 14, 244n5; in sodomy cases, 119–20, 123, 137, 141–43, 264n9, 268n86; transcripts in, 4; in voyeurism cases, 181, 182, 227; in wrong-ful cohabitation cases, 102, 104, 108. *See also* CAAF (Court of Appeals of the Armed Forces)

C.M. v. J.M., 97

Code of the District of Columbia, 194–95

Codner, S. J., 139–40

Cold War, 5, 44, 183, 188, 243n2, 247n8, 264n16

Collins, Clella R., 24–25, 26–27, 33, 35

Commander of U.S. Naval Forces in the Philippines (COM-NAVPHIL), 69, 257n54

commanders acting as counsel-ors, 73–74, 211–12

"Commander's Guide to Marriage Counseling," 49

command influence: in adultery matters, 201–2; as command control, 50, 121–22, 147, 149; in homosexuality matters, 124, 135, 147–49; in marriage, 47–50, 53–56, 62–67, 70–75, 77, 204–8, 212–13, 253n3, 258n67; in prostitution, 184, 188, 198

"commercialized vice," 189, 191

communism, 15, 19, 43, 58, 198

COMNAVPHIL. *See* Commander of U.S. Naval Forces in the Philip-pines (COMNAVPHIL)

condoms, 201–2

Conrad, H., 178
constitutional rights, 123, 212–14,
264n9
consumerism, 247n7
Cott, Nancy, 83
Court-Martial Reports, xiii, 4,
41, 129
Court of Appeals of the Armed
Forces. *See* CAAF (Court of
Appeals of the Armed Forces)
Court of Military Appeals.
See CMA (Court of Military
Appeals)
courts-martial: in accusatory
questions and innuendo cases,
146; in adultery cases, 216;
authority of, 274n60; in bigamy
cases, 66–67, 100–101, 260n44,
278n34; in command influence
situations, 149; diminishing use
of, 141; in double jeopardy situations, 142; in dual conviction
cases, 115–17, 244n6; in entrapment situations, 150, 266n29; in
extortion cases, 95; in forgery
cases, 17; gender issues and, 13–
14; in homicide cases, 82, 109–
10; in homosexuality and sodomy cases, 92, 105, 115, 120–23,
125–27, 128–33, 134–35, 137, 139,
142–43, 155–57, 216–17, 264n9,
264n16; in indecent exposure
cases, 169, 172–74, 223–26,
272n37; in marriage-related
cases, 47, 54–55, 62–63, 69–
70, 74, 76, 88–89, 104, 263n82;
masculinity culture and, 162–

63; in physical abuse cases,
42, 108; in pornography cases,
166–67, 219; in prejudicial evidence and testimony situations, 143–44; privacy issues
and, 113; in prostitution-related
cases, 183, 185, 188, 189–90, 194,
196, 228–29, 252n84; race issues
in, 243n2; in rape cases, 112,
114; role of, 4–5; in seduction
suits, 94–95; transcripts of,
xiii–xiv; in unlawful cohabitation cases, 105–6; in unreasonable searches situations, 151–53;
in voyeurism cases, 180–82;
women and, 39, 278n34. See
also *Manual for Courts-Martial*
(*MCM*)
coverture, 8, 85
cowardice, 251n80
Cox, Judge, 222–23
Cramer, Myron, 56–57
Criminal Investigations Detachment. *See* CID (Criminal Investigations Detachment)
Crittenden Report, 135, 138–39
Crook, Judge Advocate, 68–69
curfew, 185–86

DADT ("don't ask, don't tell") pol-
icy, 123, 204, 225, 232–33
D'Amico, Francine, 124
Davisson, H., 139–40
Dawson, Colonel, 134
death sentence, 82–83, 109, 243n2,
262n69
Deguzman, G., 212

Freedom of Information Act, 138
Funk v. United States, 85–86

Gallegos, X., 229
gay rights movement, 122, 156, 199, 263n6, 269n90
gender issues, xi–xv, 157, 214, 236
gender roles, 7, 13, 14, 19–20, 34, 41, 199–200, 240–41, 246n6
Germans and Germany, 49–50, 253n3
GI Fiancées Act (1946), 57
Gloeckner, Frau, 196–97
Goins case, 131–33
Goldstein, Joshua, 39
Goldstein, Seth L., 220
"good order" concept, 23, 50, 63–64, 162, 235–37, 269n13
government quarters, misuse of, 193–97
Green, V., 134–35
Greene, Private, 146
Greiner, Virginia, 33
Griffin, Judge Advocate, 70
Grogan, P., 99–100
Gross, Mary Preston, 30, 36
Guaglione, D., 228–29
guidance classes, 205–7
guidebooks: challenges to, 96; on finances, 28–30; gender roles promoted by, 26–27, 31, 38–40, 43–44, 239–40; homemaking promoted by, 24–28; on mothering, 30–31; on outward appearances, 28, 32, 36–38; on personal behaviors, 32–36; propaganda in, 26
Guidry, W., 65–67

Hacioglu, E., 194
Hack, Raymond L., 82
Hadsell, M., 101–2
Handbook for Army Wives and Mothers and All Other Dependents (Redmond), 26
Hanna, R., 93
Hawkins v. United States, 86, 90
Haynes, C., 150–51
"heart balm" acts, 94–95, 97
Hernandez, A., 69
heterosexism, 8, 11–12, 38–39, 41, 121, 179, 245n12, 251n82, 272n41, 274n60
Hickey, Dorothy Coffin, 28–29, 37–38
Hillan, C., 151–52
Hillman, Elizabeth Lutes, 6, 14, 56, 68, 106, 121
Hints from Heloise (Bowles), 25
HIV (human immunodeficiency virus), 201–3, 215–16
Hollis, Colonel, 147–48
Hollywood, Dana, 208, 209, 211–12, 278n26
homemaking, 20–21, 23, 24–28, 236, 247n10
homicide, 79–84, 108–13, 210, 261n66, 262n69, 268n86
homophobia, 225, 264n16
homosexuality: attitudes toward, 8–9, 119–21, 129, 154–57, 265n24, 268n71; classification of, 127–32, 138; criminalization of, 121; definition of, 124; discharges for, 265n23; due process rights and, 147, 233;

pandering, 183, 188–93, 228–29, 273n58, 275n67, 282n66
Parker, B., 105–6
Parker, Carol Bowles, 25, 29
Parker, H., 92–93
Parker, Seaman, 74–75
Paul, H., 110–11
Pechenino, Mrs., 106
Peeping Toms. *See* voyeurism
physical touching, 224
Pilon, Captain, 135
Plummer, F., 187
pornography, 160–61, 164–68, 199–200, 218–23
prejudice, 162, 269n13
prejudicial error, 100, 106, 115, 171, 181, 189, 224, 262n73
prejudicial evidence, 143–45
prejudicial questioning, 146
prejudicial testimony, 143–45
privacy: invasion of, 5–6, 59, 113, 203; as legal issue, 53–54, 151–54, 164–65, 167–68, 179–80, 202, 207; new technology and, 221–23, 231
procedural errors, 279n37
promiscuity, 51, 55, 60, 154, 190, 229, 256n33
prostitutes, 55, 162, 184, 189–90, 192–93, 228, 278n26
prostitution: crimes related to, 183–88, 273n53, 274n61; in government quarters, 193–97, 252n84; military overlooking, 163, 188; pandering and, 188–93, 228–29; policing of, 272n47; segregated, 243n2

Protection of Children against Sexual Exploitation Act, 219
public morals: indecent exposure and, 169–76; negligent exposure and, 176–79; pandering and, 188–93; pornography and, 164–68; prostitution and, 179–83, 193–97; voyeurism and, 179–83
public nudity, 168, 174–75, 178, 179, 224
Pullen, Staff Sergeant, 222–23
Pye, Anne Briscoe, 32

questions, accusatory, 146
Quinn, Ferguson, 63–64, 87, 90, 92, 96, 104–5, 192–93, 196

race: in military justice system, 169–73, 243nn1–2, 270n28; in military records, xiii–xiv, 243n1, 253n1, 270n28; violence and, 243n2. *See also* marriages, interracial
Ramirez, C., Jr., 224
rape, 90, 112, 114–16, 163, 216, 241, 243n2, 244n8, 251n79
Rawson, Mr., 136–37
Reagan, Ronald, 13, 156
"reasonable person" concept, 177, 271n36
Redfield, Dr., 276n4
Redmond, Catherine, 26, 35
Reese, Private, 47–48, 76, 253n1
Rehfuss, Captain, 159–60
Reitzel, Judge, 67
religious conservatives, 217

religious freedom, 70–71, 73

Republic of Korea (ROK), 183, 205–7, 208–12, 213, 230–31, 277n23

residences, private, 166, 167–68, 176, 180, 194, 196, 223, 225

reversals, 142; in abuse cases, 42; in adultery cases, 116; in bigamy cases, 101–2; of guilty sentences, 14; in homosexuality and sodomy cases, 120, 130, 132, 138, 141–43, 145–46, 150, 264n9; and husband-wife privilege, 18, 92; in marriage-related cases, 56–57, 207–8; in negligent exposure cases, 177–78; in prostitution-related cases, 185, 189, 191–92, 228; in voyeurism cases, 181–82; in wrongful cohabitation cases, 106

Rex v. Crunden, 271n35

Rice, A., 186–87

Riska, I., 110–11

Riska, V., 110–11

Royston, J., 169–73, 270n26

Ruby, Judge, 171

Russia, 278n26

Schedel, H., 175

Schick, Staff Sergeant, 1

Schneider, C., 166–67

Schoenberg, J., 182

Schoolfield, K., 202

Schroeder, Pat, 208

searches, unreasonable, 151–54

security, national. *See* national security

security clearances, 73, 150

seduction and seduction suits, 84, 93–98. *See also* alienation of affections; enticement

Servicemembers Legal Defense Network, 233

servicemen: African American, 47–48, 169–73, 253n3; homosexual, 122–23; as protectors and providers, 40–42, 251n84; role of, 44

servicewomen, 55–56, 126–28, 215–16, 225–26, 241, 282n4

sex: extramarital, 3, 106, 190, 193; heterosexual marital, 125; military standards for, 5, 7–8, 117, 235; natural, 215–17; procreative, 121, 165; promiscuous, 229; relaxed attitudes toward, 199; unprotected, 201–3; virtual, 231. *See also* adultery; heterosexism; homosexuality; sodomy

sexual assault, 3–4, 216, 244n4, 244n8

sexual deviance: definition of, 4–5, 9, 205, 218, 231, 237; military view of, 15, 84, 261n66; prosecution of, 10–14, 120, 124, 204–5, 225, 232, 252n86; as public crime, 161–63; violent crimes compared to, 244n6

sexual orientation, 121, 130–31, 138, 142, 232

Shaffer, M., 273n53

Shea, Nancy, 21–22, 24–25, 27–28, 30, 32–34, 37

Sheehan, W., 133

204; in prostitution-related cases, 184; role of, 5, 6, 141, 163, 244n5; in voyeurism cases, 180

Unofficial Ambassadors (Alvah), 36–37

unreasonable searches, 151–54

U.S. Counsel and Commission of Immigration and Naturalization, 62

USFK (U.S. Forces Korea), 207, 210–11, 214

U.S. Lady, 36–37

U.S. legal cases: *Alphin*, 262n73; *Bailey*, 103; *Bohannan*, 273n58; *Doherty*, 264n19; *Ford*, 167–68; *Franklin*, 270n28; *Gentry*, 191, 274n61; *Hanna*, 93–94, 97; *Hartwig*, 221; *Haynes*, 150; *Hillan*, 268n89; *Hodges*, 274n58; *Johnson*, 201; *Leach*, 88; *Lyon*, 97; *Maxwell*, 222; *McGinty*, 225; *Miller*, 280n52, 282n66; *Norris*, 115–17; *O'Brien*, 108–9; *Parker*, 264n19; *Perez*, 201–3, 276n4; *Reese*, 253n1; *Schoolfield*, 202, 276n4; *Snyder*, 237; *Weems*, 268n86; *White*, 270n28; *Whitehead*, 279n37

vagueness, 121, 128, 130–31, 141, 162, 190n

venereal disease, 55, 183, 256n33, 272n47, 273n48

videotaping, 182, 215, 218, 226–28, 231

Vietnam War, 218, 247n8

Vinet, Judge, 154, 155

visa fraud, 212

voir dire examination, 147, 150, 267n71

voyeurism, 176–77, 179–83, 226–28, 271n34, 272n43

W., Shirley, 195

waiting wives, 208–10, 214, 278n33

Wallace, Miss, 170–73

war brides, 52, 57, 255n12

War Brides Act (1945), 57

War Department, 56–57

Warren, R., 143–45

Webb, Jim, 207

webcams, 182, 227–28, 231

Webster's New International Dictionary, 160, 186

What Every Army Wife Should Know (Kinzer and Leach), 30

Wheeler, Seaman, 70–71, 73, 76

"whiteness," xiii–xiv, 83, 248n10, 253n1

Wier, Ester, 22, 28–29, 30, 33, 36, 37–38

Williams, J., 95–96

window peeping. *See* voyeurism

witnesses: expert, 119–20, 220–21, 263n3; prosecution, 79, 115, 119–20, 144, 151, 170–72, 191; spouses as, 17, 86–88, 90–91; women as, 85–87

wives, military: abandoned, 69–70; as ambassadors, 36–38; conflicting roles of, 23–24; employment of, 24; expectations of, 9–10, 19–22, 31–36, 42–44, 239–40; finances handled by, 28–30;

wives, military (*continued*)
historical study of, 248n18; as
laundresses, 53; as mothers, 30–
31; of officers, 249n39; potential,
55–56
Wolf, Judge, 171
women: in legal cases, 153, 215; postwar, 246n6; as prostitutes, 189–
90, 192–93; race issues and, 173;
seen as lesser beings, 34, 85–86,
96, 249n19; subordination of,
24, 83; as victims, 217, 225–28; in
workforce, 22, 148n10. *See also*
servicewomen; wives, military

Woodward, J., 153–54, 246n5
Woolridge family, 17–18, 41, 246n1
World War II, 243n2, 244n4
Wright, J., 193, 275n67
wrongful cohabitation, 102–8,
261n56
Wysingle, P., 191–92

Yeast, L., 135–38
Yoon, K. E., 210

Zablocki v. Redhail, 212–13
zero-tolerance policy, 190, 219